THE DREAMWORK MANUAL

A practical book covering all aspects of dreaming and showing how the power
of dreams can be harnessed to develop and transform our lives.

"Strephon—

Your analysis techniques are impressive indeed.
Thank you for sharing your manual.
I think I'll listen more carefully to my dream work — again.

    In Love,
    Ram Dass"

". . . a treasure trove of many ways of understanding one's dreams."

    Arthur Hastings, Ph.D.
    President, Association for Transpersonal Psych.

"Dear Friends,

 I am part of a dreamgroup that has been meeting on a weekly
basis for over three years. We have explored many methods and
systems of working with dreams, but we have found the
Jungian-Senoi Dreamwork Manual to be invaluable. Most of its
methods we have practiced successfully. It has been a rich
sourcebed for connecting our inner lives to the outer ones.

    Thanks,
    D.L., Cambridge, Mass."

THE DREAMWORK MANUAL

A Step~by~Step Introduction to Working with Dreams

by

Strephon Kaplan Williams

JOURNEY PRESS
Berkeley, California

The illustrations are from old alchemy texts, many of which can also be found in Jung's **Psychology and Alchemy.**

LIBRARY OF CONGRESS CATALOG CARD NO.: 79-90507

PRINTING HISTORY

1st printing: 200 signed copies, Feb., 1980
2nd printing: 200 copies, April, 1980
3rd printing: 500 copies, July, 1980, perfect bound, red ink mandala cover
4th printing: 1000 copies, Oct., 1980, revised edition.
5th printing: 1,500 copies, May, 1981, typeset cover and page titles
6th printing: 3000 copies, March, 1982, new three color cover by Nasrin
7th printing: 3000 copies, Sept., 1982
8th printing: 3000 copies, June, 1983
9th printing: 3000 copies, June, 1984
10th printing: 3000 copies, June, 1985, new cover by Jani, typeset, revised
German language edition by Ansata Verlag, Paul A. Zemp. 5000
hardback copies, Sept. 1984
United Kingdom edition, The Aquarian Press, 10,000 copies, Oct., 1984

Preface

We feel the publication of this manual is of great significance to the Jungian-Senoi Institute and hopefully to others. As far as we know this is the first fully comprehensive and practical dreamwork manual ever published. It contains over thirty major dreamwork techniques, many of them innovated and all of them further developed at the Institute.

There is nothing simplistic about this book. One will have to study and practise its content to get at what it is trying to convey. The chapters are written and designed to be re-read as one gains in experience.

Within these pages are the techniques described in practical format which allows the dreamer to actually apply the technique to working with a dream. Also, we have written the book in an inspirational style, both to show that dreamwork can be a work of art and that dreamwork really does reveal the Self or soul at work. This book is designed to last. Its purpose is to convey to readers everywhere that dreamwork is now an extremely practical tool for creative self-discovery and even the transformation of one's life.

The development of this manual occurred as follows. In 1977 I self-published a fifty-two page book, *Jungian-Senoi Dreamwork*, whose value travelled by word of mouth and it was used in classes at several colleges and universities. But it contained only a simple overview as to the possibilities in dreamwork.

I did not choose to make an extensive research on the dream literature but decided instead to research and organize exactly how people were working with dreams in Institute dream groups. Thus the real sources for this book are the dreams and dreamwork of everyday people struggling with their lives, plus my own dreamwork and formulating abilities.

In January of 1979 I began writing chapters which were used in a dreamwork training programme. The interchange with students produced new material ideas, issues and insights which were then included in revisions of the chapters for the next training classes. Thus the version seen here has been worked with and revised, some of it as much as three times. Examples included of dreamwork come from students with their permission.

The final writing phase of this version includes extensive editorial work on the part of key Institute people, Harriet Skibbins and Terran Daily. We have also been greatly helped by the warm support and typing of Hilary Scaife and Ursula Stehle. Terran Daily with my assistance designed the flow chart. The professional typing was done by Susan Steele.

The illustrations are mostly from ancient alchemical texts reprinted in various sources, the best collection of which is C. G. Jung's *Psychology and Alchemy*. The quotes from dreams are all the contributions of Institute dream group participants.

I should like again to acknowledge the many people who have contributed dreamwork, some of which I have been able to use. My principle editors have been Harriet Jasik Skibbins, Terran Harcort Daily, David Warren Skibbins, and Mollie Hughes. Mollie has joined us as a participant in dream groups and with a background as a professional editor. I also thank Lou Savory for his support and editing. I must add, however, that the copy is not yet perfected and, as we are still evolving the approach, we are still evolving the manual. Comments of any kind from readers are certainly appreciated.

Strephon

Strephon Kaplan Williams

JOURNEY

For every season there is a choice,
A time to die and a time to live,
A time for decrease and a time for increase.

For every beginning there is an ending,
A time for regression and a time for growth,
A time for saying goodbye and a time for greeting.

For anything new the old must go,
A grave must be dug and new seed planted,
A sacrifice made as well as fulfillment created.

The days of our years are numbered by eternity.
What was will never again be.
The songs which have been sung are only an echo.

We are as grains of sand in the infinitude of oceans.
Our consciousness illumines life for only an instant.
We are as nothing in a transcendent now.

And what we have we have not.
What we are we will not be.
What we can become is already
A burden on our shoulders.

Where is my life going? asks the seeker.
To what end are all my choices?
And for what purpose have I been born or unborn?

Yet still will I say my refuge is in what is.
My salvation is in what I do with what life brings me.
My longing is within the sacred.

When I am no more the rains will still fall,
The seasons will swirl into eternity,
And the voice of my lips will be somebody's song.

For I am not alone in my common humanity.
I am not alone in the journey towards wholeness.
I am at peace where the center guides me.

And I shall live in all my dying.

of special interest

Journey Press books have been developed through the workshops and activities of the Jungian Dreamwork Institute in Berkeley, California. A brochure is available on its programs which include,

Weekend workshops in Transforming Childhood, The Dream Journey, and Transforming Relationships.

Summer week long training intensives in dreamwork and Jungian psychology.

Weekly dream groups and individual dreamwork and therapy.

Please write for training and workshop dates. Workshops are scheduled in the United States and Europe.

We especially recommend organizing a two and one half day weekend workshop in your area for training with Strephon Williams on working with dreams. Please contact the Jungian Dreamwork Institute for details.

The Jungian Dreamwork Institute
1525J Shattuck Avenue
Berkeley, CA 94709

Contents

Contents

PART III — REFLECTIONS

Dreamwork Methods List

Dreamwork Methods List

The following is a list of dreamwork methods described in this manual. Following the method's title will be the names of the originators of the method as I have experienced it. Others, not acknowledged here, may have originated or contributed to certain techniques, but it has not been part of my own development of this dreamwork methodology. Essentially, all the methods described here have been developed further from Institute students' personal dreamwork experiences. We have not established the methodology from reading books.

Dreamwork Methods Fully Described in This Book

Other Dreamwork Methods in This Book

The Healing Mandala

The mandala on the cover of this book might just as well be called 'the Western Mandala' to distinguish it from Eastern mandalas which are usually quite stylized and partly designed to keep out demonic or dark forces.

The Eastern mandala tends to wall out certain cosmic energies in an effort to create tranquility and non-attachment within.

This Western, healing mandala, on the other hand, has been created out of an urge for emergence from chaos and darkness.

In other words, the centre is born out of chaos and does not itself contain it or keep it out! The primal ground of the unformed and turbulent is the necessity, the molten bedrock, out of which creating through the fiery torment and extreme beauty unfolds the new, the urgent, moving centre calling out for a devotional affirmation of Source.

The way to work with vital darkness and whirlwind chaos is through catalytic emergence which insists that a transformative birth is possible exactly where hope, that grey light, vanishes.

Hope is never effective. In place of hope put commitment and the active search for meaning. Go to the most energic and there penetrate and open yourself to one point, to an interior harmonizing which allows the darkness and the light together their necessary transformations.

Using The Healing Mandala

Many, or most of us, will in our lives at times feel close to the verge of being overwhelmed by unconscious forces.

It is suggested, as a healing device, that you duplicate this mandala for yourself and colour it in. In so doing you will be evoking an emergent centre within the chaos affecting you. Do at least one mandala a day until you are through the worst. Use any colours that appeal to you. Also let evolve your own mandalic shapes. Then write feelings or other reactions which are evoked by your experience. Lastly, date your creations.

Colouring this mandala is also effective for focusing, whether in a crisis or not, and for the simple pleasure of creating a harmonious whole.

No greater beauty exists, perhaps, than those artistic works which enable us to experience the mystery and power of centre. Mandala, the sacred circle, creates within the inner heart the longing for harmony which lives within every soul and every wound.

Where Source exists there mandala is.

Part I
Beginning the Journey

Story of a Dreamer

I dreamed that I was dreaming myself.

Or was it that I dreamed that someone was dreaming me?

I do not remember. But when I woke up I knew that because of the dream, a dream for which I had not asked, my whole life could from this day be different.

It was as if I had awakened because I had dreamed that I was dreaming.

This puzzled me, since up to this moment I had always thought that it was I who was dreaming my dreams. But now I had also to face that I might well be being dreamed by some other being of which I knew nothing.

This frightened me. Was I not in control of my own life? Was I not an adult who had taken charge of my life and my actions? Or was I still somebody's child, to be manipulated and directed with little say of my own?

Perhaps I was most afraid because, if it were true that somebody or

something was dreaming me, I would have to find out who or what that being was and relate to it. I would want to do this because I would want choice in the matter of what was really going on in my life.

Perhaps I did not want to be dreamed? But, also, did I have control in the matter? Perhaps my only freedom was in how I related to what was really there?

My fear was not only of losing control but also of what I would find if I looked for who or what was dreaming me.

And how would I find out? Why, through my dreams, of course! If I actively remembered and worked with them, I might achieve a freedom I had never known before, a freedom which would allow me to see into that other world which compelled me and to make conscious choices in relation to it.

My fear was beginning to evaporate under the challenge. Perhaps I needed the dream? That I needed what my dreams were trying to say to me? That my dreams were not trying to control me after all, but to set me free? Perhaps working with 'He/She who dreams me' would be my way of filling a void somewhere deep within that I have always felt but have never been able to do anything with?

Perhaps the dream? Perhaps working with the dream? And my making choices in relation to the dream? But where would I go? How would I find help in dealing with my dreams?

I knew only that because I had dreamed, and been dreamed, I needed to search.

The Dream

What is a dream? Or better still, what part does the dream play in life? And what place does dreamwork have in my journey?

This book is as much about dreamwork as about the dream. Within these pages are many techniques and experiences from people who actively use their dreams as sources of self-reflection, guidance and personal transformation.

The dream is a great mystery. We do not know where is comes from or why it has developed as an aspect of our evolutionary history. And part of the mystery is that so few people actively respond to their dreamlife. In one night, we may dream five different dreams and awaken in the morning forgetting them all. But a person who is committed to dreamwork tries to remember and write at least one of those dreams down in her or his journal and takes steps to actualize or re-experience some of these recorded dreams in certain significant ways. Such a person is not just living life in the outer sense, immersed in all the projects and functions of the day, but enters the day, with all its activities, from a base in his or her inner world. The dream and its dreamwork have made this person more conscious of outer actions and choices and, therefore, more responsive to life.

Yes, more responsive to life because, through dreamwork, this dream-actualizing person is not identified with outer activities. Should a relationship dissolve that day, the possibility might have been known and worked with in

dreamwork. Should a new and important choice need to be made that day, the different options might already have been rehearsed in previous dreamwork. Should an experience of meaning develop in the outer, it might have already been evoked by a significant dream and its dreamwork.

In dreams and dreamwork, we have the extraordinary chance to rehearse what could happen in our lives this day, this week, this year or anytime in the future. Within dreams, themselves, we are offered the opportunity over and over again to experience situations and events which may or may not occur directly in the outer.

Consider that in a typical series of dreams, we find murder, love-making with different partners, travel to new and exotic places, including other planets, extraordinary feats of courage as well as great bouts of fear, gifts large and small, and meeting with strangers as well as friends. All this and much more happens in dreams. Certainly in an active dreamlife, we experience far more than we normally do in outer life. What is going on? What is the great mystery of why dreams come to us in the night?

And then other extraordinary things may happen in relating to dreams. Events may occur in the outer which are very similar to events which have already happened in a dream. A person dreams of someone they have not heard from in a long time and then a letter from that person arrives the next day. A relationship is first dreamed of and then later happens in outer reality. The actual dream session meditation candle goes out when the decision has been made to disband a dream group for necessary reasons. Information from the outer leaps across time and space and appears in a dream and significant synchronistic events.

What is going on? What, then, is the nature of reality? Is a dream only the product of nerve synapses snapping away and discharging leftover energy in sleep after a day's hard living? Is a dream only a psychological entity, a product merely of a person's mental processes? Or is there more? Since certain outer events tend to coincide with dream events in meaningful ways, is there, then, a motivating force which produces both the dream and the life? The core reality, the reality of realities, may not be materially based. I cannot say absolutely that when my dead father returns to me in a dream, he is only an inner image of my father, a memory trace, an archetypal image within my psyche. What if some of my father's energy still exists as spirit after the physical death and chooses to visit me in dreams?

Mystery. If I am devoted to the mystery, I do not need to know answers. I approach the dream only as something which is full of possibility. And I work with the dream on as many levels — inner, outer, mundane, spiritual — as seem meaningful. I do not need to prove or disprove anything in my quest for a meaningful life. The more open I am, the more possibilities are available to me. Nor am I overly fearful that I will be divorced from reality and fall into an unconscious soup of projection and fantasy, for the dream and its dreamwork ground me. Often my present dreams seem to comment on previous dreamwork choices. And dreamwork, itself, is always opening up new insights and possibilities. And, then, nothing works if it does not work in reality. I take my dreamwork possibilities to the outer life and try them out. If the consequences are negative, then I know something I did not know before. If the consequences are positive, then I move on to a newer, fuller, richer life, and an even greater mystery.

What is a dream? We know so little about dreams and where they come from. Perhaps it is not essential to solve what may be beyond knowing. We have the dream, always the dream. And we now know from dream-sleep research that everyone dreams, even if many do not remember their dreams. But many other findings of dream research still seem tentative and open to interpretation. Certain researchers state that we dream' more about the previous day's events at the beginning rather than at the end of the night. But how can they make such a judgement from the non-literal material of the dream? Let us discover many more facts before we draw conclusions. And if we cannot obtain answers, we can create responses.

Creating Meaning through Dreamwork

What we do with our dreams, how we actualize them, becomes a major experience of meaning in itself. Thus, the meaning of a dream comes from *actualizing* a dream rather than *interpreting* it. Interpretation, the rationalizing of symbols, distances us from the dream, whereas actualizing or re-experiencing the dream brings us closer to it. So often interpretation involves one person projecting his or her own personal material onto someone else's dream and personality.

Don't tell me what my dream means, please. You will only be telling me what my dream means to you, not what it means to me. If you want to help me, give me specific suggestions that I can use to re-experience my own dreams. Then I can learn to rely on my own sources and not be forced to submit to someone else's way of looking at things.

How can we approach dreams and still preserve their mystery? In this book, you will find many self-actualizing methods which have worked for people who are seeking to find meaning through their dreams. You, also, may embark on this adventure if you choose.

You may become quite excited by the process. And you may even stop remembering your dreams for a while. You may find the going hard work at times. But you may also become much more grounded in your own life journey and the sources which vitalize your being.

Some of My Own Dreamwork History

It is always fascinating to see the different structures, the different sets of methods and attitudes, which people use to process the raw experience of life. In my own case, I have been a pacifist, a Christian with Jewish roots, an American whose father was born in Russia, a Quaker, a military-school student, and, today, a person devoted to dreamwork as well as certain other forms of personal growth. When I was twenty-one, I was kept awake all night because I was upset over a broken love relationship. I decided I needed help and spent the next five years in Jungian analysis, going once a week to talk for an hour about my inner world and my problems to a wonderful older woman who helped me become deeply oriented to life. We worked with many dreams and my dead mother's dream image changed from that of a woman with razor blades coming out of her mouth to a mother travelling ahead of me on the same path that I was on.

I then stopped analysis for a few years, obtained college degrees and launched a first marriage. When this marriage ended and I also experienced a great loss of meaning in my life I began analysis again and joined a leadership training programme with a spiritual organization which was to help me profoundly change my life.

In the next ten years I went through several changes in dealing with my inner and outer life. Within three years of my new commitment to self-growth I was faced with tremendous bouts with my unconscious, the climax being at one weekend seminar in which I felt almost utterly overwhelmed by unconscious forces. I remember the circumstances quite vividly. As I was driving up for the weekend I was becoming more and more nauseous with a headache also and the bleak feeling of ordinary reality dissolving in the face of superior cosmic forces. I was up all night shivering. No amount of blankets could keep me warm. By the end of the weekend I could hardly move, so weak was my will power. However, I did stay involved with the seminar and as I was driving home my sickness vanished completely!

My analyst was warm and attentive but there was little I could do except let the forces of the unconscious have their say. What I had learned from my analyst and other seminar leaders was to maintain a creative ego committed to healing happening within the psyche. This carried me through. I had experienced again the worst nightmares of childhood, but this time within a supportive atmosphere evocative of healing and meaning about life's journey. This example is one among many of my growth and full confrontation with the unconscious. Like a dark and shimmering stream the years of my gradual progress flowed as I also made my choices to become conscious and integrative.

During the ten years with this organization we studied many spiritual texts, but primarily the life and teachings of the historical Jesus. There was and still is great meaning in this process for me. Through this and Jungian psychology, which was also central, I became committed to a process, other than ego-directed and controlled, which is at work in the psyche and in life itself.

I had found the leadership and analysts to be very real people living their journeys with consciousness and devotion. I myself was more and more committed to this community and was myself an associate leader also training to be an analyst. I expected this to be a life-long process. But that was not meant to be.

My spiritual crisis developed in part because I found myself going in a different direction in dealing with the material than the founding leaders. This divergence, which seemed to be genuine and not rebellious, caused me considerable anxiety. For if I chose to leave this organization, I would be leaving not only my analyst and chief spiritual teacher, but also a community with its own work, relationships and celebrations which had been built up over the years. In my own mind, I questioned deeply whether or not I was even going against the 'Will of God' if I left this organization. We had been asked to commit ourselves for life, and so it was with great fear and trembling that I opened up to the possibility of leaving. For if I did indeed leave, I would have nothing left but myself. There would be no organization for me and my friends there would cease to relate to me. I would have chosen to step outside the circle and would have to accept the consequences. Nor could I fault the leaders or the organization itself in what they were doing. It was basically good work, the finest I had ever found, but mine would have to be different.

Dreamwork had grown, for me, into one of the central forms for choosing meaning and direction in my life. I would go weekly and tell my analyst my dreams and she would comment on the possibilities for meaning. Dreams appealed to me because they seemed to come directly out of my own unconscious and were not the beliefs or attitudes of any other person. But I often left my analyst's office bewildered. True, I had learned new ways to grow. But I could never quite figure out where my analyst got the things she said about me. Did she have some secret diagnostic ability which enabled her to see things in the dreams I could not see? And how was I to know that she was not projecting her own hidden material onto my dreams? During the later stages of my analysis, I found myself questioning her more and more until, finally, I had a crucial and decisive dream experience which set the stage for my choosing to end my analysis with her and my relationship with her organization.

The Crucial Dream

On the night of April 2, 1975, my birthday, I had the following dream which showed me decisively the way to go. I consider this the great dream of my life so far:

'I dream that my spiritual leader's house is being destroyed and the members of the organization have to move out. My analyst gives me permission to take some things, so I select some beautiful antiques, which are not too fancy, to put in my car. But an older man from the university and his wife are also taking things. I tell the man he has to have permission to take things and I stop him. I then select some of the things he has chosen. He has excellent taste and tells me about some of the pieces, which broadens my outlook. But after I get the things from the older man, a young couple drives off in a van with a beautiful old mirror I would have selected. This mirror had been pointed out to me by the older man's wife. I run after the van, but it disappears in a schoolyard where children are lined up for lunch. I would have liked everyone to be excluded from the leader's house while I was selecting my pieces. But this is not the way things are. One does not get all one wants in this life. And I realize I can't always be protected and have what I want handed over to me. I must assert my own authority and tenacity.'

According to my journal, I had asked for a birthday dream showing my future. Imagine my excitement when I awoke in the middle of the night with this dream. I was spiritually desperate. I needed help but no outside source or authority could evaluate whether or not I was being egocentric in questioning my further involvement with the organization which had helped me transform my life. Wherever the response ultimately came from, it had to be from other than my conscious ego and not from still another spiritual guide or therapist.

Right after recording the dream, I wrote the following in my journal:
'It seems that permission to take the valuables is not just given securely, directly, decisively, but must be taken by asserting my own authority and not giving in to another's authority . . . I am not given the overall structure, the organization. That is to be destroyed. I am given some of the fine pieces of furniture, the traditions, best values, what has been achieved that is portable .
. . So taking on the heritage is done by asserting and developing my authority and knowledge by acting promptly and, also, by resisting that which would take it away from me — the university professor, the older tradition who knows the values but wants them for himself . . . I am not a collector. I am a user. I must resist aggrandizement. Also, I must resist the younger part which would just take something and run off with it without carrying on that which is valuable. This younger part takes the mirror, the reflective consciousness versus the active, doing consciousness . . . I give and take by asserting my authority. The original permission was given, but it did not prevent others from coming in and trying to take things.'

After this journal work, I fell asleep and continued the dream. 'I dream that I return to the house. People are still moving things out. There is a long, cut-glass mantle mirror in two parts. My wife questions my taking it, wondering where to put it in the house. But I want it. Someone else already wants the mirror, so I compromise by taking one part which has its own integrity. The mirror is rectangular and has a border of twelve cut-glass squares. I leave the other half of the mirror with the other person and wake up as if seeing a woman at the foot of my bed who disappears when I am fully awake.'

Incredible. Notice the change in behaviour on the part of my dream ego, the contrast between the image of myself in the first dream and the second dream. In the first dream, I am frantically trying to get what I have permission to take, but I lose the mirror. In the second dream, I get my part of the beautiful mirror, which is whole in itself, not by trying to prevent another person from taking it, but through compromise. And I choose and get that which is absolutely essential. I do not withdraw, either, in the face of opposition. Five years later, as I write this, I am still working at living the full meaning of this dream. And after doing the dreamwork, I felt that my life and a new spiritual direction had been confirmed. I could indeed continue the spiritual path and personal growth without having to still be a part of this organization or particular spiritual form. I was enormously excited and grateful to have received these dreams. From then on I knew at the core of my being that dreams represented a great mystery to which I could respond in order to realize my life.

When I shared this dream in analysis my analyst questioned why I had chosen the gifts for myself and not for the organization? This was a forthright question but a disturbing one. For it pointed clearly to the nature of my crisis.

Was I to choose the next life direction based on the commonly accepted goals of the group and its leaders?

Or was I to strike out and develop for myself goals based on what I perceived the Self, the centre within me, was wanting?

Many leaders and ex-leaders with this organization had faced the same question. Some chose to stay, choosing what the leaders and community had developed as the best form for expressing their own individual journeys. Some chose to leave, and many within a cloud of some negativity and agony on both sides. Archetypally, leaving the known and valuable for the unknown can be extremely painful. I certainly felt pain and caused pain. I felt basically unsupported during the process and even more unsupported after the climax and transition to new beginnings.

In 1976 I stopped analysis and resigned from the organization. All my assertiveness and determination were needed to survive the agony and doubt of the separation.

The separation from any spiritual organization to new life for almost anyone who is at all passionate has the element of fresh wounding. Some never solve their negativity problem by living fully what they could not live when with the organization. I have seen it on the faces of ex-leaders of various groups. I have seen it on my own face.

I share my story, my version of reality, here because when I was going through the process I did not understand the dynamics. For each of us, wherever we are in life and whatever our communities and beliefs, we can develop a strong enough relation to inner resources so as never to be dominated by any group or vision. For myself, almost the greatest motivating force in further developing a dreamwork methodology is to enable people to follow inward rather than outward sources. We must not only become responsible for our egos, our choice-makers, but also responsive to the Self, the integrative, transformative centre within.

The years never heal wounds. They simply bury them in the passage of time. To heal the wounds we can allow them into our objectivity. We can take responsibility for everything which happens, not necessarily as of our own choosing, but as potentially meaningful and even crucial to our destiny, the larger meaning of our lives.

For me the healing from this crisis has come by my fuller devotion to dreamwork as a window into transpersonal or non-ego sources. And healing has also come by more and more living the potentials which I thought were being denied to me by others.

Incredibly, the years since the break have seen several dreams in which my former analyst becomes more and more supportive, a thing which did not happen in the outer. There is a point at which analysis, or growth under someone else's direction, can end for a new stage in the self-actualizing wholeness process.

In the last dream of the series my analyst and I are working together on a paper for the Jungians. I am doing most of the work. I awake feeling very happy.

The Jungian-Senoi Approach

The golden rule of dreamwork might be stated as follows: *To get to the meaning of dreams, actualize dreams rather than interpret them.*

Actualizing one's dream brings one closer to the dream. Interpreting one's dream distances one from the dream. The meaning of a dream comes from the dreamer's re-experiencing the dream and not from what someone else may say about it.

Actualization is the re-experiencing of a dream, or some aspect of it, with

similar or greater emotional intensity than that of the original dream. Actualization also refers to gaining meaning from a dream by doing specific outer-life projects which embody some part of the original dream. Thus we include under the term 'actualization' both re-experiencing the dream in itself and transforming the dream into specific outer-life experiences.

Interpretation is the translating of image into concept, using an outside symbol-system or reference language. The interpreters, whether of dreams, personality or whatever, seek to take the living, primary experience of a symbol and categorize or fit it into a generalized conceptual system. Symbols are fluid and can often, seemingly, be made to fit into a number of different symbol systems. But there are certain fallacies in the interpretive approach, as in the following example:

One person attempts to take over someone else's dream by calling on his knowledge of mythological symbols to tell the dreamer what her dream symbol means. The dreamer does not do her own exploration herself but accepts his authority. The authority figure may in fact be projecting his inner contents onto the other's dreams and masking, with his knowledge, his true intentions. He does not help the dreamer to go through her own process with her own dream, but tells her instead what to think about her dream. He, for his part, stays within his own authority, causing himself to become 'puffed up' and distorted with his knowledge, which he projects onto the other's psyche.

This can be a dangerous story, repeated many times with many people. In contrast, if we teach people to actualize dreams, if we give others the skills to re-experience their own dreams, we will be freeing ourselves to better live our own lives and not other people's lives as well.

Or consider this example of an analyst who would make behind-the-scenes personality judgements about his clients, but would not say, when asked, how he arrived at those judgments. By what methods and processes was he analyzing his clients? Or where in their dreams was the evidence for what he was implying? Did he really know? Or was he keeping secret the analytic process by not teaching his clients the skills to determine their own growth and follow the guidance of their own dreams?

In contrast, the actualizing approach teaches the *methods* for individuating right along with the *process* for individuating.

Developing a Dreamwork Methodology

Until quite recently, those interested in working with dreams have not seen the need for a dreamwork methodology since the chief method for understanding dreams has been the interpretive one, whether the system be Freudian, Jungian or any other 'this symbol means this.'

However, new ways for working with dreams, which are not interpretive have now been devised, such as Gestalt process or Jungian active imagination. Yet no one we know of has so far attempted to draw together material from many sources to create a comprehensive dreamwork methodology. A methodology itself does not have to be particularly tied up with a specific school or psychology. We need to distinguish the methodology of an approach from the context and personality theory of an approach.

In the Jungian-Senoi experience, our primary focus is the dream and the specific dreamwork methods which help a dream come alive. We have been able to delineate more than fifty dreamwork methods, over thirty of which appear in this manual. Although we feel the methods described here present a fully developed and varied approach to dreamwork, we have not included all the methods of which we are aware. Among the notable exceptions are Gestalt dreamwork methods which, we recognize, can give people powerful direct experiences of a symbol but may not always help strengthen the ego or integrate the energies released. When a person is asked to become or identify with each part of a dream, we feel the ego identity and function gets lost in other personality dynamics. Also, the dialogue technique presented here may get to the same dynamics as Gestalt process work but at a more introverted level, and with the ego keeping its own separate identity. Using the Gestalt technique, a person may experience a release of archetypal energy, but he or she may not have much ego function left to integrate what is evoked.

Also, we do not include some of the more esoteric systems such as Tibetan dream yoga, which attempts to create a consciousness in which ordinary dream imagery is dissolved into light, a state no different from that of a developed, non-imagistic meditation. So much for what we do not include. Now for what we are most interested in.

Producing Specific Changes in Dream States

Dreamwork methodology is the complement to dream-sleep research. Most research emphasis has been placed on discovering the many natural facts about sleep and dreaming. This research has done an important service in educating the public to the fact of the psychological necessity for dreaming in every person, even those who do not remember their dreams.

But what is also needed is extensive research and development in the methodology of dreamwork. What effects do various dreamwork experiences have on the person and on his or her future dreaming?

Recently, there has been a new movement to develop dreamwork methodology. Ann Faraday's books, *Dream Power* and *Dream Game*, and Patricia Garfield's *Creative Dreaming* and *Pathway to Ecstasy*, have been significant contributions to the field. This manual and the Jungian-Senoi approach were developed independently of these sources and attempt to give a comprehensive dreamwork methodology.

As of 1980 we have been able to accomplish in our dream groups the following dreamwork experiences:

— *Producing a sequence of changes in a dream theme* so that a person using our dreamwork methodology not only redreamed the same theme on successive nights, but also experienced a sequence of dream changes which paralled her changes in attitude in the waking state.

— Learning to *fall back asleep and continue a dream.*

— Incubating a dream. *Evoking a dream on a given subject* which will produce the theme and imagery desired.

— *Experiencing synchronistic events in relation to dreamwork.* Synchronicity, or meaningful coincidence far greater than the laws of chance, occurs fairly often in our process, especially when what the person is dealing with is of great import. We do not consciously will synchronicity. It occurs naturally, as if confirming the depth and meaning of the process. As an example, the galley proofs of this edition of the book arrived in my mail box on exactly the same day as my fiftieth birthday.

— *Inducing the ability to remember dreams* in habitual nonrememberers.

— *Changing the nature of the dream ego's actions* in future dreams.

— *Confronting adversaries* and establishing creative relationships with them in future dreaming.

— *Ending recurrent dreams and nightmares* by bringing their dynamics to resolution.

— *Changing personal laws and archetypal patterns* which previously repeated themselves in the person's inner and outer life.

The chief methods used for producing dream-state changes are the following:

— **Direct Dream Re-entry** — a method whereby the person re-enters the dream meditatively and re-experiences its dynamics visually and emotionally, a process which leads to new developments and resolutions in the re-entered dream. This method also seems to produce profound changes in personality. Guided re-entry, versus self-re-entry, seems to produce the most profound changes.

— **Following the Dream Ego** — a method in which one analyzes carefully what the dream ego is doing and not doing in a dream in order to arrive at the dream ego's attitudes underlying such dream behaviour. Once the dream ego's actions and attitudes are clearly delineated, this knowledge can be applied to the waking ego's actions and attitudes.

— **Rewriting the Dream** — using the imaginative process to rewrite a dream with more creative responses on the part of the dream ego and other characters. This method, when done regularly with a chosen dream theme, can evoke changes in future dreams consistent with the direction of the dream rewriting.

— **Dream Incubation** — a method in which pre-sleep preparation is used to evoke a dream on a given subject.

— **Dialoguing with Dream Images** — this method evokes the conceptual level of dream symbolism and thus makes one conscious of new levels of possible meanings.

— **Working in Art, Drama, Movement and Song** — expressing and sometimes transforming dream energies and images.
— **Meditating to the Dream** — holding dream images in daily meditation, often waiting for spontaneous resolution during meditation or in a new dream.

Dreamwork Results at the Everyday Level

Many dreamwork experiences occur regularly, at an everyday level, for participants using the Jungian-Senoi approach.

People learn to *deal with current relationship issues* such as assertiveness, sexuality, and attractions to partners outside the primary relationship, anger, lack of communication, and psychic awareness of what the other partner is doing or thinking but not revealing. Thus, dreamwork can make an intimate relationship a lot more honest, open and interesting. It can also lighten the burden created in relationships by the participants' projection of inner material. In Jungian terms, intimates project their opposite sex characteristics, the *anima* or *animus* onto each other. But they may also project *shadow*, or self-rejected parts of themselves, as well as *parent-child* material. In fact, we seem to be quite capable of projecting onto our partners anything we have not yet integrated. Dreams will reflect fairly clearly what we are currently projecting, and dreamwork will enable us to deal with the projections without forcing the relationship to take the burden. Clearing the psychic air frees intimates to deal with other relationship issues, and, God knows, there are always many, even in an arena somewhat free of projected material. Much more could be said about the values of dreamwork in forming meaningful relationships, and many examples are given in other sections of this book.

Dreamwork has proven to be quite effective in processing *child-parent dynamics*. Basically, leaving home at age eighteen, or whenever we do it, is mostly an outer act of considerable courage. About ten years later, many of us find that, psychologically, we never left the original family. Those ten years out in the world have been spent reliving the old parent-child syndrome in other adult situations in which our authority figures and intimates take on our parental projections and attitudes while we ourselves remain rather childlike and immature. Around age twenty-eight, major crises in relationship, vocation, spirituality and mental processes may develop. A 'second graduation' is necessary and may take several years to get through. Working actively with dreams during this period, we notice the parents appearing in various forms which are not always pleasant. And also revealed are our most childlike and defensive behaviours. But as we work with this dream material and make creative changes also in outer situations, the dream parents will change, sometimes for the worse, mostly for the better. There will also be many children in the dreams to relate to and nourish. Our own outer children, and how we relate to them, will also be part of this parental landscape. And perhaps most crucial of all, the dreams and dreamwork will reveal to us the life-limiting patterns, attitudes and expectations taught over and over to us by our sometimes insecure and mixed-up parents. We will discover most likely that we have indeed been living out our parents' worst stuff.

Shake it off. See it in dreams. Dialogue with these inner parents. Find your own values and potentials and ways for living life. Get to the anger created in you by having had thrust upon you the unlived and rejected life of your parents and even grandparents. Needless to say, the outer relationships with the parents change significantly through this kind of dreamwork. And, if a parent is dead, he or she may still be there in dreams for you to continue to relate to and work things out with. Parents also may have repressed feelings toward their children which will show up in dreams.

Gradually, graduation from the parental syndrome comes. There are periods of much uncertainty, much suffering, much choice-making and much new creative potential. And when the syndrome is basically worked through, you will emerge into adult life following your own unique direction and destiny. Such a process is deeply moving, and need we say that it might occur at any period in one's life? The choice is always there to decisively solve the parental problem and move fully into the adult world.

Another basic aspect of the dreamwork experience is *building the creative ego*. The symbol most common to all dreams is the dream ego, the image of ourselves in the dream. In a dream we can observe the dream ego's actions and determine what attitudes or personal laws are motivating or governing those actions. Each of us has a part of our personality which functions as ego, as the choice-maker and awareness carrier of who we are and what life is all about. But since we ourselves are ego, we have a difficult time finding out who ego is. It takes ego to observe ego. Dreamwork, then, gives a clear viewpoint from which to observe and work with our own ego's choice-making abilities and attitudes.

Are we usually observing the action in the dream? Do we often run from adversarial situations in dreams? The answer is a definitive 'yes' for most of us. In outer, everyday life, do we not also act in much the same way? And if we are tentative, hesitant, uninvolved and fearful toward much that is life, what must be the quality of our daily living?

Dreamwork provides a fluid arena for seeing how we do and do not make creative and life-affirming choices. Dreamwork is the arena for experimentation and change because the process happens more on the inner than on the outer level. Making certain choices in the outer before they have been tested on the inner level can lead to disastrous consequences. In working with our dream egos, through such techniques as following the dream ego and dream re-entry, we can try out new ways of creative behaviour. We can face adversaries more directly. We can express deep emotions. We can explore new territory and people. We can relate in new ways. Then when we have become more conscious, we can, in the outer life, try out new ways of acting and choosing. The results for most people have been impressive, with real and lasting changes occurring in daily life. And, as if to confirm the ongoing process, new dreams come which show the dream ego acting and choosing in new, more creative ways.

Another major aspect of this approach is using dreamwork for *changing archetypal patterns*. This is perhaps most vividly seen in working with recurrent dreams or nightmares. It is our assumption that the recurrent dream directly mirrors an archetypal pattern in the psyche which is blocking the free flow of libido, or life energy. One example would be a woman's inability to relate fully to men sexually because of a truama pattern locked into the psyche by an early rape experience. This pattern might continually show itself in nightmares in which the original rape scene is re-enacted, or in recurrent dreams of terrifying, dominant males. There are many kinds of locked-in archetypal patterns other than those induced by trauma. Dreams show us what those patterns are and dreamwork helps us change them. Dream re-entry is usually our preferred method; and what seems to happen in an emotionally powerful dream re-entry is that the person is able to experience the pattern as it is, make new choices regarding it, and then experience, without forcing it, the pattern coming to a new, more creative level. A blocked archetypal pattern is one in which a situation is being aborted and cannot come to resolution. Thus certain archetypal patterns express themselves in recurrent dreams or dream themes because our psyches want and need transformation so that the energy of the psyche can flow more freely.

Many of the most profound and basic dreamwork experiences have been in this area, which concerns not only severe traumas, but the more normal locked-in patterns caused by childhood experiences, innate dispositions and life events left unresolved in the outer. People report such experiences as bringing former relationships to completion in an inner process and dealing effectively with strong ambivalences within the psyche. Sometimes such changes are dramatic, occurring with one dream re-entry, and sometimes they occur in a more gradual process involving work on a whole series of dreams.

Another major category of dreamwork activity is the experience of meaning or *relating to transpersonal or spiritual forces* reflected in the dream state. Most of us have at least some dreams in which spiritual symbols appear. Whether it be temples, crosses, gifts, treasures, mandalas, healing guides, high mountains, journeys into the cosmos, or even terrifying dream experiences of great abysses, atomic explosions and raging hell fires, we are all faced with symbolism of a nonpersonal and transcendent nature. Something out there really seems to exist which is much greater than ourselves. But how we relate to that something can become crucial.

In working with the more cosmic dream, one important thing to note is the dream ego's relation to these larger forces. Dreamwork in this approach means not only experiencing cosmic forces, but also relating to them meaningfully without being overwhelmed. Too many of us want the path of ecstasy without the groundwork of integrating whatever comes up into daily life.

We emphasize the spiritual aspects of the dreamwork process, but not because we are religious in the traditional sense of being part of an organized religion. We work transpersonally because these elements are clearly reflected in dreams, as they are also in life. Moreover, it remains a great mystery to us as to why the dream source seems to respond so wisely, individually and specifically to how we are or are not dealing with life. Through the dream and its dreamwork, many of us find a guiding power at work in our lives and at work also in the larger community. And through dreamwork, we have the chance to establish a creative and active relation to such a source. In the sense, then, of following a direction more meaningful than anything the ego can create alone, we work with dreams to develop a spiritual life. Such a process is and will always remain a great mystery.

Using dreamwork to deal with everyday reality is our last major category for the dreamwork process. One of the central values of dreamwork is developing a relationship to one's own inner authority. Dreams come from within, from one's own sources, and not from some outer authority, however, knowledgeable. The dream, then, coupled with a dream-actualizing methodology, enables people to become self-determining and self-directing in their daily lives. To be sure, outside support in the form of a dreamwork group or guide can greatly aid the process, but there is much that one can do on one's own.

What are my choices in this life situation? What is really going on here in this relationship? Why am I depressed? What can happen between this person and myself? Why am I acting this way? These and innumerable questions about daily life can be meaningfully worked with using dreamwork as a guide. Dream research seems to be indicating that we need to dream in order to stay mentally healthy. But we may also need dreamwork to become conscious of life and to become Self- or centre-directed, perhaps the most advanced state of a healthy mentality.

A Note of Caution

What we have been describing is all based on many peoples' dreamwork experiences, and any one person may feel a bit overwhelmed, as well as excited, by what is presented here. All of us are always beginners at many things. If you choose to use this manual in working with your own dreams, take things a step at a time. In one of the next chapters will be a detailed description for how to proceed from the beginning and move along at your own pace. There is much material here. It required steady work and gradual absorption to become effective. Your dreams also will help lead the way.

If for any reason you feel psychologically overwhelmed in working with your dreams please seek competent therapeutic help. How information from this manual is used is solely the reader's responsibility.

The Jungian-Senoi Approach

At the Institute we use the words 'Jungian' and 'Senoi' to describe certain major aspects of our approach. We consider ourselves Jungian because we emphasize the fact that the dream plays a central role in revealing to a person the potentials for his or her own *individuation*, or journey toward wholeness. Within the psyche of each person there seems to be a drive to realize one's deepest self, which Jung terms the teleological principle in the Self, or central archetype. Archetypes are innate energy clusters within the psyche which reveal themselves most clearly in dreams and other visionary experiences. We also derive from the Jungian tradition the methods of amplification (symbol inherency), association (symbol linking) and active imagination (evoking the spontaneous flow of images from the unconscious).

The Senoi aspect of our approach is based on the key ideas of altering the dream state and using dreams to create projects which directly contribute to individual and community life. The Senoi people of Malaya have gained a reputation, largely through the work of Kilton Stewart, for being an extremely peaceful society who used dreams to create harmony and well-being in their culture. Whether or not the Senoi actually worked extensively with dreams has been recently questioned. However, the 'dream people' of Malaya have become a symbol for the intention of a community to make dreamwork the guiding basis for social, cultural and personal lives. And it is now known that many cultures all over the world have used dreams as a basis for cultural and personal guidance. At one time, almost everyone had daily intercourse with their dream worlds, a reality which helped to bring us culturally to where we are today, and which survives mainly in folktales which must have originated 'once upon a time' as somebody's dream.

My personal introduction to Senoi dreamwork occurred when I was a therapist at St George Homes, where a daily dream session had been started to elicit inner material from otherwise hesitant, psychotic teenagers. The chief methods used at the time were working in art and doing outer-life projects based on dream content. Later, certain American Indian-based nature rituals were included, as well as a Jungian perspective as to what the dream symbolism might mean in terms of personal psychodynamics.

Shortly after leaving St George Homes to go into private practice, I founded the Jungian-Senoi Institute to embody an emphasis on developing dreamwork further, as well as to enhance the Jungian analytic process in working therapeutically with individuals. During the next two formative years in working with individuals, and especially dream groups and training classes, many new techniques were originated and others were further developed. During this period, major techniques such as following the dream ego and direct dream re-entry were created to complement already existing techniques, such as dialogue, working in art and amplification. It was then, also, that this manual began to take shape as the training text for dreamwork classes. At present, we have a small group of new dreamwork leaders who are beginning to lead dream groups both at the Institute and elsewhere. Also, the approach is now being taught in colleges and universities.

The Need for Dreamwork in the World

Today we are experiencing a new resurgence of interest in dreams. Perhaps continual crisis in the outer world has driven some people back to reliance on inner sources. Where else but in dreams, in the primary world of the inner, can we find the renewal and creative power to transform our outer world into a state of harmonious wholeness? Dreams and other primary intuitive experiences have always been a major means of discovering what is possible but not yet a reality. Certainly most past cultures have originated from the dream world. Have we, in fact, almost lost one whole evolutionary step by our modern neglect of dreams?

What leap of consciousness is needed to help us over the brink into a New Age? Must there not be a full and total movement forward by both the individual and the community? One fundamental requirement for anyone moving into the evolving New Age is the conscious acceptance of total responsibility for one's psyche. This means developing the habits and skills for self-reflection and owning all one's projections as they become known. My own darkness as well as my own light must be taken back from where my unconscious has projected them, so that I may integrate the energies within my own centre and search for wholeness. Dreams and dreamwork can be a major tool for such integration.

The actualization approach to dreamwork, as well as to certain other growth processes, may sound the death knell for the 'old school' interpretive approaches.

When a person is given a dream, is he or she not also given the potential to actualize the dream and thus discover its meaning?

Our fundamental position is that almost anyone can work with his or her dreams. The dream and the dreamworker ego together are authority for gaining the meaning of the dream. The dreamwork leader or analyst-therapist may have more skill and commitment to the process, but, still, no one can define the truth of someone else's dream.

The Choice to Individuate

Individuation is for all individuals who choose to realize their essential selves. It is not for the esoteric few, the variegated leaders and their bliss-laden followers. We will never get to where we need to go as one people, world united, unless we break the authoritarian pattern.

Any culture, any religion, any government, any school of psychology is in its infancy as long as it maintains the parent-child, expert-student, authority-follower, doctor-patient relationship as the primary one for interaction and learning.

There comes a time when the problems of childhood must be solved if there is to be maturity and true individuality as persons. The parent-child dependency relationship must be left with childhood so that the manifesting of the real and choosing journeyer can emerge confident, alive and able to deal co-operatively and creatively with Life and its needed steps into the future.

A Transformational Journey

Strephon's Introduction

The following dreamwork, life-work episode is included here as a major

example of a healing process using dreamwork as a guide.

Hilary came to Berkeley from Scotland in 1978 and worked with me analytically and in Institute training for nine months. She had previously had three years of therapy. She was now ready, although she hardly expected it at the beginning, to go through a major life transition.

Hilary arrived here with her husband and children. At the end of the year she would return to Scotland separated from her husband, but with most of the issues of their nine-year marriage worked through individually and in relationship counselling.

The key to this life change is not the outer situation, although Hilary's decision about marriage and family became a major testing ground for her. The key was, and is, Hilary's own inner development.

With the drowning of her father at the age of six, and the overwhelming circumstances following this event, Hilary became a traumatized and blocked individual. She was largely unable to express her considerable personal creativity and suffered from severe bodily symptoms such as migraine headaches and cancer of the cervix. She also found it very difficult to stand up for herself in life, being fearful of many things as a result of the unprocessed traumatic loss of her father.

The *key to healing* is to go through and re-experience the original trauma, face it passionately and completely, and bring it to resolution. This breaks the pattern in the psyche, resolves the blockage, and allows the life energy to move forward into vital channels.

The preparation and the actual trial of going through the traumatic experience requires considerable courage. Such a courage is often born of great desperation and great spiritual searching. Almost no one is able to enter the gates of transformation who does not have this courage and inspiration.

As described in what follows, you will see that we emphasize dreamwork as a chief way of manifesting the healing source and preparing the ego for the choices which only it can make. The use of considerable dreamwork and journalwork is the basis for such a healing event. The use of psychodrama is reserved for only the most transformational experiences. The choice to use psychodrama is based on the natural movement of the psyche and on whether the ego is committed to taking the plunge. The use of ritual is one of the most ancient forms of healing, evoking and containing the archetypes. Ritual, in the form of a funeral service, was used here to effect resolution and transformation. The psychodrama was used to bring out the repressed dynamics associated with the original trauma so that they could be fully experienced and accepted as reality.

The vision quest which followed the psychodrama represents going into nature meditatively and then letting things happen. Often what occurs serves to confirm and strengthen the healing process.

As you will read, a tremendous amount of synchronistic events coincided with this process. *Synchronicity* is when inner and outer come together to produce meaning. Negative synchronicity occurs when needed to give a push into consciousness. Positive synchronicity gives confirmation that a choice and an experience is absolutely right in terms of an individual's psyche and journey. Seen in this light synchronicity is one of the direct evidences for God, for a guiding power which intervenes and confirms our lives.

Hilary was extremely, though not totally, devoted to her analysis, having on the average about four hours a week, and doing, besides, considerable journal and dreamwork. Her cancer had already stopped through an operation and her migraines have now virtually disappeared as she has grown and learned to express her feelings and her journey much more fully.

I, myself, as Hilary's analyst, friend and teacher, was and am very moved by the experience. It gives confirmation to my approach to healing and echoes my dealing with certain very traumatic events in my own past analysis.

But read for yourself Hilary's account in her own words. Correspondence is welcome. Be sure you are dealing with the feelings aroused. Perhaps something here or elsewhere in the book speaks to your own journey?

Hilary's Story — 'In the Beginning Is an End, A Transformative Journey'

On Sunday, June 18, 1950, my mother was 500 miles away in the south of England, experiencing with my baby sister, the first holiday she had had in years. A stranger, a woman whom we did not like, was looking after us. My father, a country doctor, walked out of the house like any other day and I still do not remember whether I said goodbye to him or not. A few hours later he drowned at sea, in an accident, and a week later his body was recovered by deep-sea divers and brought ashore, unrecognizable from the time it had spent on the ocean bed. I was six years old.

First Dream: (1954–1959) *'The Hand' A Recurring Nightmare*
I am standing at the top of a high cliff. Below me is a stormy sea with huge waves crashing onto the rocks at the base of the cliff. Suddenly I see a hand appearing out of the water and I hear my father's voice crying out, 'Help me, help me, Hilary, save me, please save me!' I begin crying. I am reaching my right arm as far down the cliff face as I can, without falling over. I call, 'I'm trying to, Daddy, I'm trying to' — but I cannot possibly reach him. I wake into outer life crying and shouting out, each time at the same point. This dream started when I was ten and stopped recurring at fifteen.

Second Dreams: (1962–1963) *'Returning' Two Recurring Dreams*
a)   All seven of us, my mother and us six children, are seated round a long rectangular table, out in the back garden of my mother's house. We are eating a sumptuous meal. I am seated in the left corner — I look up and see in the opposite far right corner my father. He is eating and talking animatedly, just as though he had always been with us. He is wearing his Quaker doctor's 'uniform.' I get up slowly, not taking my eyes off him in case he disappears as quickly as he arrived. I walk round the table behind him. I cover his eyes gently with my hands, and say, 'Guess who it is, Daddy, guess who it is.' He replies, 'I'm not Daddy, I'm Robert!' I remove my hands, shocked, and look down at the upturned face of my younger brother — the brother I love to hate.

b)   The whole family are in the main room of my mother's house — all eight of us — my father has arrived back after all these twelve years of separation. He is in his Quaker 'uniform' again. He embraces my mother who looks young and radiant. He is talking and laughing, as we all are. There is a shared feeling of unity between us all. Later I sit in a quiet corner with my father. I feel angry and upset. I ask him, 'Why have you been away so long? Where were you? Why didn't you come back?' He says, 'Well, you see, Hilary, I got lost at the end of the war and I couldn't find my way back to all of you. I've been wandering in many lands.' I am not very satisfied with his answer, but I say, 'Well, never mind, at least you are back now.' He leans forward and says quite quietly, 'Well, no, actually I'm not, I have to go away again.' I am now eighteen years old.

1974–1976
I enter analysis, acknowledging to myself and the analyst that my life lacks meaning and direction and I feel in a constant state of 'living death,' anxious and morose, for increasing parts of each day. I have begun to experience severe bouts of migraine. I no longer sing, draw, paint, sculpt, write, sew or make anything with my hands. I feel that apart from relating with my children, life holds less and less meaning for me. The analyst turns out to be a Freudian in a Jungian disguise. The migraines last for several days at a time and become more and more crippling and frequent. The analyst dies quite suddenly of lung cancer at the time I am just beginning to express some of my really negative

feelings for her and the process, Freudian style. My feelings of grief and anger threaten to overwhelm me. I fantasize suicide and, again, only the presence of my children grounds me, pulls me back, presents reality as they ask to be considered. The day she dies of cancer I receive a letter from the hospital informing me that I have a noticeable 'cell change' taking place in my cervix, and I am to keep an appointment there in a few day's time. Eighteen months later I undergo a hysterectomy operation due to cancerous cells having penetrated my womb. My age is now thirty-two.

Third Dream: (1976) *'Life Imprisonment'*
I am in a large house in the country, it is half familiar to me, half not. I'm being pursued by my father who is trying to strangle me to death. I run frantically from room to room, he is a few steps behind me. I feel his hands near my throat as he tries to grab it and choke the life out of me. I run into the kitchen and slam the door just before he catches me. I lean against it sobbing with terror and slam the door just before he catches me. I lean against it with my full weight as he pounds on the other side. I try to prevent him forcing his way in. Suddenly his hands come through a gap in the door, which he has partially forced open. He grabs me from behind and I begin to choke as his fingers press hard on my throat. I am screaming and screaming but no sound comes out. I see the distant figure of my mother, at the back of the kitchen, looking like she did when I was small — she has the same hairstyle. I reach my arms out towards her imploring for help. She takes no notice, it is as if she cannot see what is happening. I lunge forward to try and free myself and I manage to do so. I run towards my mother and I say, 'I'm going to phone the police as he's gone crazy — he's trying to kill me.' The police arrive. There are policemen and psychiatrists and nurses, all in uniform. The police are in dark blue and the doctors and nurses in white. A whole group of men have appeared to take my father to Carstairs Hospital for the Criminally Insane. He has been committed there for life, and will never be free again.

I am standing outside the house while they go in to fetch him. He comes out, heavily flanked on either side by all the officials. I feel like a Judas, I have betrayed my own father.

As they come past me I cup my hands together and my father pauses to say goodbye. As he does so he very gently and carefully places something tiny, something precious into my cupped hands. He says, 'This is my gift for you, Hilary.' We are both quietly weeping. He then leaves in an ambulance.

I am now, by this time, working with another analyst who is Jungian inclined and introduces me to dreamwork and a whole new way of living my life on a daily basis. Dr. Winifred Rushforth is a very wise old woman in her early nineties, and through a wonderfully alive and creative relationship with this remarkable person and, by beginning to work with my dreams and face my 'nightmares' in inner and outer life, my life takes on new depth of meaning and direction. I begin to work intensively with myself. My individuation process has begun. But there is still a feeling of a deep void within — a desperate hunger — a thirst for more and a deeper questioning — a searching for my own source, spirituality, to give this form in my daily life.

1978–1979

This leads me to Berkeley, California, and in the autumn of, or fall of, 1978, I arrive at the Jungian-Senoi Institute for my first dream group meeting there, bringing with me a dream which heralds the new beginning and I begin my biggest 'adventure' yet. This dream came in the early morning of the day I attended this first dream group. Three major gifts were contained in this great dream. Firstly, a symbol, a jade stone, circular plaque, a work of art, was hanging on the Institute wall above what turned out to be, in outer life, the sacred place. Secondly, Strephon Williams appeared in this dream and though I had not met him yet in outer life, he and the Institute were just as I had experienced them, the man and the building, in my dream. Strephon was to become my new inner-outer guide, and a creative relationship of a depth I had never experienced, but had always strived towards, began. Thirdly, my father visited me again in this dream, and in outer life his spirit-ghost began to haunt my days with a greater and darker intensity than ever before. Part of this dream follows: I am now approaching my thirty-fifth birthday.

Fourth Dream: (22 October 1978) 'The Jade Stone Plaque'

I am at the Institute in my nightie as I have just stepped out of a dream to go to a dream group there. I am in a large wooden building which I don't recognize and yet I do find it familiar. S., whom I have not met before, is showing me around the place and introduces the group to me. There are six to eight men and women. Again, I do not know any of them and yet one or two of them seem familiar. One woman, small with short dark hair and a very open smiling face says, 'My son is at the Rudolf Steiner School' — I say, 'Oh! That is how I know you' and yet even this seems unreal and unlikely to me — though I feel warm towards her and pleased that she has recognized me. An old school friend, J., materializes out of the group and is very vivacious and noisy in her behaviour. She shows me a very quiet, white faced, withdrawn-looking dark-haired man and says something personal about him in a loud voice to me which makes me feel embarrassed and upset as the man shrinks away from her remark and our looking at him.

S. shows me a round shaped jade stone plaque hanging on the wall — it is mysterious looking, beautiful, green, irridescent, light, shiny — I go up to it and touch it lightly to feel it. S. is most happy about this and says, 'Yes, do touch it — that's great!' Again, I recognize this — art form — plaque and yet I cannot say how. There are brightly coloured cushions on the floor, many brilliant red ones. Around the walls are many objects, hand-made ones and art objects of every description. There are many dark rooms leading off from the main room, almost like a maze. The whole building is made of dark wood with a high ceiling and there is a light, airy quality, quiet, peaceful.

S. leads me through a labyrinth of rooms — cool, quiet and dark — to a back garden with much green foliage and soft light filtering through. I am very happy to be here — at peace — in harmony — I feel relaxed.and accepting.

Fifth Dream: (18 November 1978) *'Preparing'*
I am lying in a foetal position with a pair of hand-made wings made out of a wire frame and fine grey coloured gossamer material — J., my husband who is standing beside me, does not have any wings which upsets me ... I am going to Australia ... Four suitcases for the family ... One is full of food ... Baby clothes are put beside another one by J., his only contribution — which is of no help as there is no baby any more and N. has outgrown them . . . There is a light blue sleeping suit and light blue outdoor furry suit — I look at them before discarding them ... I am having to do all the packing — great strain — I am no more sure than anyone else what we should take ... Great panic about only short time left before the ship leaves ... My cousin Thom is with us — he is staying behind but he knows something about living in Australia — as that is where he lives — on Thursday Island — diving for pearls — he's lived there for one year now ... He is watching me — a little amused — going through these panicky preparations — he has a record player lying on a bed and several 'island' records lying around ... I haven't enough time but I want to put one of them on and listen to the song — they are strange looking records — large coloured area in the centres and thick ridged grooved record part ... They are 'island music', he says ... I put my yellow oilskin in one of the cases — I am not sure whether I'll need it but I think I should be prepared for stormy weather ... We go into a department store — I am quickly having to look for clothes I may need ... We go up and down and I buy a white bra, which I try on first, in the basement, but I can find nothing else ... I think a thick, warm, green corduroy dress might be a good idea — J. cannot seem to help — has no suggestions, no opinions ... I decide against it ... Time is running out — I still haven't finished the packing ... We are waiting to cross the road to go back to the house where I am packing, when a dark-haired young woman who is walking with three young men on the opposite sidewalk, suddenly falls clean over into the pathway of a passing car driven by a black man ... I am terrified — the car swerves and just misses hitting her lying there helplessly in the road ... She is lying curled up in a foetal position — she uncurls and gets up very quickly and walks on with the men as if it had never happened ... I am very perturbed by the incident — Why did she fall? — I wondered — and why did she pretend it didn't happen?

Hilary's Comments
This dream came to me at the time in my outer life when I was just beginning to accept that I was largely refusing to be responsible for my own life and my inner chosen destiny. My husband and I had begun to talk of the real misery and emptiness in our relationship.

I did much work with this dream over several weeks. All was deeply significant and I include here a small part of the dreamwork.

One of the dream tasks was to dialogue with my cousin, Thom:

Dialogue: 24 November 1978

H: Why have you come to me in my dream at this time in my life, Thom?

T: I have come to show you a way of living your life which is very different from the way you have been living it up until now.

H: This scares me, Thom, because I feel you are saying to me that I am facing a huge change and I am not sure how ready I am for this yet.

T: Yes, I am saying you are facing a momentous change in your life. You are going to see things as if with new eyes, hear things as if with new ears, think things as if with new hands, smell things as if with a new nose and taste things as if with a new mouth. You could be reborn, if you so choose and this is why you need your grey wings to start you on your Journey.

H: You are saying *my* Journey — not Emma's or Nina's or John's, but *mine*?

T: Yes, that is what I am saying. The four suitcases are yours, not anyone elses.

H: I remember the other day, I had a vision that I was waving goodbye to Emma, Nina, and John as I was staying here in Berkeley and they were leaving. This worried me because I thought of it as outer reality, whereas now I see it was on an inner level. I am staying here in Berkeley because it is here I am preparing for my inner journey.

T: Yes, congratulations! I thought you would never get the message. You and you alone must pack you own suitcases and carry your own journey yourself. You have already chosen to take your yellow oilskin for stormy weather and you have chosen a white bra which fits you well. What else are you going to take?

H: I need you to tell me this. I am very confused.

T: I have come to bring your further insight to help you in the preparation for your journey. I am your father's sister's son, and you know that when your father, a Pisces like you, went back into the sea never to return on land again, he left you a gift which you dreamt about two year's ago. You could not remember what the gift was at the time, but I have come to tell you now, that it was a pearl, and that the pearl represents your third eye, the eye of insight. You have known for a long time that you could use this gift, more precious than any of the pearls I have dived for in the same ocean which claimed your father, so what are you going to do about it?

Poem: 25 November 1978

> I feel a stirring within me
> a being
> so powerful and deep
> I gasp
> in wonder when I see
> its light

Inside of me
a flower is opening
up her petals
towards my Sun
I feel the petals
soft, moist and crumpled
begin the slow unfurling
in the dark towards the light
and I thank myself for letting go
to this new age —
the age of meaning.

Sixth Dream: (24 November 1978) *'A Beginning'*

1. I am on my way — I am all alone and I want to be ... I see my husband — I either wake up or I am dreaming still — He comes up very close to my right eye — I open my eyes and I glare ferociously into his — his eyes are open and he sees my look — I shut them quickly and go on ...

2. I am in a circle — a ring — something is burning — there are pebbles all around me — I am standing as if at the shore of some water — it is very dark, very close, the air feels pregnant with something about to happen ...

3. I wake up in a dream and I know I am Journeying — I am saying to myself with real conviction and I feel free — light — almost in harmony? — I am telling myself I must write this down in my journal before I lose it — forget it — I see myself writing in my journal — it is a shock to wake up and find I am still dreaming — I reach for my journal.

Comments

This dream was a Thanksgiving dream. As part of the dreamwork I wrote out an affirmation in large letters.

'I am committed to my own individual destiny. Wherever it leads me I choose to go. I am committed to finding my own truth, my own way, my own inner wisdom and direction. I am committed to my own Journey towards wholeness.'

I also made a clay figure of myself (Self) standing in the ring of pebbles, having first gathered the stones from San Gregorio Beach. I placed this symbol, so full of meaning for me, in the small sacred area of my room.

November 28, 1978

I continue working with the 'Preparing' dream. I am to dialogue with the young dark-haired woman.

H: Who are you?

Y.W.: I am a young woman outwardly, but really I am a little girl. I am a little girl because I am afraid to grow up, I feel more secure this way.

H: Why do you feel more secure being a little girl when you could be the same age as your outer self?

Y.W.: Because when I was a little girl outwardly as well as inwardly I experienced agonizing pain in many areas and from many directions, and just as I felt I could grow up a little, in spite of the pain, I suffered the greatest pain of all. This made me feel like not growing up any more, because I lost myself and the path I was walking on gave way and I fell over and part of me was crushed to death.

H: I want to understand you but I cannot quite seem to. What are you denying when you get up quickly after falling down and then nearly being killed?

Y.W.: I am trying to deny that I wanted the driver of the car to feel what it was like to kill somebody without meaning to, and have to live a life sentence imprisoned behind bars, as a result.

H: Why?

Y.W.: Because I feel that I killed a man like the driver even though I didn't mean to. I am a child in my feelings of revenge, though this revenge is that of living death for me.

H: So when the black man driving the car saves you by swerving, you are embarrassed and get up quickly?

Y.W.: Yes, I am embarrassed. This man who looks evil and I think is going to take his revenge on me, turns out to be good and not interested in revenge. I must try and pretend it didn't happen, or I will be found out.

Comments

The young woman is a part of me. What is this destructive thing in me?

Yes, she is a part of me. She is dreadfully self-destructive. She feels unbearable feelings of guilt and anger about her own evil forces within. She is very unreasonable, because even though I tell her she often has good reasons for her feelings, she cannot accept that deep within is a raw, open wound which makes her feel worthless.

I feel, because my mother rejected me so often, and then my father died and therefore rejected me or abandoned me, I told myself I must be an awful useless sort of person to be so unacceptable. I fear this is true, I have to look around for who I can blame, who I can punish. And the person who is always available is the inner, worthless person within me — I must stop her functioning at all costs — deny her — destroy her.

Who is the man?

Is the man the ghost of my dead father? I know very little about him because I have not allowed myself or been able to look at him until now.

I ask him why he missed the young woman who fell in the path of his car. He tells me that though he looks black and evil, he is not. He missed her because he saw her life as precious and full of potential, and though she seemed to want him to drive over her, he did not want to. He wants her to live.

Seventh Dream: (12 December 1978) *'The Circle and the Square'*
Strephon and I are struggling to lift a very large circle shape into a square shape ... Both are bigger than either of us and it is demanding a lot of energy and strength from both of us ...

Winter Solstice: December 16, 1978
At the Institute Winter Solstice Christmas celebration we all made a Creche. We drew, out of many papers, our own choice of which figure we were to make out of clay, wood, twigs and mosses, etc. I picked a paper which said, 'the baby' — so I was to make Jesus — the Christ child ... What joy, humility, fear all rolled into one, and what confirmation ...

I have a dream that night and as part of the dreamwork I write a poem born from the dream and made a reality in my day. I dedicate this to Strephon Kaplan Williams and our working together:

Conception December 19, 1978

> The seed I have waited for
> has been sown through you
> in me
> In the dark moist labyrinth
> of my inner womb
> I receive and tend this seed
> more precious to me
> than any earthly jewel
> and rare beyond belief
>
> My newly discovered patience
> allows the dark mysterious growth
> towards the light
> of this most awesome birth
> With the mother's inherent sense
> of the Now the right time
> I wait
> fearfully
> tenderly
> in silence
> for the dawning
> of new life

Eighth Dream: (New Year's Dream, 1978) *'I Am Becoming'*
I am in a growth centre, like a Scottish growth centre called the Salisbury Centre, only it is in Berkeley. There is a meeting being held there, to go over what has been achieved during the past year. There are many people there, but the ones who stand out are — myself, my close friend, Mary, Mary's first

and second (present) husbands, my husband John, my two older sisters, Sue and Lisa, Winifred, my last analyst and dear friend, Strephon, my present guide-analyst and a young woman leader from the Scottish growth centre.

A psycho-drama is being acted out of a young child of six having to witness her young mother go through torment. Two actors are playing the parts of mother and child. The rest of us are participating on a feeling level. I am very upset and deeply moved. I see the child's bewildered agony — I feel it. My oldest sister, Sue, is beating the ground with clenched fists and kneeling on it with her eyes shut. Lisa is behind me and to my right, so I cannot see her, but I feel her sitting on the floor in a large meeting hall.

Afterwards, I stand up and tell them my very positive reactions to their attempts to live together and work as a community. Mary joins in half way through and agrees with what I am saying. I say that I feel they have grown considerably since I was away last year. Winifred is very moved by my 'speech'.

Then there is a small general discussion on the future running of the Centre, and an appeal is made for money to help further their future growth and existence. A young man comes forward with some hand-made badges — circular with a red emblem on a white background. We are to donate money and pin a badge on ourselves to show our commitment.

We move to a long rectangular table where there is food and drink laid out. I place all my money on the table. I have 83 cents which I count out. At first I am going to give 50 cents — then I decide to give 80. This is recorded in a book, as are everyone's contributions. We all begin to eat and drink. I am just reaching for some food when Mary's first husband begins deriding Mary, being heavily sarcastic verbally. Mary becomes distressed and humiliated in front of the other people. He gets hold of her arm and pulls her hard away from the table. She attempts to pull her arm out of his grip but cannot because she is so physically frail. I decide to try and help her straight away. I move between them and I say, 'Leave her alone. Stop bullying her. She is trying to work as I am. I am working on my Centre — I am Becoming.' He falls back rather in awe at my strongly felt statement. I see Strephon standing near me and I know he understands what I am saying.

I get hold of Mary's arm and guide her out of the room and take her home to rest.

While I am there with her, I am visited by Winifred. She tells me that the music performance is about to begin and I have my part to play in it.

I hurry back to the Centre. I sit with Emma and Nina. Emma is a little flustered, she does not know the piece of music, how will she play it? I feel quite calm and tell her she will manage. We are sitting high up in the brass section of the orchestra, among the horns. Though I think I am to sing a solo part again, for the first time for many years, Strephon is also in the orchestra, in the string section — we nod to each other, as our eyes meet.

Three hours later I dream:
John is packing a suitcase. I am leaving him alone to do it himself. My sister Lisa is a little upset at my reaction, she attempts to help John, but he does not want her help.

He comes along a corridor to talk with me before he leaves. He stands with his back to me and makes some comment about Lisa 'flapping around like a mother hen.' I say that she does not really understand the situation. ''After all, most people in marriage relationships do not ever reach this point — they keep away from their feelings.'' He does not like hearing this as it is separating me from him.

Comments
This dream arrived as a gift in the early morning of the first day of the New Year. I felt humbled and blest and moved by it — it came as a response — a clear song from the Other.

I felt there was a destiny choice involved here and the pain and deep confusion I had been experiencing about whether I had the courage necessary to respond to what I really passionately wanted and was beginning to find really meaningful in relation to working towards becoming a therapist in my own right. This had been very much in my mind and emotions when I fell asleep the night before this dream.

Two major things were to take place as a result of this dream and the dreamwork I did with it. One was, that I chose to begin the training at the Jungian-Senoi Institute a week later and secondly, I decided, with Strephon's warm support and encouragement to go through my own psycho-drama experience, re. my father's death, with four people who were also undergoing training at the Institute. I gave out this invitation:

Transformation — A Beginning

Gayle — Harriet — Nick — Hilary — Strephon

This is to invite you to participate in a psycho-drama process to take me through my childhood experience. It is a therapeutic process which will require you to follow Strephon's directions. Please would you bring your journal and a healing symbol if you have one.

Trustingly,

Hilary

Thursday, 28th January 1979
10:30 – 1:30
At the Institute

Ninth Dream: (24 January 1979) *'The Box with ''I'' On It'*
Strephon gives each of us, including himself, a box with a lid on it and a small

silver button catch to hold the lid on tight. If we so wish, we (the psycho-drama group) can use the box how we want, but he suggests we use it for our sad and traumatic experiences and that we put in writings and symbolic objects. On the outside of my box there is a capital letter ''I'' written there.

This same night, the eve of the psycho-drama, I had a vision.

I fell asleep lying on top of my bed covers. I had lit three candles, two tall white ones and a small white one in a pot container. I woke up — or did I? — hours later, because I heard and felt someone or something open the door and stand just inside the room, at the foot of my bed. At first, I decided to ignore it, as I felt very tired and did not wish to talk, but suddenly there was a very bright light from the candles and I woke up and half sat up and saw an incredible light. The two tall candles were throwing up flames of about four feet high in the air — I gasped aloud and I wondered if I were dreaming and I looked to the door which was now closed and there was nobody there. I fell back, dazzled by the brilliance of the light and in real awe at what I was experiencing. Surely this was my father's spirit?

January 25, 1979

My youngest daughter Nina, aged 5½, had a 'terrible' dream on the night of January 24th, 'I was in the desert looking at flowers and a whole lot of rattlesnakes came at me and I cried and cried and they bit me and then I woke up because I was so scared.' She drew a picture of this in her dream journal.

Just before I enter the Institute to go through the psycho-drama, I write in my journal. 'I am now so nervous I am almost being sick. Memories of my mother and father lurk around. I try pushing them away, I partially succeed. I am terrified about the psycho-drama — what I have chosen to do — and yet I know I am going to go through it, because my healthy part wants to.'

Psycho-drama: January 25, 1979

I am the first to arrive. Strephon is there preparing the room. I notice six pink-red roses in a vase. We place five cushions in a circle on the floor. I have a feeling of readiness; we are all here now sitting on the floor together. We each share our healing symbols and why we brought them. Strephon briefly states how we are working very closely together, he and I, and then hands things over to me. I say how the psycho-drama has evolved. I begin to relate a little about myself, my parents and each of my brothers and sisters, and then from there I begin to re-remember what happened on the day my father left our house, June 18th, 1950, a Sunday morning, never to return again. A few hours after he left he drowned at sea, in an accident in which two other men lost their lives. This was the sixth year of my life.

It was very easy for me to let go. I go back all those years and feel my way through those few days surrounding his death, and then the following weeks which were every bit as traumatic as the actual event. I am aware of the truly awful confusion, the shock and pain of knowing so much at such a tender age and yet no adult confirming this, instead denying me my intuitive power both in fear, a kind of embarrassment and from ignorance of how to deal with it. I knew my father had died, but for several days this was not confirmed. When I was eventually told, briefly, matter-of-factly, that was it; no questions, no answers, no more talk. Silence within and without. This was the most traumatic experience of all really. I did not see his body, nor attend the funeral service and I did not know what dead meant anyway.

One week later I was sent away on my own. I got out of the long-distance bus at the wrong stop, and in this strange place hundreds of miles away from the place and people I knew and loved, I cried with grief and terror until an elderly man gently directed me back to the right bus again for me to continue a truly hellish journey to the 'right' destination. The day I left I cried in my baby sister's ear, but kept the 'stiff upper lip' that I felt was expected of me for everyone else. While away from my mother and all my brother and sisters I experienced a daily terror that they would 'die' too; I would be left alone, be as abandoned as I felt now. When I returned it was to a new house, a new village in a different part of the country and all traces of my father ever having been alive had gone. His wedding ring and salt-encrusted watch were the only things I could find and even these were put away, in my mother's top left-hand drawer, the handkerchief drawer which smelt of oak and lavender, in the big chest-of-drawers in her bedroom.

To be able to share this deep deep pain and bewilderment and to experience four other people weeping with me was not only very moving but was deeply healing, too.

Then Strephon's voice comes through telling me that i am going to see my father die, I am going to be able to bury him. I feel very frightened, but I know I want to experience this, I always did, I need to face it.

Nick is to be my father, Louis. Yes, this is so fitting, Nick holds some of the really positive as well as the negative qualities that Louis did. Strephon is to be the two men who couldn't swim, crying out for help. Gayle is to be Lisa, aged 7½, my older sister and beloved playmate for many years. Who will I choose to be by the ocean with me watching my father's death? Of course, Kate, Kate Hill, strong, earth-bound, feminine Kate, one of my positive mother models and now close friend. Harriet is to be Kate.

Nick is terrified about being Louis. We hold each other. I gain such positive strength through being able to love him, care for him and support him.

And so we go through it. Again it was easy, no, it was not easy, it was utterly natural to let go and enter the drama, the life drama, *my* life drama. The most transforming part of all for me was when Nick/Louis had to go to try and save the two men screaming for help as they drowned, and I knew he had to, and I was able to love him, to feel that love and then to let go of him and to feel this, too. I felt Louis through Nick. And this became real for me and what transformation was felt in the matter of a few moments! To be able to help Gayle/Lisa cry and feel it, too, which Lisa hadn't been able to do at the time. And to be able to experience Kate/Harriet hold me, lovingly, and crying herself which my mother had not been able to share with me.

And then the body is brought ashore, and I can lay my head on his chest and I can kiss his forehead and stroke his face and caress him in my arms. He lies there and he is Louis again for me at this point.

And so to the funeral service. So movingly and sensitively conducted on all levels through Strephon. I choose the people I want to have present there. I light the candle, white in a red glass holder. We each hold a rose in our hands. Strephon's deep voice reading the beautiful words from Ecclesiastes, Chapters 1 and 3 and his own words about Louis the man, his qualities both light and dark, very meaningful for me, very fitting and true. We place our roses one by one on Nick/Louis' chest.

And now the ending, which in fact becomes a beginning.

We spend a fifteen minute quiet time writing in our journals and then share our thoughts and feelings about the experience we have all participated in. Everyone has something meaningful to express about their own father. It is deeply moving. I sit there feeling at one, and very close to all of them.

The Synchronicity Surrounding the Psycho-drama

1. The candle vision — my father's spirit entering my room the night before the psycho-drama.
2. Nina's snake dream that same night.
3. At the exact time the psycho-drama began Nina was taken to the school office complaining of a choking sore throat. It became so bad she had to be taken to a friend's home until her father could collect her. It lasted the exact time of the psycho-drama.
4. On January 25th, 1978, at exactly the same time that the psycho-drama began one year later, I entered an operating theatre in Edinburgh, Scotland, for a hysterectomy operation. This I only realized after.
5. My father, Louis Fitch, died on the same day and at the same young age, 35 years, as the man he had been named after, his great uncle Louis Edgar, a gifted French pianist — June 18th was the date.
6. The four people who went through the psycho-drama process with me shared in this real explosion of synchronicity.
   a. *Harriet*, who was Kate *Hill* in the psycho-drama, had the day before made up a name to test out the Institute's phone answering service. The name she chose was Jeanette *Hill*.

      Harriet's brother's birthday is the same date as the psycho-drama — January 25th.

      Harriet's baby daughter's birthday is March 9th, the same date as my father's birthday. Years ago, Harriet had her first psychic reading and she was told that in a former life she was a French male pianist who died young.

      Harriet bears uncannily similar qualities to Kate Hill and also some very similar life experiences.

Nobody, including myself, had known that I would choose Kate to be with me in the psycho-drama process and I had never mentioned her to anyone present at it before. None of them, apart from Strephon, knew anything about my father or the way he died, etc.

b. *Gayle* chose to bring a healing symbol from the ocean. She did not know how my father had died. The ocean had brought the shell to her 10 years earlier — she passed it on to me at the end of the psycho-drama, as a gift from the sea.

She holds many similar qualities to my sister Lisa.

c. *Nick*, like me, is the third member of a family of six. Again, he holds many similar qualities to both Louis and my brother James. He feels like a 'blood' brother.

d. *Strephon* experienced traumatic separation from his parents at the same age as me, six years old, had similar boarding school and Quaker influence as I did, experienced having gifted, neurotic parents as I did.

7. My other daughter, Emma, aged $7\frac{1}{2}$, three nights after the psycho-drama had taken place, on January 28th, 1979, had the following dream. Neither of my children had known Louis as he had died 29 years ago.

'Nina and me are in Grandpa Louis' shop. I ask him if we can go for a walk down the road and he says "yes." We walk down the road until we come to a huge main road with an island in the middle and then another road after that — so there were two roads which were full of traffic so we couldn't cross on our own.

I asked a man if he would help me over the road and he said "yes," he would, and he picked me up, just like this — one under each arm and walked over the road carrying me. When we got over I felt we had come too far maybe, so I asked him if he would take us back again and he said "yes" and he did. Then we walked down a hill and at the bottom there was a mother driving a car and three teenage daughters. They were baddies and they held onto our arms through the windows and asked us if we would like to go to their house and we said "no" but then the car started off and they took me with them. And they took us into their house and tied us up. And we waited and waited for Grandpa Louis to come and finally he did and Nina and me ran downstairs to him. But one of the daughters had a big axe in her hands and she hit Grandpa Louis with it and split him in two and killed him. And Nina and I cried and cried and we were left alone — we were all alone — the police came and took away the mother and the daughters. And then an old man came and we told him what had happened and he took us home to our mother and we told Hilary all about it.'

New Life — The Vision Quest

I left to go straight to the ocean for my own Vision Quest — for time to be on my own — to meditate — reflect — to absorb the last hours' experience and the significance of what I had just lived.

My day beside the ocean, January 26th, 1979, will be forever imprinted on my soul. I share a little of that day here, the rest is not for telling.

It was a journey all of its own. It began, up Mt. Vision where a small grey bird with a white streak on its left side, came up to me, cocked its head on one side and asked me to stroke it — which I did. Tenderly I stroked the frail form with its silky feathers and honoured I felt to be allowed to do this. Through this small wild bird I once again got in touch with the child of nature part of me. I was brought up in the country and as a child had run free in the hills and beside the lakes and streams and into the woods of rural northwest England — this was a joyous self and the joyful child soared free again, on top of Mt. Vision — the elevation, the intense blue sky, no other human being around — just myself, a small wild bird and huge expanse of ethereal skies, earth brown, green hills, distant purple peaks, and a breathtaking view of the ocean stretching forever into the horizon. I feel at home — at one with nature as I walk along the ridge. But the ocean calls me and I decide I must go to its edge.

Again, I am the only person there. I walk along the water's edge — white crested waves roar and crash on the sand — the tide is full in.

I find a piece of wood in the shape of a crucifix and there is a human face of despair whorled into the wood and two arms up in the air — it shrieks — I find myself singing the hymn 'There Is a Green Hill Far Away.' I keep singing the same bit over and over again — 'Where the dear Lord was crucified,/Who died to save us all./We may not know, we cannot tell, What pains He had to bear/But we believe it was for us/He hung and suffered there.' I walk along the sand and talk to my father for the first time for years and I sing him a Scottish folk song for him to hear what a beautiful singing voice is in me.

I come across death. A huge, hideous, very dead sting-ray. Part of its right side is missing. It is lying on its back so I turn it over with my foot to see what its front — top-side — is like. Even more hideous — two slit-like eye sockets, purplish coloured leathery-looking skin, and a very thick ropy tail — ugh!

I go towards the cliffs in spite of the ominous mumbles and spitting noises they emanate. Small bits of stone and rubble spew out at regular intervals and I am ready to flee if I have to!

I come upon death again. I feel heavy of heart when I see this one. A huge, blown-up, black and white cow had plunged to its death earlier. It lies on its back with its neck reared back and its head is buried in the sand. All four legs point stiffly upwards. I feel very overwhelmed and awed by the violence of its death, but I make myself go straight up and really look at it. I am struck by the fact that it is sexless, no sign of whether it was once male or female — though possibly something I saw were what remained of teats — I was not sure.

I go and sit down. I am weary by now of the inner dialoguing going on inside me. I struggle over my relationship with my husband — we are nearer to separating than ever before. I question any and every relationship I have and share with others. I question where I am going now? Where and what is my destiny, etc.

I fall asleep in the path of the full midday sun. Two and a half hours later I wake up and feel rested, calmer, full of a sense of being alive and very well.

I walk back along the water's edge. As I look out over the water, I see a crystal clear image of a large silver fish leap clean through an emerald green wave, out and up, up, up into the air, before diving back in again. I am half way back and begin to see on the horizon a few other human forms. Suddenly, right between my feet, a jet of water spurts up out of the sand and shoots up about 5–6 feet in the air — it falls away again rapidly. I gasp out loud and stand very still, just in case it happens again! Neptune, you who rule my Piscean depths, surely have a hand in this?!

I returned late afternoon to Berkeley. I had spoken to no one since 8:30 a.m. Twelve hours later my husband told me he would leave the house — we were to separate, as soon as he could find a room somewhere. One week later, he moved out — another end, another beginning.

Conclusion

1. The increasing richness of my dreams and visions. Gifts which bring great healing meaning — not always joyful — also painful — dark and light — but the two intermingling now, holding, containing of opposites within.

2. Increasing, growing ability to live what I am and am becoming.

3. A depth of meaning in my life to which I am committed from the depths, the essence of my being.

4. A greater ability to relate meaningfully, enrichingly, satisfyingly with others — not just with the ones I love, care for, but with the collective, too!

Strephon's Conclusion

There is nothing I can add, either as a person or as a therapist, except that from experiences like Hilary's I believe profoundly in the transformational process. Hilary is back in Scotland for a year and continues to pursue her journey. She writes of how strongly her experience has lasted and continues to be part of that resource which supports her as she moves forward in life.

Perhaps not everyone needs to undergo transformation in such an emotionally moving way. But I suspect that even those who have not been visited with severe trauma in childhood will experience severe trauma in adult life.

How much better it is not to wait for death and dying to do it to us? The traumatized may be the lucky ones among us. For theirs is a 'forced transformation.' Those who have it easy or seek absolute safety and security can avoid extreme pain and therefore transformation. But in the end they will either die dulled to life and its meaning or suffer trauma in the final spaces of life when they are little prepared for it.

Fortunate is the person who realizes that the time for transformation is now and chooses not to wait for accident, sickness or dying.

We have, of course, today another form of trauma besides suffering a major sickness of loss through death, and that is the trauma of divorce, whether actually legally married or not.

Major relationship breakup is a primary arena for those still in the full vitality of life to go through the transformational process by dealing fully with the reality, loss and pain involved.

How can I face the full extent of my personal suffering? How can I use it to completely come to terms with myself as I really am and transform myself into a new and deepened person?

Similar procedures as those used with Hilary can be used to guide a person through any of the major traumas of life into transformation.

But there is still one other way to go through the transformational process, the 'second birth.' And that is through consciously chosen rites of initiation and transformation, a truth recognized by most major religions.

Ongoing intensive dreamwork and meditative, therapeutic and ritual experiences are what we work with at the Institute. We are reminded of the ancient Aesculapian healing cult of Greece to which people came from all over the known world to undergo personal transformation. In those rites having a healing dream was a central part of the process.

There is much wisdom lost to us today. But the mysteries continue as we seek transformation individually and as a one-world culture. Perhaps much more is possible than any of us have ever dreamed of manifesting?

Relating to the Journey

What feelings and values are being aroused by what you have read so far?

Without a doubt, Hilary's story is moving to many people, not only because of what she has had to deal with and transform, but also because of the deep sense of journey within her life.

A sense of journey means for me living life consciously and in tune with an evolving destiny which one chooses to allow to permeate one's life. As in Hilary's story, there may be guiding forces at work within and without. Why not choose to relate to and manifest these forces in one's own living? We are concerned with dreams and dreamwork specifically because the spiritual factor, the sense of being directed by sources other than the ego, seems to show through so strongly in what comes in the night.

What Gives Life Meaning?

What gives life meaning? is always a major question. Is it not enough to live life fully? This is the humanist and existential position. From this position we might use our dreams only for solving personal problems and doing things we want to do in life. Our egos and our wills would still be dominant. We would enter the mine of our souls and take out the ore for our own use. We would then be living in a personalistic universe.

Why not instead enter the cave, sit there and wait for communication with whatever dwells there, and then emerge with a greater understanding and set of values to be manifested in our daily life?

Is it enough, really, to live life fully with life itself as the goal? Or do we live in order to experience an ultimate meaning which transforms and transcends life?

To live merely the biological and psychological life is to die from too much life. Yes, we can choose to become fully alive, but no life lived only for itself can take into account the meaning of death. Death is the great rectifier. Death is that which gives meaning to life. Death is the truth which makes of life a lie.

Consider that each night, when we give over to sleep, we are letting go of our daytime consciousness, that we are giving up control, that we are in fact dying. We die nightly to the day life. How many of us fight this little death by eating, reading, staying up late, or otherwise numbing ourselves to the fact of needing to die daily to life? And how many of us wake in the morning dead to the night, wake without the memory of a dream, that jewel of the night which transcends the little death?

Where has the night gone?

What do I bring from it to the new life of my day?

To waste the night is to waste a third of our lives. To use or neglect the night is everyone's choice. If I am so caught in my day that I neglect my night, what am I? What have I chosen? What dominates my life? We die in sleep. To awaken with the dream is to experience the rebirth which makes new life possible and which also honours death as a great transformative power.

Therefore, do I search for that which is stronger, more central than the living of life?

For me, such a quest becomes the journey. The journey where and toward what? Great epics and myths tell of it. Biographies of significant people show how a sense of journey can be manifested in an individual's life. And history itself, whether of ideas or events, can illustrate that some direction more significant than the individual guides and forms us all.

The journey toward wholeness is a Jungian way of describing individuation — the journey toward realizing my destiny, be it great or small. This journey of mine is a great urge within myself to realize the greatest meaning, to realize the greatest sense of relationship to all things which make up the universal web, the core of integration within existence itself.

On the everyday level, in the arena which grounds me, to live the journey fully means committing myself to, and working with, certain fundamental assumptions.

Some Key Principles for the Journey

Within each moment there is a potential for meaning which can be realized if I choose to manifest it and make it conscious. Nothing, not even the greatest adversity, is without its larger relation to the whole. I can, with all the strength available to me, choose this larger whole, of which each moment is only a part.

Within my life and the life of each person is an essential destiny prompted by a spiritual factor transcending myself and beyond my choosing. Something is there, a guiding force, which influences my thoughts and actions, and desires from me the greatest individuation possible. I choose, whenever possible, to become conscious of this source, and I choose also to manifest this source in any way I can.

I choose to process, rather than hide from or cut off, whatever comes up in my life. Within this context there is only one evil and that is the evil of avoiding some aspect of reality. For such avoidance leads to greater destructiveness than if I face and deal with whatever comes my way. And in order to be able to process within the totality of life, I must seek to be as real, honest and open as I can in communicating and acting with those involved.

I choose not to have my ego, with its images, attitudes, wants and needs, always come first in everything. Yet, I must not debase or weaken my ego, my choice-maker, but I must continually strengthen it for the purpose of helping to manifest a purpose and a process greater than its own.

As part of my overall commitment to the journey, I will continually seek to improve my relation to source by such endeavours as dreamwork, meditation and creative action. As many inadequate personality characteristics as possible must either be sacrificed or transformed in order to accomplish this larger journey into the fullness of personality and of life-death itself.

The journey is for those who wish to take it. Merely being spiritual, or immersed in transcendent experiences, will not put us on the journey. The journey takes us somewhere, and in order to find one's place, one must choose to centre, not on the ego, but on the larger totality.

Some Journey Sayings

— To live, die and be reborn.
— The Journey compels us. The Choice inspires us.
— Love yourself and you will love your neighbour.
— If we do not resist the good, we will not resist evil.
— Even feeling must be validated by action.
— Do not have visions if you are unwilling to be responsive to them.
— Doing is the ecstacy of being.
— To be at peace with ourselves means resolving the wars within.
— A well-made choice is life itself.
— It is hard to give up that which we would like to be doing for that which we are good at doing.
— It is hard to give up that which we are good at doing for that which we are needed to do.

— Destiny is what we choose to do with fate.
— The only cure for idealism is reality itself.
— Do not regret anything you cannot change.
— I was born to die but I die to live.

PART II
Dreamwork Methods

How to use this Manual

Welcome to an adventure!

What you see in this book is a complete and practical approach to dreams developed out of hundreds of people's most profound dreamwork.

We do not really know the source of dreams. But we do know the significance and profound meaning which can come from dreams and dreamwork. In this manual you will find thirty-five of the most central dreamwork techniques developed at the Jungian-Senoi Institute and elsewhere.

This manual is designed in a step-by-step format to introduce you to the basics of dreamwork. You may, of course, simply read this book to gain inspiration and knowledge about this field. At another level, you may return over and over again to the material here, as you dream your life onward, and use what is presented to process more and more fully your dreams and your life. You may be working alone, or with friends, or in individual therapy or analysis, or in a dreamwork class or group.

One of the most typical statements from people who have trained themselves in this approach is that they have learned an important new set of skills for processing and enhancing their own growth.

But people gain not only skill in working with dreams, but also an intensity of personal experience which puts them profoundly in touch with their own source guides. They may experience through dreamwork a whole new

development in consciousness and personality.

To process is everything.

It is not enough to live, to experience life. To be fully alive we must also reflect on life. And we go beyond reflection to integration. The dream source is always sending us dreams which point to the most meaningful potentials for transforming aspects of our lives.

We must first go to the inner before going to the outer.

We are, most of us, stuck in, identified with, outer events and circumstances, and therefore we are more reactive to, than choiceful about, whatever happens to us. Through dreamwork we use the dream as the arena for first experiencing potentials before we go to the outer life to manifest them.

Developing Your Dreamwork Methodology

The sequence for presenting dreamwork methods in this book has been designed to launch you gradually deeper and deeper into dreamwork. We suggest that you follow the sequence to the best of your ability until you have re-experienced a number of dreams. You may wish to use a few techniques on one dream or take a different technique for each dream. After you have worked with the techniques for a while, you will find most effective the use of a combination of them with each dream.

Each major method has a chapter devoted to some of the issues surrounding the method. This is usually followed by a detailed example of how someone used the method on a dream. Next will be a separate section called 'Dreamwork Entry.' This is a specific step-by-step procedure for using the method and evaluating the results.

The Central Techniques

We have found that the most central and basic dreamwork techniques are the following:

— The Jungian-Senoi Dream Task
— Dream Incubation
— Objectifying the Dream
— Key Questions
— Following the Dream Ego
— Dialogue
— Symbol Immersion
— Bringing Resolution to the Dream State
— Direct Dream Re-entry
— Outer-Life Dream Actualization or Outer Dream Tasks

Let us call these the 'basic ten'. If you learn these well by using them over and over again with your dreams, you will be well into your dreamwork. We note also that there are many other important techniques in this manual. We have, for example,

— Remembering Dreams
— Symbol Amplification
— Rewriting the Dream
— Choice-Making from Dreams
— Dreamwork in the Arts
— Carrying the Dream Forward
— Journalwork and Dreams
— The Method of the Four Quadrants
— Metaphorical Processing
— Transpersonal Dreamwork
— Dream Meditation
— Transforming Nightmares

Please be aware that it is best to use a variety of dreamwork techniques as well as to work on a variety of dreams. The ten basic techniques should be used regularly and often in combination.

For fully developing a dream's potentials do combined dreamwork. The standard sequence is usually as follows:

— Objectifying the Dream
— Key Questions
— Dialogue
— Dream Re-entry
— Outer-Life Dream Task Actualization

This sequence may take one or two hours. Considerable time is needed to get into fully re-experiencing your dream. But it will be worth it in terms of new consciousness and the changes in your personality and life which result. You will want to do combined dreamwork with what you feel to be your major or high-energy dreams, which may occur once a week or at least once a month.

If you have only half an hour for working with a dream, using one or two of the following methods usually seems to work best.

— Key Questions
— Dialogue
— Dream Re-entry
— Outer-Life Dream Task Actualization

When you have only a few minutes, what do you do?
Write the dream down, if possible.
If you do key questions, simply list the most important questions or issues raised by your dream.

If you choose dialogue, pick the dream symbol with the most energy and ask it questions and write automatically whatever comes into your mind. This method seems to be the preferred one for many people and the one which most easily produces new consciousness.

If you use dream re-entry, sit quietly in a meditative state, with eyes closed, and see again that part of your dream which has a lot of energy for you. Your dream may then come more alive and the resulting experience will produce meaning and insight for you.

If you take outer-life dream task actualization as your method, choose some dynamic from your dream and formulate a specific action you will carry out during your day or week.

Is this helpful? There is a tendency, when faced with so many methods and experiences, to feel overwhelmed. Where do I start? Can I really work on my own? Will I be successful? Will I get overwhelmed by something coming up which I feel I am not ready to handle? So many questions and so few answers. Do not get lost in your doubts, your resistances and your ability to sleep through anything. Let your natural enthusiasm for new life be evoked and use that energy to move yourself to new levels. Get in there and start somewhere. There will be a response. You will most likely find help for what you are doing.

Certain techniques will have more appeal to you than others. Also, some techniques feel safer to many people. For example, dialoguing with a dream figure takes some letting go by your ego, your conscious directional side, but not as much letting go as in dream re-entry. Dream re-entries can bring up fearful things as well as such outer symptoms as a feeling of being overwhelmed, dizziness and various strong emotions. Do only what you feel safe with, and risk more as you become grounded in what you are doing.

If you study the material and use the procedures on your own dream, you should be able to actualize your dream with good results. Of course, sharing the dreams and doing the dreamwork in a small group helps give support and deepens the process. Institute dream groups are limited to four or five participants in a two and one-half hour session each week. Other sections in the book provide background and inspirational writing.

One obvious way to work with what is here is to follow the progression of the book and to process your dreams with each new technique as it comes up. However, once you get a feeling for the basic approach, you might want to skip around and choose techniques which appeal to you.

It is important to let the natural psychic flow happen as you work with a dream. This is why dreamworkers often find themselves using more than one technique with a single dream.

After you are familiar with all the techniques, you will probably find that certain techniques appeal to you most or seem more productive.

This may or may not be positive. Conceivably, by concentrating only on certain techniques, you are limiting the possibilities for your own wholeness. The ego is often narrow-minded in its views and therefore neglects or opposes certain other aspects of the larger personality. All the techniques have their place in the transforming process. Creativity is the vitality of life, and no one can become vital whose choice-making is toward limitation without expansion.

Therefore, we suggest that after you have become familiar with all the techniques, you yield, at least sometimes, your ego's 'right to dominance' to the deeper, more central interests of the Self as represented through synchronicity.

The procedure is to write the section numbers of all the techniques on slips of folded paper and choose, without looking, as many slips of paper as you want for techniques in working with your dreams. We are not suggesting this be done all the time. Of course the ego with its own power of consciousness should be choosing what it needs and wants at least some of the time. And sometimes a combination of the two approaches might provide the most meaning.

If this book is not for you, you might pass it on to a friend. Its natural audience is those who seek meaning and direction in life through following the inner guidance which comes through dreams and dreamwork.

Dreams which are born in the night manifest in the day. No person is entire unto the known part of him or herself. Wholeness comes through the completion achieved through exploring the unknown, the greatest mystery. In a sense every fact becomes a lie, every value expendable, in the face of that which is yet to be known and manifested in reality.

Without the dream we are poor indeed. Without the dreamwork we are in abject poverty.

A dream actualized is like a priceless jewel flung at the eternal void. And as simple as an opened hand.

The Dreamwork Procedure

Let us introduce you to the dream journal. Any blank-page book will do, either loose-leaf or bound. In choosing to use a dreamwork journal, please take yourself beyond the stage of simply remembering your dreams or only writing them on scraps of paper. Now is the time for more organization and structure. You may even want to buy or make a bound journal and decorate its cover. This adds to its symbolic value and shows the amount of care with which you are approaching your dream world.

There are a number of ways to organize your dreamwork journal. One structure is always to write the dream, with a title and date, on the left-hand page and then to use the right-hand page for doing dreamwork. Whether you do dreamwork right after recording the dream or later, that right-hand page is left blank for the dreamwork and evaluation. Also, if dreamwork is not done with a particular dream, lifework may be put in its place. The basic divisions of the dreamwork journal are as follows:

Left-hand page:
    Dream Title   Date
    Recorded Dream

Right-hand page:
    Dreamwork-method title
    Dreamwork
    Evaluation

The evaluation is usually a free-flowing summary of what you have gained from the dream and its dreamwork. It is often important to add a specific commitment to carry out the meaning of the dreamwork in your daily life.

Lifework is any non-dreamwork journalwork which may or may not be related to a specific dream. Thus we might write up a particular relationship episode, some philosophic sayings, or a dialogue. Journalwork is more fully described in a later chapter.

Another way to structure the dreamwork journal is to record dreams with title and date and then turn the journal upside down, recording on what is now the first page the dream title and date and the dreamwork and its evaluation.

You may also choose to create a special section for symbols in the back of your journal by alphabetizing pages and recording there only primary symbols and dream-wisdom statements.

Making a Symbol Book

When we consider that in the span of a year we may record three to five dreams a week or a total of 150 to 250 dreams a year, we are faced with what to do with them all. One alternative is only to record and think about them. But is this satisfactory? How much is missed by not being able to gather together at least some of the most important dream material?

A symbol book is one way of organizing the richness and meaning of one's dreamlife. At the Institute we are using a beautiful symbol book in our dream groups. After sharing a dream or dreamwork, the person can then write into the symbol book a brief description of a major symbol or saying from that dream. Individuals are also beginning to work with symbol books of their own.

First, obtain a fairly thick blank book. Then decorate its covers and alphabetize its pages by writing the letters on the outside upper corners of each page. Then whenever some major symbol, action or saying comes to you in a dream, record it in your symbol book. Write first the name of the symbol, then the date and year of the dream in which it appeared, and then a description of the symbol as revealed in the dream. You may also want to record a sentence or two on the significance of the symbol.

A year later, or even months later, you will be able to browse through your own symbol book and recall with meaning the dreams and significant events in your year's journey.

Evaluating Your Dreamwork Experience

How do we evaluate our dreamwork or any life experience? Do some of us really evaluate? Or are we so absorbed with living that we have no time for reflecting except, perhaps, when we are sick?

Reflecting on life does not take away from the living of it, but in fact adds to it. If I am constantly living or reacting to whatever is happening, I am like a ball tossed by innumerable players. I am not myself one of the players in my own game of life. I am only the ball. What could be more helpless and non-determining?

Thus, learning the skills for evaluating becomes essential for learning to play the game of life, a game in which we are both the ball and one of the essential players.

Reflection is at the seat of consciousness and action is the desired result of and testing of consciousness.

If I am reflecting on what I am doing while I am doing it, I am developing the observer ego as well as the interactive ego. If I do not reflect on the patterns, attitudes and issues which moderate my actions, then I am caught in my patterns and caught in the environment itself. I am thus completely subject to the fates. I cannot act. I can only react. And to be governed by one's patterns means also that one tends to repeat over and over the same old behaviour. What a bore! Is that really living?

The Values of Evaluating

Evaluation becomes a ritual necessary to the living of a meaningful life. We discover who we really are and can become. We are better able to tune into the nature of reality and its potentials. We establish a context and a breathing space within which to establish a set of values consciously chosen. We tune into a source destiny larger and more meaningful than that which can be created by the ego alone. We enlarge the arena of personal freedom by freeing ourselves gradually from unconscious patterns which govern our lives. We become a lot more interesting to ourselves and others. In recognizing ourselves, we will become recognized by a source superior to and transcending our personal selves.

The Skills of Evaluating

All evaluation must occur within a context, and we can choose the context within which to process our life experiences, inner and outer.

A context then becomes a set of values and insights about previous experiences. How does this dreamwork relate to similar dreamwork a few months ago? What are the ongoing major themes in my dreams and in my life?

In other words, what are the ongoing themes, sequences and developmental stages within which my dreams and dreamwork seem to be happening?

And what place does my ego, the choice-making function, have in all this? How do I feel about what is going on? What does it all mean? What new insights and values can be gained from this experience? What new, further steps can I take out of this experience? And how can I express gratitude for what has happened?

In evaluating, apply yourself to these questions, and in responding, let it flow. Your unconscious, as well as your more conscious side, will do the work.

In summary, evaluation means developing the context, the values, the ongoingness, the newness and the relatedness of what you are experiencing in your life. And out of such an awareness comes consciousness — awareness plus appropriate action.

Evaluation is the primary necessity for future action. And reflection is the preparation for action.

Jungian-Senoi Journalwork

Using a journal for the evoking of *integration* and *consciousness* seems fundamental to the *individuation* process as practised in this approach.

What is consciousness? What is integration?

There are no easy answers to these questions. Yet if they are not asked and dealt with, we may live our lives and never know truly that we have lived.

Let those questions stay as questions which your ongoing journalwork may help make clear.

No one can teach you how to do journalwork. You simply do it and gain its skills through experience.

No one can learn what journalwork really is by reading about it.

Read only what you are willing to practice and your life will be radically different.

What follows are some principles, guidelines and tasks for deepening your involvement with journalwork. They are the distillation of many people's experiences. Share in them and you will be in good company.

You will be in the company of those perhaps who have grown up always feeling at least a little different from the group or society. You will be in company with those cursed and blessed by something intangible which pushes for realization, for becoming truly an individual. You will be in company with the sometimes lonely whose only option is themselves and not running to the crowd. You will be in company of journeyers, known and unknown, whose mission in life inspires them forward to participation in the growing edge of a more universal destiny.

Your journal is your secret. It can be the basis for your manifestation in the world. No one need know what you write in it but you. Within its pages you communicate with yourself. You are no longer as lonely. You are alone with yourself.

Principles and Definitions

— Consciousness is awareness plus appropriate action.
— Questions produce consciousness. Answers without questions produce stasis.
— Reflection can only be tested by action, not by further reflection.
— Consciousness leads to consciousness. Unconsciousness leads to further unconsciousness.

— Consciousness is the basis for evoking the powers of the unconscious.
— To become a totality we must acknowledge in thought and detail all our parts.
— To integrate we must synthesize all aspects of our lives into one multiple whole.
— True maturity depends decisively on developing one's own inner authority towards outer things.
— No one can teach oneself as well as oneself.
— No one can teach us what we do not already know.
— No guru or teacher has the answer for another.
— The teacher teaches only him or himself.
— The therapist aids healing by being evoked to his or her own self-healing.

Discussion

Journal processing means fundamentally developing the inner authority for one's life. You can form a commitment to creating the book of your life. For as many days or years as you are involved with the journal process you will be living life and creating life from that living and reflecting upon it.

Journal writing frees us from identification with outer reality so that we may relate to rather than be dominated by it. The reflective life frees us from the outer and therefore prepares us for more creative involvement when we return to the outer.

The creation of consciousness is crucial to the integrated life. We are not whole. We have enormous splits and conflicts within ourselves and within our lives. Through journalwork we can learn the skills for dealing with our unintegrated life.

There must be a goal for the consciousness process in order for consciousness to develop. That goal is the integration of personality.

It is not enough to merge into some 'super awareness' through drugs, meditation or the like. Awareness alone is a false consciousness if it does not lead to action. The journal then is the place of reflection and the inner and outer world are the places for action. Action tests awareness like no heightened awareness can do.

No outer teacher can teach one. Let your journal be your teacher. Only in your own work will you find your own truth. Resist running to anyone for answers. Be content that there is no truth that anyone else can give you. And were it possible for it to be given to you, you would not be able to receive it anyway.

The only skill worth teaching is teaching people to teach themselves.

Writing It Out

Why write something down rather than just mull it over in your head?

Basically what seems to happen for most people is that in writing about or feeling an issue they discover new insights and possibilities. If this is not happening for you, you are probably blocking or being too analytical or factual. Write faster perhaps. Let it flow. Do not read as you write. Later after it is finished you may return and read what has been said.

Dialoguing with Parts of Oneself

A dialogue is a giving and receiving of feelings, thoughts and action between two people. Both listen and both talk. And in dialogue there also seems to be a loose progression which develops with some resolution ending it.

We dialogue by choosing some part of ourselves, some inner being, and having a conversation with it. This is usually best done by asking questions of your dialoguees and listening for a response. Do not censor whatever comes but actively listen and interact. You may question or react to what has been said. Or you may ask another question which develops things further. You may also give feeling reactions, instead of questions, to what is being said to you, such as, 'I love you', 'that makes me feel bad', 'I take you into my heart', 'I hate you', 'I hate everybody', and so on. You might even meditate a moment before hand on what feeling reaction you would like to convey.

The ego, the choice-making part of ourselves, is, in most people, used to hearing only itself. Letting go, listening to other parts of oneself speaking, challenges the ego to realizing it does not have the only truth.

Central to the integrating process is developing connections between various parts of oneself. Thus dialogue can become a major technique for aiding personality integration.

The marks of authentic dialogue, or dialogue in which other than just the ego is doing some of the listening and talking, are again that there is new information and acceptance of other points of view. You may also feel a powerful effect in general from good dialogue.

We talk to hear ourselves and in talking we are also heard by the deep centres within.

The Central Dialogues

What follows is a list of the central entities to have inner dialogues with as you progress on the journey.

— One's death. What must I do to have really lived life?
— One's birth. For what was I born?
— One's body. What am I doing to you?
— One's wounded side. What must I do to evoke healing for you?
— One's inner guide or guardian spirit. What do you have to say to me? I will listen.

— One's dream figures. Why are you in my dream?

— One's enemies. What purpose do you have for my life?

— One's shadow. Where are you? What must I do to reconcile with you?

— One's destiny. What must I do to achieve myself?

— One's lover. How may I accept and care for you?

— One's parents. Why do you still hang onto my life?

— One's source. Why have you forsaken me?

— One's journal. How am I doing, both the positive and negative?

— One's children. What are the ways I can let you grow more in freedom?

— One's passion. What is it to which I can give my total commitment?

— One's greed. What agony creates my need?

— One's teacher. Tell me the way you are not perfect!

— One's symbol. What must I do to honour you more?

— One's birthday. What is in store for me this coming year?

— One's own ego. Who are you really?

There are, of course, more special beings with which to dialogue. Perhaps you can think of one of your own.

Go down the list and select a respondent with which to dialogue. What is the result? Eventually you may complete dialogues with all these entities. Do not rush things. This is not an exercise. This is life itself.

Another task would be to go down the list and formulate other questions for each of these entities.

And you may find that dialoguing with the same entities at different times could produce different results.

Feeling Expression in Journalwork

Any feeling person is on occasion going to express him or herself in emotionally uncontrolled terms. We note, obviously, the relation of swear words to the four, not two, great instincts: sex, elimination, anger and the spiritual.

But these words, even if deeply felt, are not always able to be expressed in the outer appropriately. The journal then becomes the place for your feelings.

Write large and flowingly sometimes. Let the words be as big as your feelings really are.

There is also a sense in which swearing may stop for a developing individual, not through conscious repression, which is the traditional religious way, but through expression of one's feelings fully everywhere, every day. If we are not repressing our feelings there may not be extra energy to break out into swear words when we have reached an emotional breaking point.

Distilling the Essence of Your Experience

You could just write down in your journal what has happened to you today or this past week. This would be the narrative of your life. But what you put down is not really your life but your bias towards how you select from experience.

You are not your experience. You are that which processes your experience.

What are the contexts within which you process your own life experience?

This is a crucial question because it shows the state of your own consciousness even more than who you really are. Do you describe your experience by paying attention to details, or to feelings, or what so and so is doing to you? Do you describe more often nature or erotica? Are you philosophical or spiritual in your perspective?

Do you write mainly from your own point of view or from what others are doing in your life?

'Yesterday, Jim came over and we got into a fight. He was quite upset and carried on ...'

'Yesterday I fought with my boyfriend again. When will I ever learn? Does there have to be so much fighting in our relationship? ...'

'Distilling the essence' means in journal writing responding to any of the following questions:

— Why did this experience happen to me?
— How is this experience necessary to my life?
— What is this experience to teach me?
— How can I change as a result of this experience?
— What is the essence, or chief value, to be gained from this experience?

There are perhaps many other focusing questions. What is obvious here is that the raw experience of reality gets translated in the journalwork processing into some form, context or relation to a larger whole.

Journalwork has as one of its primary values discovering and creating relationships between things, people, etc.. The discovery of relationship is the experience of meaning.

In writing down an experience, let it flow, let it carry itself. A basic journalwork tenet is that in the writing we write beyond our known selves. What seems to develop, to come into consciousness as you write? What might you be including? When does the energy seem to taper off? Is this due to reaching a blockage in what you are trying to express? Or does the experience seem to be coming to a natural end or resolution? How would you state this resolution or overall value in one sentence? How will you live this value in the coming week?

The Unsent Letter

Letters are a form of communication less ephemeral and elusive than most forms of direct communication.

But how many of us write what we truly feel regardless of the recipient's attitudes or feelings? We know better. The cost of an upsetting letter can be great. Do not open doors unless you yourself are willing to pass through them. There are some doors, once opened, that may never be closed again.

Yet by writing the unsent letter we can express feelings we may not want to or are afraid of sharing directly. You write your letter openly as if you were going to send it. What is important is that you censor nothing and that you have a recipient for your letter.

Letters may be written to those we love and those we hate. Letters may be written to the dead or to those as yet unborn. I may write a letter to my eleven year old daughter for when she reaches eighteen. I may write a letter to be read after my death. Some of these letters can go to their recipients. Other letters we may choose to hold back, keep in our journals, or even destroy.

I usually write a letter to a person after they die. The most recent time I did this I received a 'reply' the next morning in a dream in which the dead person came to my bedside and gently reproved me for something negative I had said in the letter about him. I had chosen to present the good and the bad of our relationship and he had responded appropriately. He had expressed anger which he had not done much of in waking life.

Ultimately, whether sent or not, we may never know how far into the mystery our letters go. Perhaps there is always a response and what is required is a consciousness capable of perceiving it.

Journalwork in Relation to Dreamwork

Both journalwork and dreamwork are major and usually necessary avenues for the individuation journey. Many dreamwork tasks go into the journal and journalwork may directly influence dreaming.

In terms of dreamwork, feel free to use any journalwork methods appropriate to dream content. Thus if a dead parent appears in a dream, have a dialogue with her or write a letter.

Journalwork is, in effect, dreamwork applied to other life experiences besides, but including dreams.

Journal Work as Question-Asking

It is more important to ask the right question than to receive a right answer.

A question is the central response to life.

A question is a great mystery. It opens up possibility. It creates freedom to choose. It prevents closure and thus affirms life. When you find yourself about to give someone an answer, see if you can turn your response into a question and experience what happens.

The appropriate reaction to a question is a response, not an answer. Answers rarely answer anything. The only questions worth stating are those which generate responses, not answers.

These statements are not answers to 'What is a question?' They are merely responses which relate to a mystery.

The more questions we ask of ourselves and of life the better. When caught in a dilemma, ask questions, do not seek answers.

Questions create consciousness. Answers limit consciousness.

The more ways we can ask questions of ourselves, the more possibilities we will have for living life.

Let my life end in a way that it ends as a question, a mystery, and not an answer. Answers end reality. Questions begin it anew.

What is the next question for my life?

The Goal

Perhaps the core focus for journal work is the building of a reflective and active consciousness which sees as its task the forming of one's personality into a unified and passionate whole. We look back to look forward. And even at the end of our natural cycle, will we die awake or asleep to the meaning of what it is to have had a realized life?

What is a Dream?

Let us assume we do not know what a dream is. Let us start from the beginning.

We have only the dream. Yet we do not have even that. We have only the remembered dream. That is where we start.

Already the remembered dream has been filtered by some ego process. The 'remembering ego,' that choice-maker and focuser of consciousness, has

brought the dream into the waking state. But already the dream has begun to change. After all, the ego has its point of view and is not a clear vehicle. The ego filters the original experience through its own attitudes and abilities.

Never mind. In the remembered dream we still have much which is beyond the conscious ego's will and ability to distort. How do we know this? Partially because when a dream is worked with, it will reveal things the ego does not particularly want to face.

Task

Look at the following dream before reading further. Describe in writing what you think/feel the dream is about and what its internal structures are. You will then be able to compare your comments with what is written here about this dream.

Dream Title: The Silver Car
Date: February 5, 1979

A black-haired, Indian-looking man, tall and slimly built, drives his car and parks it outside a building, a Victorian-style building, a hotel. I am standing outside it, waiting for him, as we have an arrangement that I am to drive his car somewhere for him. The car is very modern looking, a dull metallic-silver colour with a dashboard like an airplane's. He asks, quite quickly and coolly, that I drive his car to Centre Street for him. He says that this is where he lives and he wants the car returned there for him to use again in the morning. I feel scared. I am intimidated by the modern appearance of the car. But I say that I will drive it, because I know I have already made a commitment to do this earlier.

I walk off the sidewalk to go around to the right side of the car where the man is opening the driver's door (British side) to let me in. I suddenly find that I have dropped to my knees; my lower legs have given way and I begin to panic a little. I want to get to the car door before the man leaves because I want to ask him about some of the complicated-looking knobs, switches, and lights, etc., on the dashboard. How do I work them? I find I can move along on my knees quite well, and I reach the car door and the man just before he turns to leave. I stand up and ask him, "How does this car work? I have never driven anything like this vehicle before." I am saying this lightly, slightly jokingly. He is unimpressed! He says that I will really find it quite simple to drive, and then he goes inside the hotel building. I pursue him because I am still not satisfied that I will be able to drive such a complicated-looking car.

I get inside the hotel lobby. The interior is dark wood and there are huge, green plants standing around. I look around for the man but can see no sign of him. I decide I will go and make an attempt to drive the car and trust that the man was right to believe I could do it. I go outside and start the car slowly, calmly, turning the lights on, because it is night-time; and I drive off carefully. I find out that he was right; so far, anyway, it is not difficult.

Comments
I woke up with a feeling of strange excitement.

I was interested to find such a powerful car image entering my dreams. I have never been much of a "car person" in inner or outer reality!

Developing the Nature of a Dream

Perhaps you are thinking that this dream is about the dreamer's insecurity or dealing with power, or that a man will come into her life who has a special car. Or, if you are orthodox Jungian, you may think the dream contains a fairly typical animus figure, represented by the dark, male stranger and the car.

Perhaps you are thinking the dreamer is male. Or female. And perhaps you feel that the dreamer's sex is important to know.

You might feel you would need to know facts about the dreamer's life and what happened the previous day before you could begin to make sense of the dream.

These are some of the typical bits of information required in certain dreamwork systems.

Our concern for the moment is *the dream and only the dream*. Why go to outside contexts in order to develop the dream's meaning? Some psychologists and writers state that information about the dreamer's outer life is necessary for working with dreams. But where do they get their authority for this? Is it from God? Feel free to challenge any claims made about dreams in this book or elsewhere. Dreams are, and will always remain, a great mystery. We probe to the core and yet another door opens. We wonder what is to come next.

A Basic Principle

Let us return to the dream. Always the dream. *A basic principle is to start with the dream itself and objectify it*. Do not leap off from it to some foreign context which is not the dream itself. Outside contexts may have their value in developing a more total picture. But first there must be an objective reality to leap off from. Get involved with the dream itself using questions such as these:

— What is the dream ego, the I, literally doing in the dream, starting from the beginning?

   The I is standing waiting. It has an arrangement.
— What is this arrangement? Is this arrangement realized in the dream?
— How does the dream ego feel in the dream?

   The dream ego is scared and intimidated.
— But how do we know this? Is the dream ego having these feelings or is the waking, remembering ego having these feelings? How can we tell? What is the internal evidence?

We know how the dream ego feels because we see how it acts. The dream ego's legs have given way.

— Are feelings ever in dreams even? Or only actions? What is the difference?
— What is the relation of the dream ego's feelings to its commitment? What does it mean when it says commitment? How does commitment show itself in the dream?
— What does the car symbolize? Something other than itself? Or does it symbolize itself? What is the car like in the dream? Describe its literal characteristics. Why does it seem such a challenge to the dream ego? What is the challenge in terms of the dream?
— How would you describe the Indian-looking man's response to the dream ego? List his responses. Do not say anything which is not in the dream.
— In view of how the dream ego responds, how is the man's response helping or hindering?
— How would you describe the dream ego's accomplishments in the dream?

At the beginning we see a dream ego afraid of what seems like an enormous task. But the dream ego has a commitment, a conscious willingness to stick with the task no matter what. The man's 'neglect' and confidence are in fact supportive of the dream ego's need to accomplish the task by itself.

There is resolution in the dream in that the dream ego accomplishes the task of driving the car. However, at the end of the remembered dream, we still do not know where it is going.

Do you see how staying with the internal structures of the dream actually helps objectify it, helps us discover what it is in itself?

As with dreams so in life.

Are we just as misinterpretative of our outer realities as of our inner ones? Are we any more objective in the outer? Perhaps, but most of us still have much to learn about the nature of our own consciousness.

The Dream Tasks Related to the Dream Example

Together, the dreamer and the analyst evolved a series of four dream tasks for the dreamer.

1. Talk with the dark man.
2. Think up ten ways I can earn a little money in outer life.
3. Write out my negative statements and then rewrite them as positive ones three times a day. Then on the right side of the paper, put what comes into my head — negative stuff as well as positive. I may want to rewrite the affirmation to include the negative side also.
4. What affirmation out of this dream can I construct?

In my therapy session I re-entered the dream and described the silver car in detail. Later this helped me more than I had realized at the time, in that I found it very easy to open up to further creative dreamwork, particularly the really moving dialogue I had with the man.

1. *Talk with the man*

Man: Would you drive my car back to Centre Street for me?

H: Centre Street, where is it? Why do you want me to leave the car there?

Man: It is over there, in front of you (he points). I live there and I want the car parked outside my house so that I can use it in the morning?

H: But why me? Why do you want me to drive or even think I am capable of driving this car? I have never driven anything so complicated or modern looking.

Man: I think you will find it quite simple to drive and you are certainly capable of doing it.

H: I am so scared. I feel intimidated by such a complicated-looking dashboard. It looks like a computer. How will I know which knobs to turn, which button to push, where the lights are?

Man: You do know, but you will only find out that you know by climbing into the car and driving it.

H: You are so cool, so calm, so unemotional. How can you know that I will manage such a task when I am such an opposite kind of person from you?

Man: Because it is *my* car you are going to be driving from here to my house. I can guide you if you will only get into the car, steer the wheel, drive, and, most of all, trust me. Put your trust in me and have a bit of faith.

H: I suddenly have a feeling that you are right, and I will try, because actually a part of me really does want to, you know.

Man: Good. It has been a very long time since you and I met and you decided to trust me so we could work together when it became necessary.

H: I still feel scared, but I feel gratitude toward you for coming into my dream and challenging me this way. I am very moved and I feel close to tears, tears of joy and thankfulness.

Man: Drive my car in this dream and have more faith, more courage, more trust in me as well as in your other dream figures.

H: I will try. *I commit myself to more trust, more faith, and more courage.*

Man: Good!

H: Could I ask you one more question? Why am I to drive to Centre Street?

Man: If you will trust me and trust yourself you will experience, through me, my part in the centre. You remember that about a week ago you had a fragment of a dream come to you? In the dream you were feeling terrified and a voice spoke to you and said, "Neither walk on the right nor on the left, but walk in the centre." Well, you drive the car to Centre Street, and you could do just that.

H: I feel suddenly overwhelmingly excited by what you have just said and I see some of the inner mist rising and I can see a tangible form appearing and I get the feeling you are a guide and a heroic figure. I am going to paint you if I can.

Man: You *can*!

2. *Think up ten ways I can earn a little money in outer life*

   1. Rent the room vacated by my husband for more money than I had originally intended. This way I can earn some money apart from just the amount needed to recoup J's rent money for his room elsewhere.
   2. Teach a children's creative clay class which would include making pots by hand and modelling dream figures — people, animals, witches, monsters. One class a week to start with, ages 5–9, to be held either at our house or at the Youth Hut because I may need the publicity they can offer in the beginning.
   3. Lead an open dream group at the Youth Hut for publicity to draw a small group of women to a continuing dream group.
   4. Lead a women's morning dream group in my house once a week for $2\frac{1}{2}$ hours.
   5. Model again for art classes.
   6. Do more work for the Institute to help continue to pay my way.

3. *Evaluation*

I also did a lot of work on the third task which is too lengthy to go into here, but which illustrated how riddled I am, and have been, with negative stuff. So the dreamwork in this area proved to be very helpful and, in part, healing.

4. *What affirmation can I construct?*

I have painted the man and the car, and I have written out in large lettering:

I **CAN** *TRUST, I HAVE* **MORE** *FAITH EVERY DAY AND I* **GROW** *IN COURAGE.*

The dream about the silver car has proved to be quite an important dream for me. The dreamwork has helped me to make it so. 1) I have let my separated husband's room for the extra amount of money I had hoped for. We now have a family of three living with us; they desperately needed a place to live and have added much that is positive for both my own and my daughters' daily living experience. 2) I begin both classes, the creative clay class and the open dream group, within two weeks. 3) My positive animus figure's image hangs on the wall opposite me as I type this dreamwork. He has a wonderful quality for me, and I draw positive strength and courage from his portrait each time I pause and relook at him. The painted silver car glows with a metallic sheen as it did in my dream. 4) I do more work for the Institute every day! My work comes from the heart and, in addition, helps to pay my way. All this is helping me greatly in my inner and outer life. The necessary emergence of the masculine in me, one of my underdeveloped areas — my creative energy — deserves honouring and constant recommitment. this dream and the dreamwork have vividly reminded me of this fact.

Relating the Dream to Its Dreamwork

Now that we have objectified the dream and reviewed some of the dreamwork done on it, we can ask questions about the relation between the dream and its dreamwork. For example:

— Why do we need dreamwork? How does dreamwork add to or detract from the dream experience?
— Is, in fact, the dreamwork related to the dream? How and how not? Why even do dreamwork?

We may also ask questions about the dreamer's comments following the dream report.

— Is the dreamer's strange excitement found also in the dream itself?
— How does this feeling compare with the feelings expressed in the dream?
— The dreamer mentions inner and outer reality. Is the dream necessarily

connected to outer reality. How and how not?

In general, after responding to questions about the dream situation and the attitudes in the dream, we may look for similar attitudes and situations in the outer reality. For example, we might ask:

— How do the outer-oriented dream tasks relate to the inner world of the dream?

— What does the dreamwork add to the experience of the dream?

Much more could be said about this dream and its dreamwork. We have stayed only with the essentials. No interpretation has been necessary because much actualization of the dream has occurred. The inspiration, the meaning, and the motivation have come from within the dream. What could be of more value?

The dream exists in itself, ready to be found.

The Basics for Remembering Dreams

Memory is itself a key component of *consciousness*. It is not the lack of mental capacity to recall past events, inner and outer, which causes forgetting. It is a defensive part of ourselves which blocks us from re-experiencing what we have chosen at some level to consider negative.

Thus, if you are not recalling many dreams vividly, analyze your own shut-off mechanism. It could be involved with any of the following attitudes:

— I do not really want to know what my unconscious is saying to me because it might be painful and require change.
— This bizarre, angry or sexual stuff is not really me.
— I would rather act out my stuff than see it as inner.
— I'm too tired to work on my dreams with all the other stuff I have to do.
— I must have eight hours of uninterrupted, peaceful sleep or I will not be able to function the next day.
— I'm too fearful or limited to be able to be really successful at anything.
— I must remain in control of my life at all costs.
— I am afraid to wake up because my waking day may be traumatic.
— I must remember or others will judge me inadequate.

These are only some of the more common possible memory-denying attitudes. See which ones fit for you and write further attitudes which apply to you.

For of course we are not only dealing with forgetting dreams but also with forgetting people's names, exam information, appointments and what we did yesterday or even today.

A basic principle to check things out with is as follows:

— If I have forgotten something I have wanted to forget it.

Memory is one of the blessings to the conscious life. We do not forget what we really want to remember. Without memory we cannot bring the past into the future and transform both the past and the future.

A developed memory is the mark of a conscious being. Those without passion are the great forgetters.

Accordingly here are some possibilities for creative attitudes for remembering dreams and other life events:

— In order to love the totality of life I must seek to remember everything impartially.
— It is creative to have my sleep interrupted or ended by remembering and working with a dream or other thoughts which come in the night.
— My passion for life means letting life in totally.
— When I give over personal control to the life sources I truly live.
— I do not remember by will-power but by letting go and becoming a vehicle.
— I am able to forget as part of the imperfection of life.
— That which I love I will truly remember.
— I am never too busy if I choose what is essential to life.
— I can work to accept life rather than control or hide from it.

Having explored your negative forgetting attitudes earlier, then you are able to contrast with them these positive attitudes and other positive attitudes which come to mind for you.

Remembering Your Dream

Why not wake to each new day as a new adventure in life, sometimes difficult and sometimes flowing? And why not wake to the day excited and committed to capturing The Dream, that product of the night? To waste the dream in forgetfulness is to waste a third of our lives, perhaps the most creative third at that.

A key question then for you to answer in your dream journal is:

— What are my attitudes towards sleep and waking up and how can they be changed towards greater consciousness?

In order to better remember your dreams you will need to do all or any of the following:

— Keep a pen, light, and dreamwork journal by your bed.
— Write anything that comes into your head, whether a dream or not, the first thing on waking.
— Always do something with your dream so that remembering your dreams will be worth the effort.
— Wake yourself up at one-and-one-half-hour intervals, the normal time between dreams. Thus, wake yourself up in the morning, either at six hours or at seven-and-one-half-hours. Not eight hours. But find your own time. It is important to wake to the dream.
— Make a commitment to writing down all dream fragments and not just the most vivid dreams.
— Increase your awareness of detail in writing down your dreams.
— As you fall asleep give yourself the intention of writing down your dreams the next morning. One person wrote her intention on an imaginary blackboard.
— Do not wake yourself up with music, or even the alarm, if it changes your consciousness. Train yourself to wake up just before the alarm. And you have to want to wake up to The New Day.
— Usually write quickly without trying to organize or first recall in your head the whole dream. Some people prefer to organize the dream first, however, before writing up their dreams.
— Do not get out of bed, exercise, or think of outside activities upon waking.
— Let yourself fail. Anxiety kills accomplishment.
— Clear your head in recall meditation by reviewing the events of the day before falling asleep and you will more likely have a clear head for a dream the next morning.
— Write down any and all dreams, even the worst! We are not good beings. We are total beings. Dreamwork reveals all! What we most avoid is what we most need to face.

— Be in tune with your bed partner. It is more compatible if both of you keep dreamwork journals. The propensity is in everyone. And neither one reads the other's journal. This is a violation of individual rights. In addition, what you read is what you take on. Are you willing and able to deal with another person's psyche?

— Be aware of and write down feelings and emotions in the dreams.

— Be ready for strong events from the previous day evoking a dream.

— If you are not recalling vividly enough you might change your sleep pattern in some way.

— To aid recall, think of significant people or events in your life and see if that clues in a dream in which the person you thought of appears.

— As you are writing your dream tell yourself what an important dream this is so that you can defeat any negativistic attitudes.

— Fight the regressive pull by struggling to become conscious of yourself and your dreams rather than falling back asleep.

— What we remember is what we live. Memory is life!

Objectifying the Dream

The central factor is the dream itself. The dream. Always the dream. Always return to the dream.

— Where is that in the dream?
— What else might the dream be saying?
— What other points of view besides your own are in the dream?
— If you already understand, why did you have this dream?
— Why have you not dealt with such and such in the dream?

The plain fact is that many dreamwork teachers, therapists and other 'helpers'

often quickly leave the dream far behind in their work and get into other things such as feeling states, life problems, childhood stuff and interpretations. These processes may evoke much energy but they are only remotely dreamwork experiences.

Dreamwork means getting closer to the dream, not further away from it. Therefore we must learn to first objectify the dream itself.

— What are the dynamics, its symbols and the relations between symbols?
— What issues seem unresolved in the dream?
— What situations seem unresolved or only begun?
— What are the contrasts and similarities?
— What is the dream ego doing or not doing in the dream?

This approach is a very direct way of doing a literary analysis on the dream in the manner that a form critic would approach a poem. Without this level of *objectification* there is little chance for re-experiencing the dream as it really is.

For the forces that would 'subjectify' the dream are exceeding powerful. They include:

— Those who would put their own psychological or religious theories onto the symbolic material that a dream is.
— The personal ego of the dreamer or dream guide. This ego usually does not want to be challenged out of its own assumptions, so it seeks to control and direct the 'dream truths' with interpretations.
— The power of other unconscious material not reflected in the dream which would try to take over in any symbolic experience. 'But we are talking about an unknown dream figure crying and not your mother's hysteria, which I see no direct reference to in the dream,' would be an objective response.

Is this enough for indicating the problems and the necessity for staying with the dream? The issue is clearly to be aware of using dreams for dreamwork versus using dreams for other things such as group process, theorizing, creative projects and spiritual awareness. In the Jungian-Senoi approach we try and start always with the dream, objectify it, and then move out into levels of manifestation.

We are not overly worried as to whether an analysis of the dream's structure is ultimately objective or not. Everything filters through our consciousness and therefore receives a bias. But given this, cannot we still establish levels of objectivity? Perhaps, even, our own subjectivity is the greatest objectivity we will ever have? The inner world is no more subjective than the outer world. They are only different. The outer world is no less perceived through assumptions than the inner world is perceived through assumptions.

We are always labouring within the context of unconscious assumptions which we work towards objectifying through the processes of consciousness.

All that is required is that we have the attitude that a solid degree of objectification is possible, and that we have the skills and the devotion for doing such work.

In actually giving suggestions to a dreamer the dreamwork guide may do the objectifying within his or her mind and not put it out directly to the dreamer. This saves time in order to get to other central dreamwork issues, such as what to do with the dream and how to do it.

The method of objectifying the dream also makes less important the need to know what happened in the dreamer's life, and which may have stimulated the dream. If we really objectify the dream's dynamics as an internally consistent experience we may not even need to go outside the dream to previous day, outer life material.

In general *the sequence for objectifying a dream* is as follows:

— Delineate the dream ego, the dreamer's self-image. What is it doing or not doing in the dream?
— Seek out and list major contrasts and similarities in the dream. How do they interrelate?
— What sequences are in the dream, if any?
— What are the major symbols and what are the relations between symbols?
— What are the issues, conflicts and unresolved situations in the dream?
— What are the positive symbols, resolutions, relations, etc. in the dream?
— What relation does anything in this dream have to any other thing in other dreams?
— What are the possibilities for relations and resolutions which have not yet materialized in the dream?

Objectifying the dream then prepares the setting for determining which dreamwork methods are most appropriate for developing which dream dynamics. If there seems little relation between various symbols in the dream we might do a dream re-entry to establish more relations. Or if a conversation is only begun we might continue the dream conversation using the method of dialogue. The possibilities for dreamwork tasks are as great as there are dynamics in a dream. Thus, having established an objective basis from which to work, there is no limit to the possibilities for creating with a dream.

Dreamwork Example — Objectifying the Dream

Strephon's Comments

The following example of objectifying the dream was done by someone new to dreamwork at this level. What is clearly points to is that almost anyone using the procedures as described in this manual can do as thorough a job with their own dreams as any outside analyst or therapist.

In essence what is illustrated here is what this book sets out to demonstrate, that anyone can work effectively with their own dreams. The experts are only useful as supporters and teachers in developing the process for each individual.

Democracy has come to dreamwork!

Dream Title: A Ship on the Ocean   *Date: September 29, 1979*

I'm out on a ship in the ocean with other people on board. We've joined in a circle and are all involved in sharing. One person has just finished reading for the group. I'd like to go up and lead some yoga exercises or dance steps. But for some reason instead I read from an old poster on the wall. It's in a different language — perhaps German or Old English. I read it slowly and haltingly, taking my time with the words. When I've finished the short passage, I still have a desire to lead the yoga but someone else stands up right away (assuming I've finished I guess) and prepares to make their contribution to this ritual or whatever it is. This actually feels okay to me. I go and sit down.

Now, I'm near the back of the boat with almost all the other people. There's some kind of joyous, festive flavour or tone to the group — sort of hanging around a swimming pool at a party. It makes me nervous to hang over the outside of the boat so I'm still on the inside of the rail. Other people are cooling their feet this way and the sea seems relatively tranquil but it still makes me nervous. Almost all the people on board are back here — so the front of the boat is tilted up. And it doesn't seem that anyone is in control of the ship.

Now I see off to one side a huge ship coming in our direction. There's another coming on the other side of us — the formation of the three is sort of an arrow or wedge. But the fear of collision is paramount in my mind. I ask the person (a woman) next to me if we maybe should have someone go forward and control the boat. She doesn't seem alarmed though.

Things become vague for me here ...

But all of a sudden there are only a few of us in a small crude wooden dory and we're up on dry land — all the people gently tossed out of the boat. My first impulse is to right the boat. So I turn it over and drag it in the direction we've come from (where the water should be). But all around now is just dry land — hills and weeds like the dry brush of the summer hills in Tilden Park.

Comments

I woke up feeling nervous — like something wasn't right.

I'm frustrated that my dream ego doesn't act in the initial setting; and then when action finally comes, it seems irrelevant to the situation.

Dream Tasks

1.A.   What is the dream ego doing or not doing in the dream?

The dream ego joins in a sharing circle. Would like to share movement but instead reads old poster. She reads this slowly and haltingly. Then accepts someone else's gesture to share as her cue to sit down. So does so without sharing the movement. The dream ego is on a boat with others. She feels nervous amidst their festive flavour. She remains on the inside of the ship's rails while others sit outside the rail cooling their feet. She sees two ships on collision course with the boat she's on. She fears the collision. She asks a woman next to her if they should have someone go forward and take the controls. Since the woman doesn't seem alarmed, she does nothing. Then the dream ego is with a few others in a small dory. She and the others are tossed from the dory onto dry land. She immediately turns the boat over and drags it in the direction where she believes the water should be. She sees dry land all around.

1.B.   List the major contrasts and similarities in the dream. How do they interrelate?

1) Ocean-dry land
2) Sharing movement-sharing reading (active-passive)
3) My movement vs. someone else's words
4) Nervousness vs. festiveness
5) My desire to continue sharing vs. someone else's gesture to share.
6) Similarity of shape — an arrow or wedge to the three boats
7) Large ship-wooden dory

The relationship of most of these contrasts takes the form of the dream ego's desires versus the desires or actions of others in the dream. Me-them.

1.C.   What sequences are in the dream, if any?

1) One person reads; I get up and read; another person shares.
2) From a ritual sharing circle to a festive gathering on the back of the boat.
3) From general nervousness about being on the outside of the rail to concern over lack of control and fear of collision.
4) From fear of collision to being tossed onto dry land from a small wooden dory.
5) Going from the ocean to dry land.
6) Turning the boat over and trying to drag it to the water.

1.D.   What are the major symbols and what are the relations between the symbols?

1) Ocean
2) Ship
3) Ritual circle
4) Ship rail
5) Arrow or wedge
6) Small wooden dory
7) Dry land and hills

The ship is on the ocean. The ritual circle occurs on the ship. The ship rail is a boundary between the security of the ship and the waters of the ocean. The arrow or wedge shape is formed by the course of the three ships on the ocean. The wooden dory is much smaller than the big ship. It seems less threatening as does the dry land.

1.E. What are the issues, conflicts and unresolved situations in the dream?

1) Though the dream ego says she feel okay about not sharing the yoga or dance, this seems unresolved.

2) Rather than sharing the movement, the dream ego shares something she's unfamiliar with. This seems somehow conflicting with who the dream ego really is.

3) The nervousness of the dream ego and the festiveness of the others on board the ship exemplifies some kind of conflict.

4) The fact that no one is apparently in control of the ship seems to be an important issue.

5) It's suggested by the dream ego that perhaps someone should go forward to control the ship. But this is not resolved within the dream.

6) There is tension or conflict in the image of an impending collision. This is not resolved in the dream; as the dream ego is suddenly in a small dory on dry land.

7) The attempt to drag the dory to the water when all around is only dry land seems to exemplify some kind of situational conflict.

1.F. What are the positive symbols, resolutions, relations, etc. in the dream?

1) The ritual circle for sharing seems to be a positive symbol.

2) The small wooden dory and dry land seem more manageable for the dream ego. Despite the ludicrous appearance in this setting, the dream ego is at least able to act and so this is somewhat more of a positive symbol than the large ship and the ocean. The positive aspect of this relationship is that the dream ego acts. The negative aspect is that the action is ludicrous and ineffectual.

3) The festive attitude of the others on the boat could be a positive symbol (if seen as a celebration to the ocean).

1.G. What relation does anything in this dream have to any other thing in other dreams?

1) I've had frequent dreams of the ocean and ships on the ocean —

sometimes out of control and being tossed wildly, sometimes being controlled by another person.

1.H. What are the possibilities for relations and resolutions which have not yet materialized in the dream?

1) The dream ego could actually share the intended movements.
2) The dream ego could understand the reading presented.
3) The dream ego could climb over the rail and cool her feet in the ocean.
4) The dream ego could go forward herself to control the ship.
5) The dream ego could send someone else forward to control the ship.
6) The impending collision could occur.
7) The impending collision could be averted.
8) The wooden dory could be dragged back into the water thus making the dream ego's actions relevant.
9) The dream ego could feel festive along with the others on board.

2. What possibilities are there in experiencing the impending collision? Unity-Explosion-Big Bang-Expansion-Change-Transformation-Melting Together.

In my journal, I wrote a fantasy of what could possibly happen. The dream ego took no action but allowed it to happen and watched curiously.

3. How do I (the dream ego) make choices? The easiest way? What's handed to me or expected? The hardest way?

The dream ego seems to *do what's expected* in joining the sharing circle.

The choice to read the poster rather than leading yoga is perhaps *based on fear*. She takes the *least risk* and does something *unthreatening*. Also she hasn't seen anyone share a movement so may be going along with *what's expected* — the *traditional* way.

Again, instead of leading the yoga, she sits down — going with the *expected*-least threatening.

Fear and nervousness keep her on the inside of the rail.

She's at the back of the boat because everyone else is — *expected*.

* I did additional work on this task but it's not necessary to include it here.

Evaluation

The particular process of objectifying the dream has been incredibly rich for me. I think I've seen other therapists do this silently and while listening to a dream. But it seems really important to realize that its a process. In doing this assignment, I realized as I was going along that many tasks came to mind that would address a particular issue or help to enhance resolution. My sense is that this is a key step in working with one's own dreams or in guiding another in their dreamwork.

Dreamwork Entry
— Objectifying the Dream

Objectifying the dream prepares the setting for determining which dreamwork methods are most appropriate for developing which dream dynamics. If there seems to be little relation between various symbols in the dream we might do a dream re-entry to establish more relations. Or if a conversation is only begun, we might continue the dream conversation using the method of dialogue. The possibilities for dreamwork tasks are as great as there are dynamics in a dream. Thus, having established an objective basis from which to work, there is no limit to the possibilities for creating with a dream.

The *procedure* for objectifying a dream is as follows. Analyze and record your responses to these questions:

— What, briefly, is the dream ego doing and not doing in the dream?

— What are the major contrasts and similarities in the dream, and how do they interrelate?

— What are the major symbols and relationships between these symbols?

— What sequences are present in the dream?

— What dynamics are revealed by generalizing the major symbols?

— What is the dream ego's relationship to the major symbols?

— What are the issues, conflicts and unresolved situations in the dream?

— What are the resolutions or healing factors already present in this dream?

— What are the possibilities for relationships and resolutions which have not yet materialized?

— What relationship does this dream, or the symbols in it, have to other dreams?

— How would you summarize the particular character or identity of this dream?

— What have you learned so far?

Good, perhaps just by following the above procedure you have already begun to experience the meaning of your dream. The next step would be to now design dream tasks for yourself based on your analysis of the dream's dynamics. Design tasks which expand the content of the dream and which also establish fuller relations between its parts. Also work with what needs resolution in the dream and what in it can apply to your outer life and personality.

Objectification of any experience is one of the major tools for relating to reality.

Applying Key Questions to Dreams

What is a question?

A mystery ultimately? When is it more important to seek the right question than to have the right answer?

Without questions there can be no consciousness. Facts do not awaken us half so much as uncertainties do. Answers are fallible, limited in time and place. With the right question we transcend the limitation of the purely factual.

Every answer can lead to a new question or we become bound in by time and its consequences.

Could the single greatest step so far in evolution be the discovery of the question? Imagine the dramatic moment way back on the dim horizon when some lone individual asserted him or herself with the first question.

A dream is a question, not an answer.

We must look to our dreams as inner potentials for outer possibility. To look to dreams as god-given answers to the way we should live life is to substitute still another dogma for the last outmoded one. People do this. They take their dreams literally as the truth, never facing that even within a single dream there are contradictory points of view. And always you as choice-making ego are responsible for making decisions. No dream, only you, can suffer or enjoy the consequences of your choices.

Study this list of the following questions. Yes, they will produce tentative responses. Such 'little truths' are worth working with. Try out your responses in reality. Most likely they will lead to new questions with the result that you

will have gone on your journey a little further and, having stepped forward in life, also increased your consciousness. As you work, new questions may occur to you. These are your own questions that come from your own unconscious.

It is important also to let your intuition have full rein by writing whatever comes up in responding to the questions.

And there are no 'right' answers. No one else can judge for you the quality of your own consciousness. You alone, for better or for worse, determine the integrity and sense of reality with which you respond to life.

Key Questions for Responding to Dreams

Respond to as many questions as you choose. In selecting, usually go with your greatest positive or negative energy response.

— How am I, as dream ego, acting in this dream?
— What symbols in this dream are important to me?
— What are the various feelings in this dream?
— What are the various actions in this dream?
— What relation, if any, does this dream have to what is happening right now in my life? To something in my future? To something in my personality?
— Who or what is the adversary in this dream?
— What is the helping or healing force in this dream?
— What is being wounded in this dream?
— What is being healed in this dream?
— What would I like to avoid in this dream?
— What actions might this dream be suggesting I consider?
— What does this dream want from me?
— What questions does this dream ask of me?
— What choices can I, and will I, make as a result of working with this dream?
— Who or what is my companion?
— *Note*: Why have we not asked: What does this dream mean to me?
— Why did I need this dream?
— Why am I not dealing with this situation in this way?
— Why am I not doing this in my life?
— What do you want to ask of us as your dream spirits?
— Why are you sometimes afraid of us, your dream spirits?
— Why have I dreamed of 'so and so' now?
— Where are my helpers and guides in life and in my dreams?
— What is the difference between a 'why' and a 'what' questions?

— What can happen if I work actively with this dream?

— What is being accepted in this dream?

— What new questions come up from this dreamwork?

Suffice it to say that these questions discriminate between those who dream and those who dream and know it. Only the awakened dream and know they dream. Dreams that are born in darkness must live in the light.

Dreamwork Examples — Applying Key Questions

Strephon's Introduction
This example pretty well explains itself. We note that the dreamer chose a variety of questions as contexts for response to the dream. There are aspects he did not cover in the dream but what he did yielded rich material. This dreamwork was entirely self-motivated. No one interpreted his dream for him. No one led the way. We each have this same capacity to work with and understand our dreams.

Dream Title: The Odd Man Out   *Date: March 25, 1979*

I'm driving my bus down a main highway resembling Jackson Street and make a U-turn. I see someone at a gas station stumbling over some spare tyres where an air outlet is. I notice it's Anna Youls. Driving past, I look in my side-view mirror to see whether she also has noticed me. She has, and is looking toward me, smiling.

I'm next in Guy's and Mary's apartment, a little uncomfortable because I don't fit. I'm conscious of our differences. Mary has her hair in a tight natural and I notice grey hairs in it [the rest is brown, which is not true in the outer world]. She is going to go out for a while and I wonder whether she will drive, knowing she has no license. She stands outside the door a while [it's like the door of Ron's apartment]. Then she re-enters, laughing — didn't we notice anything strange? She was still in her bathrobe (long, faded, turquoise) and wearing her 'natural' wig like a cap over her long hair. I had noticed, though I said nothing. She laughs at us for being so unobservant or inattentive and dresses to go out. When ready, she is wearing red and a tall, cone-shaped hat that is also red and has crescent moons and stars on it. I joke to Guy that it resembles a witch's cap. He says seriously that he likes it and appears himself well-dressed to go shopping, wearing a cone-shaped hat himself. Embarrassed, I agree with him that they are indeed attractive hats. They resemble hats I have seen Shakespearean players wearing:

With Guy and Mary are others — among them Nora with perhaps her family, for there are children and teenagers [though in the outer world I know Nora to be too young to have teenage children]. I notice that they are all extremely well-dressed, even Guy, who is wearing a flowered dress shirt and a vest. I make a mental note: in Mexico they dress better when they go out, regardless of what they are going out for. I think of talking with Guy about this.

At a balcony railing that they all pass by to exit, one of Nora's teenagers lifts a foot and says to me, smiling, 'Sandals. See?' I can't see them well in the poor light where he is standing, but I acknowledge his comment. He seems happy to be wearing what I normally wear. Nora, behind him, is smiling to me.

Left alone in the apartment, I feel more uncomfortable than ever. What am I doing here? The place is not mine, and is different from what I would have.

I look around. The floors are all carpeted nicely, even Tom's room, which has more than one carpet. It has patches of different colours. Everything seems lushly comfortable, in pinks and blues. In the bathroom are rolls for towels, rolled up like the tissue paper. The towels look good, obviously expensive. I wonder, "How much did Guy pay for these? They're so expensive, how does one bring himself to pay for them?" In Tom's room I pass a mirror and notice myself: I can't see my head unless I bend down, for the mirror is in a child's room. I do bend down, however, to see an overall image. I am surprised to see myself looking attractive. I'm wearing a light blue pullover shirt, the neck of which is unzipped so that it is casual. It hangs loosely. My pants are white, bell-bottom, tight at the hips. I'm barefoot. The clothes are 'comfortable,' because the shirt has no tails and is short so that I can't keep it tucked in. I consider going out — I seem prepared for it.

I wake while still attempting to tuck in the shirt. I'm walking around in the living room, still feeling out of place and thinking that I should go out since I don't look too bad.

Comments:
The 'mirror' of myself is important. I don't remember mirrors in former dreams. My head cut off — an aspect of me commonly not accepted, which is important enough to me that I stoop to see it. In the world of others, my intellect is not valuable or desirable.

The dream seems to comment on my relationships with others, my feeling of estrangement. Lately I have spent most of my time with people I would not consider similar to me. I'm generally the odd one out among people who strive for happiness by being playful, gay, sociable, lovable. Their lives seem divided between their work, which consists of money-making activities not generally creative for them, and their play, after which they burst out gaily. Guy's house reflects the outgoing, modern life — they have been shopping and keep up with modern merchandise (which is expensive). I can't possibly talk with any of them. My difference is understood simply — I'm reduced to the adolescent's grasp of things: he wears sandals to imitate me.

Dream Tasks: Applying Key Questions
— How am I, as dream ego, acting in this dream?

I am reacting, not initiating. I observe the others, almost as if I were watching a film, and I note the furniture, etc., with an active curiosity, as if to translate it all into some sort of statement. The other dream characters also behave almost as if I weren't capable of responding — Mary's not noticing how observant I was; the teenager's comment inviting no significant response other than simple recognition for his sake. I watch myself in the mirror and react almost to a stranger. Thus, dream ego is responding as one detatched, alienated.

— Why did I need this dream?

It responds to an outer life problem that I am doing nothing to solve. It responds by offering definition and outline to what I have neglected to organize.

— What relation does this dream have to what is happening right now in my life?

See 'Comments,' above.

— What choices can I (and will I) make as a result of working with this dream?

I can — and will — be less easily compromised by others who need to simplify what I take seriously. It is possible for me not to demand of them that they adopt my values and concerns; it is possible, then, that they not demand that I adopt theirs or sacrifice mine to make their world simpler. I can enjoy their world by allowing myself to expand in a sort of sympathy; they can take the opportunity to use the same process to expand when with me. Or they can resist and be challenged. Either way, for me it has become a matter of self-respect.

— What is the difference between my working actively with this dream or simply dreaming it without any conscious attempt to do anything with what happens?

To ignore the dream is to perpetuate a frustration that could create more severe problems in the future. By doing nothing about it I could risk wandering far from what is important to me, moving little by little into a life that has little meaning for me, little significance.

Simply to acknowledge the issues raised by the dream is to provide me with an understanding and an affirmation of the significance of my values that can help me not to lose sight of them. By taking some action I could go further, perhaps creating a milieu in which I can live a productive, rewarding life. It is not to forget Keats' dictum, 'that which is creative must create itself.'

Questions I have ignored
— What are the various feelings in this dream?

I have ignored a question whose answer must come from a part of me that is poorly developed. I commonly ignore my feelings. In the dream I feel abandoned, ridiculed, outraged, alienated. But I face it calmly. These feelings, in the dream as in life, stir imperceptibly within.

— What would I like to avoid about this dream?

Its suggestion of vanity that is encouraged when I submit to the desires of others to please them. I stare in the mirror admiringly and think to go out where others can see me.

— Where are my helpers and guides in life [and in my dreams]?

The dreamwork answers this, and I have to face the answer: My helpers and guides now are my own instincts and training (Yoga, I Ching, Tai Chi) and knowledge. I have put myself in a situation where there are no outer guides whom I contact, and no helpers. The dreamwork offers itself as guide and helper, to put me in contact also with the others.

Evaluation
Common themes — The conflict between the individual and his society that both needs his individuality and struggles to resist and destroy it. Consciousness of the them, now, is not enough — I must actively assert my own individuality — Arjuna against his own family in the Bhagavad Gita.

Questions — Why am I not seeking outer helpers, individuals in sympathy with my way and goals?

How much can I expect from myself if I surround myself with individuals inattentive to the matters important to me?

N.B. The *dream* I understood fairly well immediately, and this satisfied me too much. The *dreamwork* proved useful, and was *necessary* for me, in order to know the dream's lesson and *offering*.

Dreamwork Entry
— Key Questions Applied to a Dream

Instructions

— After writing your dream down read over the list of questions. Select a question which appeals to you, write it down, and start writing a response to it with your dream in mind. Write fairly quickly so you are getting material from your spontaneous self.

— Select another question and respond to the dream with it. Pick as many questions as seem relevant or you have time for.

— Check out the list of questions for the one question you have avoided. Your ego naturally avoids things which may be painful or which may further purify it. Now use this question as a basis for responding to your dream.

— After you have written out your answers check for common themes and new insights. Summarize and write these down. How can they be used in your everyday life and in your future dream life?

— What new question or questions have surfaced for you from doing this work? Write them down and perhaps leave them as questions which permeate your being. At some future date you may want to review this material and see what answers have come for you to your questions.

Following the Dream Ego

What could be more practical than seeing how your dream ego is or is not acting in your dream?

Your *dream ego* is usually the image of yourself in the dream.

You may find your dream ego observing the action. Or running from something. Or taking a journey somewhere. Or exploring. Or in a car.

Very seldom will you see your dream ego actively choosing, actively aware of alternatives in the dream and choosing which to do or not to do.

Most people starting dreamwork find that their dream egos are not very active or assertive in dreams. Most of the action is happening to them or other figures.

As in dreams, so in life.

Life itself is a reality, is a waking dream every day. Most of the time our outer oriented egos may not be all that initiatory in what we do.

Depressed people tend to have depressing dreams.

The experiences of hundreds of hours of dreamwork point to the fact that dream sharers find it more fulfilling to get their dream ego active, assertive, initiatory in dreams. This speaks well for outer life as well. The more assertive we are in outer life, the waking dream, the more we will exercise choice and actualize the potentials possible to us in reality, and a creatively assertive ego

also usually knows when not to choose before the time is ripe.

We learn to activate the creative ego by activating the dream ego in dreamwork.

If you really want an accurate picture of what your ego is like follow what it is doing or not doing in your dreams.

Yet dreams often picture the dream ego doing things it would not dream of doing in outer reality.

If what you are doing in your dream seems positive, creative, new or meaningful, why not try out the new behaviour in outer reality as well?

If what you are doing in your dream seems negative, different or destructive, why not see whether you are also doing just that in outer reality as well? If you observe in dreams do you also observe in life? If you run in dreams do you also run in life? If you kill in dreams do you also subtly kill in life?

If what we are doing in a dream seems uncreative or destructive we might look into the dream and see what other kinds of choices we could have made. We could even re-enter or re-write the dream having our dream ego deal with the situations differently.

When 'following the dream ego' describe as descriptively as possible what the dream ego is doing or not doing and then list the attitudes that govern the dream ego's actions. Describe also the feelings the dream ego may be having. Feeling is internal action. Feelings may also be evoked by attitudes as well as evoke attitudes.

An *attitude* is a personal law. We all have sentences within our heads which we use to make our choices. An attitude is usually a judgement, or evaluative statement, about oneself or the 'other'.

When I choose to run from an adversary I am saying to myself something like 'it's safer to run' or 'life is out to get me' or 'if I don't choose it I don't want to do it' or 'I'm not strong enough to confront the adversary.' I am also feeling *fear*, a state of tension and perceived danger of annihilation.

What personal law or attitude governs your specific action or feeling? Let go to your own thought patterns and see what comes up.

When you have seen closely what your dream ego has been up to and what attitudes seem to govern its actions then decide which actions and attitudes seem appropriate, meaningful and assertive and formulate ways in which you will act thus in further dreams and in outer reality.

For those actions and attitudes which seem inappropriate or destructive see how you would reformulate or change those attitudes.

One real change in working with dreams is to change the attitude which automatically says 'it is safer to run from adversaries' to 'it is often safer to confront adversaries and demand help.' This is a basic attitude of Senoi dreamwork. Confront the adversary and often you will get help. Run from the adversary and the adversary will gain further power over you.

Some Characteristics of the Dream Ego

In dreams we characterize the dream ego as usually the image of oneself. But this may vary. For even more central than image is the awareness of an 'I' or centre of awareness and action. Thus people have reported themselves in dreams as being the opposite sex, animals and inanimate objects such as chairs and dinnerware.

How many egos are there involved with the dream state? We have the dream ego itself, the image of ourselves as interactant in the dream. We have a 'non-ego' in which we experience a dream but without ourselves in it.

We have the observing ego, that centre of awareness which sees and remembers the whole dream and maintains it in consciousness into the waking state.

We may have in the other characters in the dream aspects of our egos. Certainly these characters embody attitudes, sometimes quite contradictory ones, to the dream ego's attitudes. And other characters may make choices or have feelings in the dream.

Is there an essential difference between the dream ego and other beings in the dream?

We do not know enough about this, yet there seems to be a significant difference. It is one thing to experience a murder in a dream and quite another to experience yourself doing the killing.

Perhaps this is due in part to the waking ego's identifying with the dream ego. This identification becomes clear in dealing with *nightmares*. Which ego wakes the dreamer up in fright? It must be the dream ego, the direct receiver in the nightmare of the threat. What if the observing ego remained dominant and did not let the dream ego take over volitional control?

Then the dreamer would stay asleep and complete the action. This is the preferred way to deal with nightmares. To stay asleep and get the dream ego to remain in the dream and deal with the threat, either by letting the threat do its worst and seeing what happens, or by confronting the adversary and transforming it. Another technique which helps this process is to re-write every nightmare by dealing with the threat and bringing things to a resolution.

It is quite possible that loss, death and trauma dreams are an attempt by the unconscious to get us to differentiate our ego functions better. For instance, most people call the waking, outer oriented state the real world, while dreams, feelings, fantasies, etc. are implied as not being real. How much better to use the terms 'inner' and 'outer' reality and to differentiate the waking ego from the dream ego.

Characteristics of the Fully Functioning Creative Ego

Questions such as 'Who am I?' (Ramana Maharashi) or even 'What am I?' (C. G. Jung) fall to the wayside when we ask simply 'What does the ego do?' or 'How does my ego function?' The ego in this view is not a static being but a highly creative entity which is always acting, however weakly or strongly.

If you asked me right now 'Who are you?' I would reply 'I am listening to you. I am observing you and myself. I am processing the energy between us.' And if you were to respond, 'Yes, but who are you anyway?' I would have to reply, 'One who considers your question irrelevant. Let us not waste our time here. Let us do something together.'

No enlightenment is needed where there is action. Enlightened action is enlightenment. Enlightenment without action is void.

The ego in its purest form functions as choice-maker, or director of the energy available to it. It also exercises memory, or the ability to recall the language of past events. And the ego is the centre of consciousness, or awareness plus appropriate action. The ego also seems to exercise an organizing function. It sorts out things and creates or discovers relations between them. It also formulates a set of values which become the context within which to live life and make choices. And finally the ego may choose to form a commitment to certain values, the ultimate of which is to manifest the deepest, most meaningful sources available to it.

The weak or uncreative ego is not even that aware of its essential functions. Its choice-making and awareness is usually governed by unconscious attitudes and feelings. It is full of identifications with rather than relations to various archetypal entities, like mother, child, priest, therapist, writer, etc. It has not faced the problem of its own annihilation yet and so usually acts out of fear and anxiety.

Creating the Healthy Ego

To change the weak ego into a creative ego involves a lifetime of work and development. Perhaps the fullest arena for observing the nature of one's own egos is in regular dreamwork. Through such work we learn to differentiate various ego states, inner and outer, and we work to develop wholeness within ourselves.

For example, in using the method 'following the dream ego' on a whole series of dreams you will discover many formerly unconscious attitudes which govern your choices. You will also notice that a number of these attitudes are not merely contrasting but contradictory. In other words, you have been actively and continually defeating yourself with your own choices!

As you process these attitudes, sacrificing some, transforming some into positive values, and actualizing creative ones even more, you will be developing and organizing your personality and life more in line with your own wholeness potential. To integrate we must develop creative interlinkings between attitudes as well as between the more archetypal parts of ourselves. One might go so far as to say that one changes attitudes through consciousness into values. In this sense, values are attitudes consciously realized.

'Following the dream ego' is one primary method for working with any dream. No matter how unintelligible other symbols and actions are, we can gain in fundamental insight and action by processing the dream ego.

And there is an aspect of hard work to such a process. *It takes ego to have ego.* Most egos prefer sleep or ecstasy rather than the quiet but vital satisfaction of manifesting strong and committed choices. Yet no ecstatic or unconscious experience builds ego. In the last analysis, when left to it, the ego has only itself to create itself. If this is so, then let's get on with it and develop!

Following the Dream Ego — An Example

Strephon's Comments
This could well be called a dream about dealing with relationships. What is one to do? So often these days, and perhaps always in the history of humankind, there are outside influences on a relationship. One person has feelings for more than one other. Jealousy, the emotion of possessiveness, hangs heavy on relationships. Human relationships seem to be a major and difficult area in which to find fulfillment, if not security. What does dreamwork add?

Dreamwork adds reality and working to accept it. We cannot control the outer but we can certainly creatively work with our own responses to what is happening in reality.

Thus, in this dream, we see an actual outer relationship situation directly reflected. And then what? Is this the purpose of the dream, just to reflect the outer? No, it shows also, in the symbol of the dream ego, how we typically react to the outer. When we find out exactly what our reactions, attitudes and feelings are, we can work to sort them out and change them. So the focus shifts from concentration on an outer situation to concentration on the inner situation. This dreamwork, then, is a good example of getting clearer on attitudes influencing relationships and what can be done creatively about them. Personal names have been changed into role names to hide identities and help the flow. 'S.H.' refers to the 'separated husband.'

Dream Title: A Dream of Relationship   *Date: November 25, 1979*

I dreamed of calling my lover, and asking her how her day went. She was sort of weepy over the phone. She had had a good, warm and sensitive visit with someone.

'Was it S.H.?' I asked.

'Yes, he is really changing,' was her response. 'And he is studying his dreams.'

'With whom?'

My friend does not answer and I repeat, 'With whom?' a second and third time, saying, 'You can't objectify a dream without a guide.'

She said he took her dreams about him and his dreams about her and really studied them. He was unable to stay long and visit with her since the man he drove down with in a truck had to leave.

Note: This dream reflected the outer life situation in the sense that my friend did have feelings about both her separated husband and myself. And all three of us had recently gone through a crisis of her having to no longer be ambivalent.

Comments

This dream came on the night I slept alone after two beautiful days with my friend. S.H. was returning the day after that day and I was anxious about whether they would talk or not. After the visit from S.H.'s sister, who has self-reflection, I could feel insecure that S.H. would suddenly mature and my friend would then want to relate to him. Was she in fact in bed with him now? I had gone to bed wanting to incubate a telepathic dream. So I called my friend. No, she had not talked with S.H., but her daughter had shared one of S.H.'s dreams about her with her. An image also came of splitting my friend right down the middle with a sword and her still living.

Dream Tasks

— Do following the dream ego to get at the basis for my insecurity. Not what actions but what feelings is the drego (dream ego) experiencing in the dream and what are the attitudes behind them? Am I really responding to my lover or a feeling level in the dream? Re-write the dream sharing all the feelings.

— Write a relationship meditation on the nature of insecurity. What are the forces bringing a relationship together and what are the forces pulling it apart? The relationship stays together when the +'s outweigh the −'s? The element of competition with others and performance to meet the other's expectations. Note: This dream task was not directly done since the energy seemed to be focused on certain anxiety producing attitudes rather than on the relationship itself.

Following the Dream Ego

— Calling my lover and asking her how the day went.

- Hidden anxiety — did anything happen with her separated husband?
- o Attitude that when I am not in control fate is going to come in and rob me of that which I most cherish.
- o Attitude that I am so little lovable that the woman who loves me will easily give me up.
  Hidden feeling coming out as anxiety that I really do love her more than I objectively want to now because of the difficulties.

— Drego responds to friend's appreciative feeling state over another man with questioning, superiority, anger (suppressed) instead of statements of feeling. The drego tries to control the situation by passing judgement and persistence. The drego also tries to get information to ground its fears in the factual world. It tries to use authority and logic to dominate and therefore win over his friend in the situation.

- Hidden anxiety that friend is rejecting him for another man.

o Attitude that a positive response to another person automatically means that the drego is no longer first and therefore is last or rejected. No recognition that his friend can respond positively to her separated husband and still respond positively to drego.

o Attitude that the way to prevent rejection is to try and dominate the potential rejector. This can be done through anger and logical argument which convinces the other person to make certain choices despite what he or she is feeling.

o Attitude that the rationale of logic and facts can win over feeling.

o Attitude that feelings are not to be trusted since they cannot be explained, chosen or be subjected to logic.

Note:

drego = dream ego	● = feeling state of drego
− = description of drego	o = attitude of drego

Re-writing the Dream after Following the Dream Ego

I dreamed I called my lover and right away told her I was anxious about her having met with her separated husband and wanted to know all about it if she would tell me. I also told her I was feeling very related to her lately and was quite afraid of having her separated husband back on the scene to perplex her and upset our relationship.

My friend then told me that she had a warm sensitive visit with her separated husband and that he had been studying his own dreams about her and her dreams about him which she had given him.

At this point I blew up and said I could not take the tension of her being intimate with both him and me at the same time, that I considered sharing dreams to be as intimate as sexual intercourse and that I was also worried that she would go back to him if he changed and really started working on himself the same way she and I were working on ourselves.

She said she could still have positive feelings for S.H. as well as positive feelings for me and could I accept that.

I said I wish I could but that I was human and it always came down to me or him whatever the context and that I did not feel secure relating to her if she was going to be at all intimate or holding the door open to him. I told her I wanted to be loved and appreciated despite S.H. and I did not want to always be placed in this comparison game.

My friend said she heard me and appreciated hearing my feelings.

We left it that way, with no decision made on her part about what she was going to do about dual relating. My decision would have to wait for hers.

Afterwards I wanted to scream. Why was I placed in a position like this in which I could never feel secure?

Perhaps I needed to just let myself be loved and love?

Should I really pull out completely and find someone else? Or would all the interesting, vital women have another man? Perhaps I was not feeling enough and that was what could change in the situation?

I knew this much. I wanted to get over my anxiety. If it could not be resolved in the outer, could it be resolved in the inner? Perhaps the inner was where it was all at anyway? With that I woke up!

Evaluation

This really gripped me. As I was doing the whole thing I could feel the tension and the feelings. I was right in it. Even after doing it all I am not clear on everything. But I am clearer and the issues seem well raised.

— Can one ever be secure in relationship or is there always someone lurking just around the corner? (How can I state this more positively? Is it true that someone I love will always have so much love that she will respond intimately to others as well as to myself?)

— What decisions and processes need to be made in terms of the outer relationship?

— How can I be much more directly feeling regardless of circumstances?

— What inner anxieties and defensiveness are there to be transformed around this issue?

Dreamwork Entry
— Following the Dream Ego

The technique of following the dream ego is sometimes difficult, but it can create a powerful and meaningful experience. So please persist and complete this process despite any resistance. The ego dealing with difficulties is the ego-building ego. You will feel the extent of your achievement by the end of the process.

The Conscious Work

— Starting from the beginning of the dream, describe literally what the dream ego is or is not *doing*.

— Describe what the dream ego is or is not *feeling*. Doing is action. Feeling is being.

— Choose certain key descriptions and redescribe them in generalized terms. Thus, 'My dream ego is running from a tiger' might become 'The dream ego is avoiding confrontation with an adversary.'

— List possible underlying attitudes which may be governing the dream ego's actions or feelings. Thus, from the dream with the tiger adversary, we might obtain these possibilities for attitudes. 'It is better to avoid threats than to face them.' 'When I am afraid I have to give in to my fears and run.' 'I am too weak to deal with certain negative forces.'

— Choose which attitudes are positive, valuable, and life-affirming for you, and which are negative. The context for this evaluation may be the goals in the dream itself, or other goals or values for you. For instance, in the above example from an actual dream, the tiger was about to eat the dream ego and the person woke up in fright. Thus, running from the tiger was ineffective. There must be some other way to cope with the total situation without having to escape from the dream.

— Choose which negative attitudes most seem to fit you and change them through doing *affirmations*. To create an affirmation take a negative attitude and re-write it as a life-affirming, reality-affirming statement. For example, the attitude 'It is better to avoid threats than to face them' can be changed to 'It is better to face threats than avoid them.'

Then write it several times on the one side of the page and write whatever comes into your head on the other side of the page. This will usually be the 'negative mass' evoked by the new attitude. You are re-training yourself in new attitudes, which are now really values and which are more integrative and life-affirming. Keep doing the affirmation until it wins out over the negative mass. Or write a new affirmation which includes the new and the negative attitudes evoked together, if this will make your affirmation more realistic.

An example would be as follows. 'It is better to avoid threats than face them' becomes as an affirmation 'I am more and more able to face directly the threats in my life.' If the voice of the 'negative mass' says strongly enough, 'no, you're not,' then re-write the affirmation as 'I am more and more able to face directly *some* of the threats in my life.' This style of doing affirmations comes from Leonard Orr, founder of 'rebirthing.'

Unconscious Process Work

— Rewrite the dream imaginatively with the dream ego going through the same scenes but this time interacting with dream figures, using the new, more creative attitudes. Let your words and feelings flow.

Grounding the Experience

— Compare your dream ego's attitudes with your waking ego's attitudes in the same area.
— List those attitudes you will let go of and transform.
— Formulate intentions for specific actions, which embody the life-affirming attitudes. As you carry out those actions during the coming weeks, look for dreams and synchronistic events which confirm these new attitudes.
— Formulate what dream ego changes you hope for and will intend to make while in the dream state. Watch for results.

Summary Evaluation

— From your dreamwork, what have you learned about life and yourself? What attitudes are you using as a context for this evaluation?
— Be welcomed more fully to the arena of life! Why do we loathe reality so? Reality is what we have to create our lives. Reality tests all our attitudes; the consequences which reality creates teach us which attitudes work and which do not.

Dialoguing with Dream Images

The Nature of Dialogue

The life of dialogue is one of the chief accomplishments of humankind. Everyone talks daily all over the world, except in the most silent of contemplative orders or the most isolated of prison cells. But even there, *in extremis*, the isolates must hear themselves in internal dialogue. Why so much conversation? What's it all about? Processing? Not only the living of human experiences but the processing into meaning of those experiences? What else?

We talk to hear ourselves, that is the lesson of any confession. It is we ourselves who must accept whatever we have done or not done in life.

And who is there who does not talk with him or herself? Or who does not hear voices or bells ringing or some long lost memory or the rhythms and tunes of the cosmos?

Are we any better at listening than at talking? Some are too busy talking, stating their point of view, to listen. While others absorb, listen, remain tentative and almost never assert themselves. Is any of this a dialogue?

The life of dialogue means a 'respondent' and a 'responded to'. The life of dialogue means a 'thou' talking to an 'I' and an 'I' listening at least as much as 'it' talks.

In terms of the dream here is an actual outer life scene: We are now observing an interpretive dream-sharing group. A dreamer shares a dream in which someone she knows is flying. She receives from half a dozen other

participants possibilities as to what flying can mean. The dreamer is to pick the possibility which makes the most sense.

But wait. Who has been left out of this interaction? All we see is a bunch of egos each giving a different point of view on a symbol. None of these egos have been in the reported dream so how can they possibly know what is going on?

And why has no one thought to ask the figure in the dream why she is flying?

When we need information why not dialogue with the being directly affected?

The dialogue with dream figures and situations is one of the major techniques of Jungian-Senoi dreamwork. Spending a few minutes in dialogue after writing the dream down will almost always produce new information about the dream. Dialogue can often replace conscious amplification for obtaining meaning from a dream, even when there is only a short time available within which to do dreamwork.

Discovering the Issues

The first phase in doing dialogues is *discovering the issues* in the dream. Perhaps every dream has aspects which are unclear or puzzling to the conscious mind. There seems, even, to be an intention on the part of the 'dream originator' to present situations which require activity by the conscious and unconscious sides of our personality in order to clarify them. Discovering the issues can be based in part on using the following *central questions* as the focus for beginning your dialogue.

— What, or who are you?
— Why are you in my dream?
— Why are you acting the way you are in my dream?
— What do you have to tell me?
— Why is such-and-such happening in my dream?
— What do you think/feel about such-and-such?
— What do you want from me? What do you want me to do?
— What is your gift to me?
— What questions would you ask of me?
— What do you think/feel about this dialogue?

Perhaps you can formulate other questions? It is usually desirable to have questions with which to begin the dialogue. As it proceeds, further questions may occur. At some point a flow may happen and the dialogue becomes almost automatic.

In asking questions we are not fishing for answers. However, 'fishing for answers' may be one level of dialogue in which one might ask each dream character, why are you in my dream? But this is a somewhat rational level of dialogue. The more unconscious flow level is when the dialogue gets going between the dialogue ego and a dream entity, and to attain this level, persistence and letting go on the part of the questioner is required. In such a dialogue the 'I' not only asks questions but listens, gives responses, positive and negative, and becomes really involved.

A frequent issue people new to dialogue raise is, 'How do I know this is not just myself speaking? I already knew the answers I received.'

Yes, the ego may know the 'answers' but not have trusted or practised them. In doing dialogue we start where we are. Many people have a pattern in which the ego only listens to itself. If what comes out of a dialogue you already know, then persist, tell the dream figure you want new information and be ready to really listen.

Always bring up your problems about dialogue with the dream figures involved. They are best equipped to help you. They will tell you quite honestly what you may need to do to open up the flow.

Another important issue is in the question, 'How do I know the information in the dialogue is real and not made up by my imagination?'

We could take the position that anything you produce comes from the unconscious and is therefore relevant to how your psyche is expressing itself. But we go a step further and suggest that there are differences in levels of working with the unconscious, or even differences between the imaginative powers and the directional powers of the deeper self.

If the flow gets going for you, if the information coming your way contrasts with your own consciously chosen point of view, then most likely you are not 'making up' the dialogue.

We are not seeking to create our unconscious, but to let it speak for itself.

We have the crucial issue here as to whether the conscious ego is able and willing to give up its self-imposed and self-believed mastery of the psyche. Such dominance by the ego is a false mastery at best. Which personality entity dominates the psyche is a crucial factor in the individuation process.

Is not the interpretive school of psychology and dreamwork based on the ego's trying to maintain mastery over the unconscious?

If the ego can tell itself what a symbol means, it will not have to face the fact that it might well be told to change by the non-ego directive power in the psyche. *An ego-threatening message cannot get through an ego-interpretive approach.*

How painful it is for a being who in actuality does not like to give up its self-deceptive false sovereignty!

The issue is one of integrity, perhaps the single greatest issue for those committing themselves to any spiritual or psychological growth process.

'How do I know that I am not fooling myself, that I am not merely playing the game so well that I fool myself as well as others?'

The art and life of dialogue lends a corrective to the problem of self-deception. For not only do we let go to listening to new information. We make, also, a commitment to at least consider seriously following that new information wherever it might lead.

What an exciting possibility it is not to have to always try and be in control of everything, but to be able instead to follow, to work with, to create together a life direction superior in meaning to anything the ego can consciously manufacture itself!

Developing the Feeling Level of Your Responsiveness

Question-asking and responding to what comes is one central level for doing dialogue. But still another level is giving feelings. In one of my own dreamwork dialogues I began with 'I love you,' to a hysterical dream figure who had lost her daughter. This changed the whole quality of my response. I was not after information, understanding or knowledge. I was actively creating acceptance.

So before beginning the dialogue you might spend a few minutes meditating on the feelings you would like to give your dialogue figure.

'I love you.'
'I need you.'
'I hate you.'
'I'm upset by you.'
'I'm confused and need your help.'
'I don't know how I feel about you.'
'I open my heart to you.'
'I'm scared of you.'
'I'm in despair, can you help?'
'I'm amused by you.'
'I'm intrigued.'

There are many more feeling responses, of course, Make up your own list.

The crucial point is looking at our own dialogues, inner and outer, and seeing if we ever give a feeling response. There is a difference also between the feeling which is expressed as reaction and the feeling which is given as choice.

By my choices I determine my life and this applies on a feeling level as well.

Choosing the Dream Being with Which to Dialogue

Any figure or situation can be chosen for dialogue. A person, the mountain, the dream ego itself, the monster, the friend, the battle, the ritual, and so on. Usually go where the most energy or perplexity resides. Also choose, if possible, an entity which has a lot of specificity. We may choose also to dialogue with more than one entity.

Generally, the emphasis here is on keeping one's own ego active in the dialogue. There needs to be someone who is listening and who is committed to dealing with the information received. If, as in Gestalt dialogue, you have two different parts of your psyche in dialogue you may produce some creative experience, but still, where is there a conscious ego to integrate the experience into everyday life?

To develop more than one point of view we can have separate dialogues with opposite entities in the same dream. Or we may have these opposite entities dialoguing with each other and with our own ego coming in to help process what is happening.

Dialogue is a major feature of journalwork. Some of the 'life dialogues,' which may also appear in dreams, are as follows.

— Dialoguing with one's birth. Why was I born?
— With one's death. What is the resolution of my life towards which I am working?
— With some person who has died to re-establish or complete the relationship.
— With one's own spirit guide, that presence which may know our essential life direction better than we ourselves do.
— With one's worst enemy, living or dead.
— With one's friends, lovers, and antagonists as inner figures as well as outer figures.

Through dialogue we reconcile the opposites of our lives.

In choosing the being with which to dialogue look for someone who may have a different viewpoint from your own. We do not become conscious by knowing what we already know. We become conscious by discovering that which wants to be known through us.

Launching the Dialogue

Before launching the dialogue we must, of course, be dealing with such issues as degree of openness, commitment to listening and willingness to persist until one has had an emotional experience and resolution has occurred.

The dialoguing ego must have a position about its own ability to censor, avoid or distort whatever comes up from the unconscious, the landscape within which our inner beings reside. The ability to distort or censor is different from the choice to yield to a resistance when the going gets too intense, painful or all-consuming.

And so within the moment before beginning we meditate freely upon our own position.

— Are we really open?
— Do we have sufficient strength to go through it at least part of the way?
— How great is our passion for truth?
— How much do we really want inner psychological and spiritual healing?
— To help free ourselves we might even have a dialogue with our censor and come to terms with him or her.

In doing dialogue are we not bringing the opposites of our personality together? Are we not establishing more harmonious relations between different parts of our psyches? Are we not letting the repressed sides of ourselves, as well as our dominant sides speak? Are we not, even, letting the spirit world speak to us?

Is there perhaps a psychic connection established in a dialogue with the essence of other persons, living or dead? Several Institute participants have had dialogues with parents, spouses, etc. who have died, and they have been deeply moved. Something besides an exclusively inner spirit seems to be present. Who knows ultimately all that is going on?

In beginning a dialogue we may choose to start either with questions, or just listening, or repeating, even, the conversation in the dream and continuing it.

Put yourself into a meditative state, eyes closed, and visualize the figure or entity with which you are to talk. You might even start with a question about your dream spirit's appearance or action. Why are you only half-dressed, and so on?

Usually, people write the questions and conversational flow as fast as they can so as to bypass the observer-commentator ego who could become too active and say things like, 'This is crazy' or 'not true' or 'I already know that' and so on. Others do some dialogue meditatively, write it down, and then do more. Writing the material down is necessary for consciousness. For you will be asked to process the dialogue just as you would a dream.

At any point you as ego can choose to end the dialogue. You also have choice as to how much you wish to direct the dialogue. Often persistence is a necessary quality. There may be silence. The respondent may say it does not have the answer or does not know the answer, etc. Persistence is the ability to maintain a goal in the face of any adversity. There can be no dialogue without opposition. There must be distinction before there can be reconciliation.

Let the conversation flow. Let it develop. Let it go where it wants to go. Yet, stay active. Bring up the issues. Question what is being said. Agree where you can. Give your own response as dialogue ego. Keep going until you choose to stop or the dialogue comes to a natural resolution.

Evaluating the Dialogue

If you have become really involved and moved by the dialogue you may end in deep feeling and not know exactly what has happened. Perhaps you feel gratitude for being given new possibilities for wisdom? Or confusion? Where did that come from? Perhaps it is unclear as to what it all means. Or there is a sudden burst of clarity or confirmation and the necessity to make decisions.

Read over what you have written, perhaps saying it out loud. Let the feelings sink in. The following questions may help to bring the experience to consciousness.

— How and what has moved you, or in you, from doing your dialogue?

— What insights have you gained?

— How have you as dialogue ego acted and what attitudes are behind that?

— What is the essence or character of your respondent?

— What is the message?

— What choices can be made from such a dialogue?

— What tasks can you do to actualize its content?

— What further questions or issues arise for you?

— What effect does this dialogue have in terms of the original dream?

— How has this dialogue affected you emotionally?

In many, many dreamwork classes and groups, people have become deeply involved in their dialogues, sometimes moved to tears, or awe, or realization of truth. Who can say where such an experience comes from, or even what its meaning is? From my own experience as well as others' experiences, I can say that dreamwork is soulwork. That somehow, somewhere there is a more central part of ourselves than we usually know who welcomes the chance to speak to us. It is a rare occasion when we first listen, and so we are moved, often profoundly. Yet what could be more natural than knowing oneself? And this means using the known self to learn and relate to the unknown selves. To know ourselves we must know the various parts of ourselves.

A dialogue is a relationship between a known and an unknown. Dialogue penetrates mutual isolation. We have the choice to listen perpetually only to our known selves, or to take the leap towards a relationship with the stranger

who stands in the corner waiting for us to wait no longer.

Every dialogue is a reach into the unknown where we listen to more than the echo of our own solitary being.

Dreamwork Example — Dialoguing with Dream Images

For a good example of dreamwork dialogue see the chapter entitled 'A Transformational Journey.' In it you will find an active and committed dialogue ego learning some essential things from a dream figure. The dialogue 'works' because of the flow and because the dreamer's ego is open to internal direction from other parts of the psyche. This same ego probably would find itself more resistant to external direction from other people.

Dreamwork Entry
— Dialoguing with Dream Images

Instructions

— After writing your dream down look for:

— Any conversations barely begun.

— Actions or issues which seem unresolved, or which have special energy or concern for you.

— Formulate questions which state these issues.

— Pick out a significant figure or situation in the dream, positive or negative, to dialogue with. You might even dialogue with the 'you' in your dream, your dream ego. Personalized figures are usually more responsive than impersonal figures or inanimate objects.

— Visualize your fellow conversationalist as he/she, appears in your dream and start your dialogue, asking key questions, persisting and writing down whatever comes into your head.

— Stop when you have run out of energy or some resolution or resistance on your part has happened. Or you may choose to push through a resistance in order to confront what you may be avoiding.

— Re-read your dialogue for its meaning. Have any of your questions been answered? What new questions arise out of the material? What new information is at hand?

— Formulate specific ways and actions you will act on what you have learned. What attitudes or inner laws and beliefs need changing?

— Have you honoured what happened? Do you feel gratitude to the dream figure who dialogued with you? Why or why not and what will you do about it?

— Ask your figure for a dream task and be willing, if appropriate, to do it. Appropriateness means following the laws of reality or humanity.

— What is your dialogue ego doing and not doing in the dialogue?

— What specific dream wisdom can you list from this dialogue?

— What choices and tasks will you do as a result of evaluating this dialogue?

Expressing the Dream in Art Forms

Image laced with feeling and emotion is the primal language of the unconscious, that primordial ocean out of which emerge all thought forms to manifest a language of symbol which all peoples can understand, not so much through analyzing as through direct re-experiencing of the symbol as it echoes core energies from its depths.

On an evolutionary scale of increasing consciousness the archetypes first manifest themselves as channel and energy, the functional or 'essence' aspect of the archetype.

Then next on the scale we have the archetypes yielding out of themselves clusters of images, feelings, and compulsive or automatic actions.

Which leads finally to the borderlines of consciousness and the manifestation of the archetypes as concepts and predispositions to action. These manifestations form the basis of conscious choice-making and reflection.

The reflective consciousness-creating process is absolutely necessary for dealing fully with reality and for developing and integrating the personality. However, an over-loaded, over-rational consciousness has its drawbacks as well. Too much reflection and rationalism can dry up the personality with the result that we lose at least a part of our essential vitality, flexibility and openness to change.

When we are 'too' conscious, when we are too rational and organized, our essential being needs a return to primal experience, or the level of the archetype which manifests symbols. Thus in symbolic experiences, whether with certain drugs, rituals, music or instinctual experiences such as sex, we return to 'source ground' to find renewal in the primal universal energies. After participating in such experiences we must again assert conscious direction and development and manifest these energies in concepts, feelings and actions. Not to do so leaves the ego identified with the archetypal level of reality, and woe then to its ability to function and manifest on an everyday individual level.

In working with dreams and other visionary experiences we may choose or need to express certain symbols in one or more of the art forms, such as in graphic or plastic art, poetry, music, meditation, ritual, or dance.

What we are usually trying to do is re-express the archetypal energy of the dream in a kind of 'distillation to essence.' Once we have captured some of the image and feeling of the original dream symbol we can again experience it and feel the energy within overselves evoked by the symbol.

When we put dream symbols into an art form we are consciously re-directing energy back to that part of the unconscious from which the symbol originally manifested. The ego uses some of the energy from its own energy store, energy which it has previously won from the unconscious. The ego also redirects energy from other parts of the psyche. Thus a man choosing to paint his feminine in art rather than chase after still another woman is re-directing the energy of the unconscious and reducing the compulsive nature of his archetypes. The same would apply for a woman in dealing with her own inner masculine instead of always projecting it onto outer men.

Once the symbol is manifested in an art form it is 'out there' and available for us to experience and re-experience until we have consciously integrated the energy back inside ourselves by withdrawing the projection.

With the love projection, as an example, the person's contra-sexual component is projected onto the beloved. This is a natural process. For, as Jung has stated, we must first see the energy as outside ourselves before we can integrate it back within. This integration of the archetype destroys its compulsive dominance over our lives and shows itself creatively in our increase ability to express the archetype functionally.

Thus for the man the more he ceases in projecting his own feminine onto a woman, the more he will express as coming from himself feminine functions of receptivity, warmth and flow, to name only a few of the attributes.

Expressing archetypes in art forms is an intermediate step in the whole process of integration. Art and culture were probably invented as symbolic forms in order to help disengage us from the complete identification with outer forms that the compulsive nature of projections require. When we go to the theatre, as an example, and see our relational lives re-enacted as a farce we are bound to reflect more on how our own relationships are going and all we project onto them.

Cultural arts may also serve to evoke archetypal energies, thus enriching our actual life experiences by creating more possibilities for expression.

Dreams and dreamwork can play a crucial role in this manifesting and integrating of the archetypes because dreams also manifest or reflect archetypal energies back to us. Dreams have, however, an advantage over most cultural products in that they manifest the universal energies of the psyche in specific ways unique to each individual in a developmental process. Dreams usually reflect those archetypal energies with which we are most ready to deal. With cultural products we may get too much energy evoked. This is the 'museum effect' in which I as observer can only take in so many paintings before I must go outside and sit on the grass and process what has been evoked. The same would be true in seeing dramas or movies of violence or sensuality.

Do not evoke more than you can contain or transform. Either you will get overwhelmed by the archetypal energy and your choice-making power reduced or you will close off your feeling function and become less sensitive to life's energies.

Working in the arts oneself is quite different from participating in other people's artistic expression. Both experiences have their value but it is clearly more integrative for a person to express his or her own archetypal energies in specific projects.

The Issue of Innate or Projected Manifestation

Do objects themselves only become symbols because of what we project onto them? Is the energy all from within the psyche or is it also out there inherently in the object? And how can we ever tell?

This issue is important by virtue of the fact that there are certain more or less universally recognized symbols which continue to have great archetypal power over our lives. The mandala, or sacred circle, is one symbol manifested over and over in the world's great religions and architecture.

A religion can be described as a symbol system, like architecture or other cultural forms, for expressing the archetypes. No religion is a 'truth' in itself but only a symbol-system for manifesting the reality, the universal energies of the universe and their ongoing transformations, all of which we call God. Some religions, perhaps, are richer than others in their symbols, myths and dogmas, but the 'mystic' in any religion always seeks to get past the form, the symbol-system itself, to the original experience behind the form.

Dreams and dreamwork give us this capacity to penetrate to original experience of life energies. But to leave dreams only as dreams and not to manifest them also as cultural products ignores the wisdom behind the necessary creation of symbol systems.

We must have cultural forms within which to evoke, contain and transform the archetypes.

In this sense every journeyer must in some form become an artist with whatever medium seems most natural, whether it be in the traditional arts or in some aspect of life experience itself.

You as 'Artist'

Certain attitudes must be challenged and transformed in order to work with dreams and other archetypal manifestations in art forms.

One is that you have to be a professional artist, or have talent, in order to create.

Within each of us is the archetypal role-function of artist which is probably somewhere very close to the central archetypal of the Self. Ability to express oneself vividly comes more from being in tune with the flow from the unconscious than from any lessons at art or dance school. We are not concerned here about your developing an artistic proficiency in the aesthetic, cultural sense. So you can relax.

You are not performing for others.

You are not even performing for yourself.

What you are doing, hopefully, is letting yourself be moved by your own archetypes and your own need for wholeness.

Let go. Give up completely all those childhood attitudes, given to you by teachers and parents, that you have to be talented and skilled to be an artist.

You are not an artist.

You are a journeyer on the way. Your only commitment is to letting the Self express itself through your creations.

Do not let others' criticisms or comments get to you. Do not identify with your own productions. Mostly people project their own stuff anyway. They do not observe.

It is fundamental that as part of the individuation process you develop, not only growth and consciousness, but also personal creativity, without which there is little vitality and fluidity of personality. The Self is both the source of growth and of creativity. Without a developed creativity there is great danger of intellectualizing the process.

The challenge is clear. We must also work with our archetypes in symbolic-creative forms to get ourselves out of the rational mind and into more feeling and creative states of consciousness.

Working in the Graphic and Plastic Arts

Primarily this includes painting and sculpture with variations such as working with wood, creating ritual objects, etc.

Essentially you have as your focus putting a dream symbol in art, but what can develop as you let go to the flow is that you will be creating a symbol right in the moment which may express dream elements, and other elements as well, of your psyche. This is productive since often dreams act as evokers for archetypal energies needing processing.

Let yourself get involved. Let go to the fullness of the symbol and create spontaneously without regard to rigid definitions of what should happen. Simply let yourself go to 'intunement' with your symbol.

It may add to your experience to do a symbol immersion first around your symbol and then draw, paint or sculpt it in clay.

Do not worry about colours but let the colour come to you. Basically you are trying to work at a feeling level rather than a conceptual one. Do not interpret colours. That is for the rational mind. The creative mind is much more fluid.

You can either be very loose or very focused in your letting go. There is a place for both in working with symbol.

Working in clay sometimes has the advantage of feeling more basic and substantial than drawing or painting. Putting symbols into clay also gives the solidness of the third dimension.

Dream symbols may be painted as they appeared in the dream or they may be extracted and placed within a symbolic context such as within a mandala or circular-square form.

Composing a meditation or writing a dialogue after creating in art adds a conscious dimension to the experience.

Expressing the Dream in Poetry and Story

Poetry is the language of feeling.

For some people, writing poetry helps bring resolution to feeling states which cannot find adequate expression in the outer. Love poetry and American blues music are two obvious examples of expressing symbolically feeling states from life. But poetry can be used to express any archetypal energy if the flow is there.

Poetry, as well as other art forms, uses one of the consciousness principles, 'distilling the essence.' Essentially we cannot take a whole experience with us into the next segment of time. But we can, through the creative act, express the essence of an experience symbolically. It is this essence which we take with us as a value and resource to enliven and deepen what is to come next.

To write poetry throw out everything you know about language or technique. You have been expressing yourself for years verbally. You do not even need rhyme or sophisticated imagery. Just let your feelings naturally flow into imagery.

Poetry uses symbol to contain and evoke feeling. What you are after is a sense of the essence of the dream, or any aspect of life for that matter.

To put a dream into an art form also has the value of actualizing or re-experiencing the dream. You do not need to know what a dream means to express it symbolically. You need only to let go to it and out of the re-experiencing will come the meaning.

Another technique is translating your dream into a story, a parable or folk tale. Using the basic folk tale structure is a way of taking a culturally evolved pattern for structuring archetypal energies and using it on yourself. We may know the old witch or the innocent child within us. But do we know the other various parts of our own psyches as revealed by dreams?

Look at a traditional folk tale to get its basic structure. How does it begin, develop and end? See if your dreams can fit into such a structure. Another task which might be suggested by a dream is to re-write your own childhood as a folk tale. This is usually a powerful experience.

Parables are perhaps harder to write, but once in a while a dream will seem to be almost a perfect teaching story or parable. Who knows how many of Jesus' parables started as dreams?

The Dream Re-entered in Music and Dance

Music is itself the energy of the archetypes. When we break down music into its primary components we find beat, or regular repeated structures or intervals. Time itself seems to be based in part on such a patterning and rituals often achieve their effectiveness through repetition. Certain rhythm states can put one in a trance, or suspension of ego consciousness, in which the pulsating energies of the archetypes predominate. In psychosis there is much repeat, ordered behaviour and experience of primary energy. The regular drip of the faucet evokes the archetypal pulse at an overwhelming level.

In music we have tune, which is also primal progression but whose structure is not based on the repetition of sameness but diversity. Whereas rhythm may be basic to the Journey archetype, tune may be basic to the Death-Rebirth or cyclic archetype.

These structures combine in infinitely complex ways in music to produce immense variations of archetypal feelings. Whether it be the soft rounded sounds of the Feminine or the sharp staccato sounds of the Masculine, the triumph of the Heroic or the clashing of Adversity, we are involved in music as still another language of the archetypes.

As you re-enter your dream state in active imagination let the images translate automatically into feeling states which you express as music. Let yourself get involved and, if you can, record the music so you may listen to it later and process it into consciousness.

Dance also can be used in a semi-trance state to let go and express the archetypes in your dreams. You will probably find that certain primal scenes or patterns develop from experiencing your dreams through dance.

— What are the primal gestures and scenes?
— Why are these the ones unique to you?
— Are they expressive of your total personality or only a part?
— What other primal gestures can you create to balance out your dream scenes?
— How can you dance your dreams to resolution?

After your experience:

— What meditation, sharing or journal work is needed to bring the experience to consciousness?
— If you are a rational person, how can you dance your dreams to get your body more fully into its archetypal energies?

Working with Dreams in Mythic Drama

What we see mostly on stage these days is a far cry from what drama can be as a symbolic expression of the archetypes.

Putting one's dream into drama has an extremely powerful effect and therefore is best done within a safe context of effective leadership.

Various people take different characters from the dream and re-enact them using the dream scenes as context.

However, in order not to evoke energy for people and leave it hanging the mythic drama itself should be created as embodying a strong resolution, whether such a resolution is in the dream or not.

Do not evoke what you cannot contain.

Do not evoke what you cannot transform.

All mythic drama sessions should be preceded by discussion among participants about their roles. And then after the drama there should be discussion and processing of what was evoked.

The term 'mythic drama' is used rather than 'psycho-drama' or 'Gestalt Theatre' or even regular drama, to make a definite distinction. The mythic drama always has a primary structure of expressing the conflict *and* bringing it to resolution. This is the nature of all myths. They do not end in tragedy but in healing. This is an ancient wisdom which goes back thousands of years. Nor does mythic drama end happily. Happiness is not a resolution to anything. To withdraw from a scene either through tragedy or idealized positivism does not bring creative resolution. Hamlet would not have died tragically if he had had the capacity to bring creative resolution, rather than bleak acceptance, to what were admittedly terrible circumstances.

What if Hamlet had lived to rule and to create a united kingdom purged of too much greed and inaction? Tragedy creates the necessity for resolution but such a necessity comes too late. What we can learn from our tragedies is not stoic acceptance but the necessary consciousness to perceive conflicts accurately as they happen and to deal with them when the full potential for resolving is still present. Look at the history of your own tragedies and evaluate them for yourself. One cannot be too cautious in using mythic drama to work with dreams and heal splits in the psyche. But it is a powerful healing technique when used effectively. It was not without reason that the ancient Aesclepian healing centres had theatres as part of their temples.

Having people enact myths and folk tales is also a powerful experience and requires the same cautions as for working with dreams.

Another form of enacting dreams is to only take a key action or theme in a dream and enact it by yourself or with one or two others, limiting the time to around five minutes. Firstly you enact the dynamic as in the dream itself. Then you re-enact the same dynamic but this time bringing it to creative resolution. Very powerful, yet capable of being handled in a conscious way.

Expressing Dream States through Sexuality

It is time to include sex as one of the cultural arts and not just as a biological or even relational urge. Great lovers have always known that sex was an art as well as an instinct. Art is in fact one of the great transformers of raw instinctual power.

Sexuality appears regularly in the dream state. On the physiological level men have erections frequently during REM dream states and women moisten in their vaginal areas. In dreams we may find our dream egos in all sorts of sexual postures with either sex. This is not something to be afraid of but to enjoy or come to terms with if the dream behaviour seems negative.

On one level sexuality is the urge for unity with a split part of oneself.

On another level sexuality, and its image states in dreams, expresses our relation or lack of relation to the life force. How warm, how vital, how alive am I? Or am I inhibited, cold and afraid to express my basic animal nature?

Our dreams will show us sexual behaviour we might need to change and sexual behaviour we might need to actualize for further wholeness.

Or the sexual experience in a dream might be actualized for dealing with inner states of being.

Using art processes with dreams can happen on various levels.

— One might describe one's sexual dream to one's lover and both work on how they might actualize it. If the dreamer finds himself making passionate love to a woman other than his lover, he might describe in great detail to his present lover how he fantasizes it and they can then share that together.

Note clearly that the conventions of the inner world are somewhat different from the conventions of the exterior world. If we have energy moving in our psyches which might be destructive if acted out in the exterior world, we can still act it out on an inner level in the realm of fantasy in order to accept and transform that energy.

Sex is not sex. Sex is the vital energy, the *elan vital*, of life. Sometimes this energy manifests directly through sexual activity. Sometimes it can be expressed directly in symbolic activity.

Thus even religious celibates can be creative or uncreative. If a person practising sexual abstinence turns cold and dry as a personality, then the celibacy is merely a form of repression rather than transformation. If, on the other hand, sexual abstinence is practised and the person becomes a more vital feeling and flowing human being, then transformation to a more evolved level would seem to be occurring.

Essentially, whether celibate or engaging regularly in sexual activity, the goal in both cases is to acknowledge and accept the sexual energy as being in itself the life force and therefore necessary to the full expression of personality. The goal is not to abstain from sexual climax but to express the grand climax in everything we do. Whether we engage in sexual intercourse or not are we truly sexual in everything we do?

Dreams seem to be always presenting the next possibilities for transformation in our life journeys. Through art we can help this process by symbolizing it and therefore taking it out of its literalistic identification to the outer.

For instance, following the practices of the ancients, it might be important to make the genitals in clay and put them on one's personal altar. For the genitals themselves are forms of the gods, the archetypal energies.

To disengage ourselves from identification with the outer we need to practice symbolic activity.

Who is there to say what sex really is? Lovers practise it. Great lovers do not identify with sex's sexual power, and thus achieve the freedom to turn sex into a fine art.

Dreamwork in Relation to Ritual

The practice of ritual can be one of the healing arts. Ritual is potentially the most powerful art form for evoking and transforming the archetypes. This is why ritual has been traditionally the perogative of government or organized religion. At some level the savants of these organizational forms know that the greatest power they have for evoking and containing the archetypes of the masses is in the use of ritual.

Ritual, in its ability to evoke unconscious forces, can unleash energies which easily overwhelm the individual ego's skills for conscious choice-making and reflection. State and religion use this fact to perpetuate their own forms of power, belief and organization.

We find this same process occurring within so-called primitive or pre-literate cultures which are often rife with ritual practices.

What is needed today is a conscious approach to ritual which sees it as perhaps the most powerful of art forms and seeks to use it in the service of the individual journey as well as for forming various types of community.

Negative reactions to ritual seem to arise from two areas. One is the individual's reactions to overly organized religions or governments in which ritual practices were forced on participants and given as beliefs, but without meaning. The other negative reaction is due to fearful feelings about the power of the unconscious. Black magic is the using of the power of the archetypes for self-centred purposes. The dangers involved in dealing in the 'black arts' is in either evoking too much archetypal energy or in evoking primarily the negative side of the archetypes.

One needs to caution even those who would do powerful positive and healing rituals because they might in their one-sidedness evoke the opposite, or they might evoke too much archetypal energy and thus overwhelm individual consciousness and values.

Simple rituals are used at the Institute as part of the natural process of working with the unconscious and seeking renewal from its source energies.

With the dream session ceremony itself we keep a candle lit during the session and ring the bell at the end for a sense of the transcendent. We also work with relating to symbolic objects, usually from nature, which might embody 'spirit in substance' energies. The effect of such a process is to create a deeper more meaningful level of dream-sharing and to evoke *the central archetype*, inner and outer. This cannot be stressed enough. The 'black magic' people probably direct much of their ritual activity towards the Adversary Archetype by using their hexes and other expressions of the principle of evil. While governments, especially in time of war, direct their rituals towards evoking the Heroic Archetype in their people.

Most religions would seem to be devoted to the central archetype but in actuality are really focused on the Saviour or Herioc Archetype to the exclusion of the Adversary or archetype of evil. True integration is the integration of opposites and to this end we need a renewal of religion which includes all the opposites of life.

In regard to dreamwork itself, certain rituals can be designed and used to celebrate the gift of a major or great dream. Sometimes there will be ritual acts illustrated right in the dream which we can choose to re-enact in the outer. The Institute itself uses rituals first suggested in dreams.

What would it be to be so open to the dream source that one did not use the rituals of any organized religion but only did rituals suggested in dreams of community members? Would this not be bypassing the ego creatively?

Dreamwork Entry
— Your Dream in Art

— One basic level is to draw or paint your dream scene. A variation on this is to draw-paint contrasting symbols in dreams. Or take the most central symbol and draw this fully. Having a series of 'dream paintings' heightens the whole process. You may want to make a commitment to doing one dream painting a week, or to drawing a recurrent symbol every time it arises. One person does this with certain negative figures in order to better face them and depotentiate their energy. Also painting a figure before dialoguing with it can add to the energy evoked. It is helpful to title the pictures you do and write in basic descriptions at the bottom.

— As a means of processing dream content in art you may choose to take a number of symbols from the same, or different dreams, and cluster them in a *mandala* or circular painting. Mandalas symbolize integration and wholeness, so a painting of this kind can evoke for you potentials for wholeness. Be especially aware of what you place in the centre of the mandala. What for you represents the centre? Do you place yourself there? Or some negative figure? Or a healing symbol?

— To acknowledge your symbols in art keep them and place them on your wall. Also date them with reference to your dreams.

— For developing a complete dreamwork experience with one dream do a number of dreamwork techniques and follow them with putting your dream and dreamwork into art in such a way as to bring things together.

— Be aware of *the central healing figures and symbols* which appear in your dreams and put them into art. You will gradually be developing the landscape of your own unconscious and, by emphasizing the healing factor, evoking integration and individuation. It is also important to put your major dream adversaries into art. And how do you portray your own dream ego?

— In *working with clay* take the healing symbols and figures from your dreams and materialize them. In many ancient religions the penates, or household gods, were probably originated in this way. What would it be like to have symbolic figures all over your house to remind you of the true nature of your soul?

— Another exciting method is to form in clay your own ''dream theatre,'' an actual symbolic miniature room with various half-hidden areas in which you place figures and symbols from your dreams. The effect of this technique is that of looking into the interior world of your own psyche. Also you can re-arrange the figures and symbols to produce different effects and meaning.

— As part of symbolizing psychic and spiritual energies in art you might create for yourself in your room a *sacred area* in which you put your 'spirit symbols' or 'power objects'. We are so one-sided in this culture that most of us only have functional space in our apartments and houses. How is the soul to be fed if all it sees is clean windows, a toaster and a T.V. set? Use special cloth and use the space also as a place for meditation.

The Jungian-Senoi Dream Task

A task is a specific project requiring a commitment to its realization within a specific amount of time by the ego or conscious side of the personality.

Tasks are what ground and test the spiritual life.

It is one thing to have beautiful and moving experiences such as can happen in receiving a vivid dream. It is another thing to commit oneself to concretizing and testing out that experience in everyday reality.

Insight is not enough. Action is required. It is not only what you say but what you do that counts. It is action which re-connects work to feeling. If I say only that which I am willing to act upon then I will be capable of feeling. It is thus that feelings become actions.

When caught in perplexities and surfeits of insight, so that you do not know which way to go, begin choosing, choose, choose, choose your way out. Do and do again. The path is one of action. Action tests reflection. Dreams need actualization in dreamwork to be truly manifested.

The task is at once the medium and focus for action.

For every dream there are a large number of possible tasks or dreamwork projects. Tasks may involve suggestions for inner reality and outer reality projects. Whatever helps the dream come alive again is appropriate. Here are some examples:

— A woman who was concerned as to whether ghosts appeared in dreams or were only inner figure-symbols asked for a dream with a ghost in it. When this dream came she dialogued with the 'ghost' to find out from it whether

it was really a ghost or not. The results were insightful and enlarged her perspective rather than narrowed it.

— An older woman, who dreamed of being on a train with two suitcases and four suitcases worth of stuff, cut down on her outer life commitments, more appropriate to her advancing age. She received a new dream in which she packed in only two suitcases of stuff into two suitcases.

— A man received a dream in which he and his ex-wife were relating. He acted on it and it changed both their lives.

— Another person upon waking from a nightmare put herself right back to sleep, without fully awakening, to continue the dream and realize resolution.

— A woman in search of her spiritual destiny received a dream with a beautiful healing symbol in it. She made it in clay and pebbles from the beach and placed it in her meditation area.

— A man re-entered his dream meditatively and re-experienced its imagery and dynamics. From this he was able to go through the emotions of a loss, process them, and let them go so that he could be free to seek new life.

— A man wrote a letter of reconciliation to a former guide and teacher based on having a reconciling dream. He also included the dream in the letter.

Other examples, each as meaningful as any of these, could flow a thousand times over again. When we consider that one person working on only one dream task a week would at the end of the year have around fifty dreams well processed in tasks accomplished, this method becomes a major resource for living. And many of the tasks are repeatable throughout one's life.

The procedure is basically that the dreamwork guide or leader makes a number of suggestions for the dreamer to do as tasks. The dreamer chooses what seems right, often doing more than one. In the course of accomplishing the task it may change or a new possibility for a task arise. This is appropriate because the creative flow from the unconscious continues.

In dream groups the leader makes many of the task suggestions but occasionally another member of the group may suggest one. The challenge is not to give interpretations as to what a dream might mean, but to turn such intuitions, projections, etc. into questions for tasks.

Give the person questions, not answers.

This is crucial. I remember one Freudian analyst who was dead set on giving his projections to a dream as answers. He could not turn his stuff into questions to save his skin.

When we truly ask a question we are admitting we do not have an answer. How many of us are willing to get down off the throne of authority and humble ourselves before the mystery?

My life is my answer. Your opinion is not the answer for anything. I will accept your questions if they evoke the search for truth in me. And how do you yourself respond to your own questions?

The first part of every Jungian-Senoi dream session is devoted to the sharing of previous dream tasks or projects completed. This is as important as the sharing of new dreams. Then the second half of the dream session is devoted to the sharing of new dreams and receiving suggestions for tasks concerning them.

Dream tasks are given as suggestions, not as opinions about how one should live life. A real danger would be for a guide to give someone a task in the form of a directive in which the guide is choosing for the person. This is a difference between a dreamwork guide and most spiritual guides.

'You should break-up that relationship. You will get nothing but grief from it,' would be a biased life-choice opinion and not a task.

'How does your dream show you two relating? Contrast your dream relating with your outer life relating. What are the differences and similarities? Out of all this, list the values for continuing or not continuing the relationship.'

These last suggestions are truly in the nature of task-making. For they open up a person to the power of his or her own discrimination and choice-making, which is really one of the ongoing goals of the whole process.

Would you believe it? There are still many therapists, analysts, gurus, guides, teachers, parents, friends, etc., who go around telling people what to do rather than helping them make their own choices. Where this is true, we are still living in the dark ages of one person judging another.

Perhaps you also are somewhat caught in this? My own analysts and teachers were. I am always having to re-look at myself for this tendency.

But then how many of us know the skills for doing otherwise?

Issues Related to Task Making

Does insight produce change? If I know what is causing a certain destructive behaviour, will I change it? What creates the kind of integrity that when I know something is true for me I will act upon it despite the suffering involved?

What is a life of endless reflection versus a life of endless action?

The *Task* combines both reflection and action. The task grounds and tests reflection with action. The task creates experience as the basis for reflection.

Creativity is the taking of whatever happens in reality and realizing its full potential into a meaningful whole. The task is the medium within which creativity can manifest.

Consciousness is awareness plus appropriate action. Without the task I cannot ground my awareness in relevant action.

Completing, or dealing with, the task gives me experience. Without the task there is little context for action.

What is healing if it is not dealing with that which seems split apart or incapable of realizing its full potential? The task helps create the context without which healing cannot take place. The task makes us co-responsible with the healing source for the healing involved.

We must work in order to play. *Work* is the re-enactment of the specific commitment to attaining a goal. *Play* is the disengaging from the goal in order to celebrate its accomplishment. In task-making we balance out the nature of the work involved with the nature of the play involved.

In *Task-accomplishing* we are building real ego, which is different from creating ecstasy by dissolving ego. We are working to manifest the potentials of archetypal energy in the outer world of concrete forms.

There are those people, Jungians among them, who ask. 'Can we know the underlying influence of our unconscious by working with our dreams in dream tasks?' 'Is it not better,' they say, 'to leave the dream alone and interpret what it is saying for our lives?'

For this interpretive position the unconscious is a vast ocean and you, the dreamer, must stay always on the pier observing it. In contrast, the Jungian-Senoi approach often has you get into the boat and sail the waters of the unconscious and interact vigorously with it.

To get involved is to suffer. To get involved with something other than ourselves is to change. And there can be no change without pain or without vital ecstasy. Pain is what frees us from the rigidity which prevents new life. When I am suffering, I know at least that I am real. No one exists, no one knows he or she exists, who does not exist in pain. Pain and ecstasy? Joy and suffering? What are they ultimately in the scale of things but mutual opposites? Do we not need them both to lead a full and meaningful life? Ecstasy, well earned, lets us know we have broken through to vital, new resources.

Tasks which involve work as well as pleasure make us suffer. And suffering is the tension between what is and what is not. Of course, we need to suffer in doing our tasks. If there is not the pain of change in them, how can they be real?

And then when the task is accomplished and we are experiencing the results, what a celebration and a feeling of vitality there can be!

The Nature of Tasks

A key emphasis here, which should be opened up to all interpretive psychologists, psychoanalysts, therapists, spiritual teachers, etc., is that in using the task approach we give up diagnosis.

Yes, throw all the psychological tests and personality profiles into the abyss of the past. Throw out the diagnostic mental disturbances handbooks, that linguistic garbage used to condemn so many people, patients and doctors alike, to mental hospitals.

To try and interpret someone else's personality from the outside is a gross fallacy and an exercise in subjective stupidity. So much of it is projection on the part of the observer with the patient trying to survive by conforming to the doctor-authority's world view as to what his or her role should be.

The task and its accomplishment does away with the need to attempt personality descriptions. If we give a person the concrete tools to realize him or herself, there will be no need for diagnosis. What is essential is that each person has a grounded experience of a further development of him or herself.

After this diatribe, which is admittedly political in nature, we add that certain tasks have not only a dreamwork base, but also a personality base. If a person seems one-sided in terms of feeling, we may suggest some thinking type dreamwork tasks. Or if they are good at art, perhaps they might try poetry for a while. And so on. These tasks, while they refer to the personality, are functionally oriented and so not based on calling someone neurotic, paranoid, introverted, over-achieving, or any broadly categorized typology which is supposed to cover the whole personality.

All tasks have a goal and a plan for action. All the methods in this book are task-oriented and have as their goals the actualization, or coming alive, of the dream state in some specific way. Certain tasks may be repeated in each dreamwork experience. Generally, as can be seen from the flow chart, we first begin by:

— Working with the dream itself in bringing out issues and dynamics, or generally, expanding the dream.
— Then we may do tasks which bring resolution on an internal level of the dream conflicts involved.
— Then how does what has been discovered, created, etc., relate to the inner life?
— Then how does it relate to the outer life?
— And, finally, how does the dreamwork relate to future dreaming?

Usually, there is a generalized task level which is more philosophic and sometimes easier to start with. A 'could you write a page on what place suffering has in life and share it with us next time?' is a more general task. 'Describe all the specific elements of suffering in your dream and why your dream ego seems to be in such agony.' This second, more specific level is important, but more emotionally loaded. Is the person able yet to face this level of dreamwork? How are they showing suffering? If they seem easily overwhelmed by it, then perhaps a more generalized task would be productive.

General Principles for Suggesting Tasks

— Go where the most or least energy is.
— Usually present tasks in the form of questions.
— Use a broadening or holistic approach with which to balance things out.
— Make the task suggestions specific enough to be accomplished.
— Make clear the values to be possibly gained from doing the tasks.
— Give many task suggestions of varying character. Eight or ten with each dream. To give only one or two tasks allows too much chance for bias on the part of the task assigner. The task doer has choice as to which tasks and how many to do.

— To ground the tasks make sure that they are specific to the dream.

— Make sure the task receiver is open and participating in developing the task suggestions.

— Leave time in the process for sharing task results.

— In evaluating tasks the value is that something has been done experientially with the dream. The results do not have to conform to the dream or to the task suggestions. Was the experience alive with positive or negative energy and did it lead to new consciousness? This is a central question. A person evaluates his own task experiences. The task suggester only expands on the meaning of the experience and does not seek to evaluate positively or negatively.

The Dreamwork Guide

An open dreamwork guide can free him or herself from the burden of being looked to as an authority by someone else for making life decisions. When someone wants advice, suggest tasks instead.

'I cannot possibly tell you what you are like or what you should do. I cannot make your choices for you or suffer your consequences. What I can do is give you some suggestions for working with possibilities. Let's formulate together some questions to give a focus to what you are dealing with. There are, probably, no right or wrong answers, but only consequences. And by your choices you become what you are.'

The task suggester may have more knowledge or only a different outside perspective. But what is central is that opinions about another person or a dream do not get conveyed as the truth.

Translate all feelings and intuitions about someone or something else into questions and not into definitive statements. Not to do so can rob the person of their own chance to gain perspective. What is mine is not yours and what is yours is not mine.

Usually have the task suggestions relate to a multiplicity of levels rather than close down to one definitive statement that is the truth.

— No truth is definite.

— All certainties are bound to be lies.

— Only that truth can be trusted which is not definite.

— All truth is the recognition of possibility.

— Certainty is the death of certainty.

These paradoxes are a blow to the authoritarian personality. If you find yourself putting out truths in an absolute way rather than stimulating others to find their own truths, then you are probably an authoritarian personality. But do not despair or get too angry. We are all authoritarian personalities, and what a burden this is!

True freedom is the freedom not to have to tell someone else what to do all the time.

Yet we need task givers as well as receivers. Perhaps the best task givers are those who themselves have carried out many tasks of self-exploration. When we make suggestions to someone else as to new possibilities for living life, it can be thought of as 'lending one's ego' to another who is not quite at the new stage of development needed.

For an example of a dream, and tasks suggeted to actualize it, see the dreamwork in the chapter, 'What Is A Dream?'

Finally, we have the issue, 'Ultimately, who gives the tasks?'

— Is it the task giver or receiver, or both together? Or is there still another source behind all this?

— In what sense is the remembered dream itself a task, a need for completion and fulfilment?

— What tasks seem directly embodied in the dream itself?

— What is the task of this life-time?

— How will I ever know this task, if such a question really exists?

— Have I come into life with certain central tasks to accomplish?

— Will my life always be a question for which there are no answers?

— What question is my life an answer to?

— What question will my life end with?

A task is always a question and never an answer.

My efforts to relate to the questions of my life are, perhaps, the only answers I will ever know. And may my answers always be further questions to myself and to the universe at large!

Perhaps in this existence there are in fact no answers to most central questions.

There are only responses.

Symbol Immersion

Symbol Immersion is an unconscious process technique for expanding or re-experiencing a symbol. Through immersion in the imaginative and meditative process we let the symbol reverberate into the layers of consciousness. We walk around the symbol. As 'dream ego' we interact with the symbol. We go into a relaxed state, focusing on the symbol with our eyes closed, and let it come really alive for us. We plunge deeper and deeper into the core of the symbol. But certain distinctions are in order.

In *symbol immersion* we stay with the symbol in its present state of being.

We do not let it develop further as in *symbol evolvement* where we focus on the symbol meditatively and let it go wherever it wants to go.

In symbol immersion we do not let it go backwards, either, as in *symbol regression*.

An example of symbol immersion is when a dreamer took a black telephone in her dream and meditatively focused on its nature, and then had an interaction with the telephone's functionality by letting it ring, answering the telephone, seeing who answered, hanging up, letting it ring again, seeing

what happened and so on until the essence of that particular dream telephone became clear to her.

An example of symbol evolvement would be taking that new car of your dream and visualizing where it might go or what would happen to it.

Symbol regression would be, for example, re-entering a dream in which a house is on fire, staying focused on it, and visualizing in stages what went before which led up to the house being on fire.

The value of symbol evolvement is in creating a flow out of a particular symbol into new material. We are, in effect, evoking a progressive or developmental dynamic. Symbol evolvement is not symbol association where one leaps from one symbol to another. There must be a progression occurring for the experience to be symbol evolvement.

The value of symbol regression is to discover 'first things' or the 'originating condition.' How did it all start? What has led up to this point? What is at work in my life? Again, regression is not associative linking. There must be a sense of continuity and character-similarity to the process.

These three processes taken together would do much to develop the particular vitality of a symbol. But of the three techniques symbol immersion is the preferred technique. Symbol regression and evolvement can be considered forms of symbol immersion.

Which is preferred in working with dreams because it maintains focus on the present reality of the symbol. Why is this particular woman in my dream? In my dream she acts a certain way and I act a certain way towards her. But now in my symbol immersion I will try to experience her in her overall potential and interact more fully, if not differently with her. Symbol immersion helps purify the dream context. This has value in that the symbol gains greater vivacity and completeness and provides a contrast to how the symbol is originally experienced in the dream.

Symbol immersion may either be done as a guided or as a self re-entry into the symbol state.

What is perhaps most important is getting the flow of feelings and images, the spontaneity of the symbol, going. A guide aids this process by helping the person through blocks and by having another point of view about the symbol.

But self symbol immersion has its own value in a person's developing his or her own fluidity between the conscious and the unconscious.

Symbol immersion and other unconscious process techniques differ from *psychosynthesis* in that psychosynthesis is a more rational approach to experiencing the unconscious. In dreamwork each person has his or her own major symbols to work with. Outside symbols from some system do not have to be imposed.

Symbol immersion differs from Gestalt dream practice in that the ego-Self axis is maintained throughout the process of evoking the unconscious. The Gestalt therapist tells the client 'be your ocean in your dream' and the person responds, 'I am an ocean, I flow, I have great fish in my depths, I am fluid and moody, I rise and fall,' etc. This technique can be a powerful experience but it can also habituate the person's ego to identifying with, instead of relating to, unconscious contents. In symbol immersion a person can have just as powerful an experience yet keep the interactant, the ego, present.

One does not identify with life but relates to life. One does not identify with love but relates to love. One does not identify with country, work roles, maleness or femaleness but relates to these experiences. And so on. To identify is to become that entity. To identify is to become or remain unconscious. When we identify with one experience we close the door to other experiences. Symbol immersion is not symbol merging.

One function of symbol immersion is to be selective about which of the many symbols in dreams we can make more conscious through re-experiencing them. We cannot possibly deal with all dreams and their symbolism and so we choose, we select, and in that process we structure our approach to the unconscious.

The goal of symbol immersion is to evoke meaning by going deeper and deeper into the archetype. The resultant experience has an effect on our consciousness. It may produce insight, attitude change, a good feeling or even a philosophy. Symbol immersion also has an effect on the unconscious because we direct our energy and focus into a certain aspect of our unconscious, whether it be an aspect of the centre, an unresolved trauma, an anima or animus problem or whatever. This directed energy seems to produce changes in the unconscious and releases a new flow of life energy.

Dreamwork Example — Guided Symbol Immersion

Strephon's Comments
In this dream and its dreamwork is a central spiritual issue for the dreamer and anyone else becoming spiritually aware at this time. The dreamer is very involved with various forms of mysticism including a relationship with a Hopi spiritual teacher and another relationship with a psychic. They both appear in the dream as well as her three-year-old boy, the recipient in the dream of the bead necklace.

This dream is a natural for symbol immersion since it has a central symbol in the necklace and what happens to it. The goal of this immersion was to bring out the full characteristics and issues surrounding this symbol and then help the dreamer to respond creatively to the issues already there.

The issue is getting the necklace back together again and in what order. And also there is the issue of the necklace transforming into more mundane, less sacred objects.

In guiding the dreamer the focus remained on the nature of the bead necklace and interacting with that until resolution is created. In a general sense symbol immersion is a form of dream re-entry but the term 'dream re-entry' is reserved for experiences in which we explore in the dream many symbols and let them unfold.

Note the tension between the guide and the 're-dreamer'. This experience is written from the re-dreamer's point of view. The value of and detriment to having a guide is the having of another point of view from the dreamer's.

To help resolve the remaining tension the re-dreamer did another symbol immersion on her own in which she honoured the traditional and the new.

For many of us, as old cultures die out in the face of mass technology and communication, we can feel the great loss and rootlessness. With the dying of the traditional culture goes also a rich symbolic-spiritual tradition built up over thousands of years. What are we to do?

Perhaps the possibility is to become again a vehicle for archetypal experience through dreamwork, ritual, meditation, music, movement, relation to nature and commitment to the spiritual quest. We can, if we reach emotionally the archetypal base inherent in all life, create a new, more viable culture. We have no alternative. Evolution means adapting to reality exactly as it is and transforming it into what it can also become.

Now for the dream and its dreamwork in the dreamer's own words. This dream was originally 'dream incubated' at a native sacred site in Hawaii.

Dream Title: The Beaded Necklace   *Date: 24th April*

Carla, a Hopi elder friend, gives Elie, my son, a necklace — she takes it out of her bag or pocket — at first I just see the heishi but the front has what looks like different size stones or beads (remember, being blue) hanging along the front of it. She puts it on Elie.

Somehow (perhaps Elie takes it off or pulls on it) some of the hanging beads come off — they seem to each be different with the same filler beads or stones (smaller) in between. At first I try to put it back together by lining people up and having each hold a different bead and then trying to string them together. It's hard to get them back in order. I have to keep rearranging the people and beads. At some point my spiritual counsellor is there, not Carla, and I finally try to put the necklace back together alone. This time the different beads seem to be like plastic 'stained glass' type decals of hunting scenes — different aspects, showing hunter (perhaps on a horse) with rifle and hunting dog. I keep rearranging them. I talk to Iris about it (Elie wakes me up at this point, he's having a dream, shouting no, no).

Comments
This was an important dream. I had sat in meditation that afternoon at an Hawaiian Hula temple in Kaui and before falling asleep that evening I asked that the spirit of that temple come through in a dream and plant a new seed for me to take back with me.

Dream Tasks — Symbol Immersion

Strephon asks me to go back to before where the necklace appears. Carla is sitting on a bench, her black handbag next to her. Elie is standing nearby.

Carla reaches in and pulls out a necklace made of light brown-grey heishi with eight irregular shaped blue and brown stones hanging down along the front. She holds it in her hand — the heishi are twisted around and folded over in her hand. She takes the necklace and puts it over Elie's head. He starts to touch it and begins to pull on the longer beads trying to look at them. The necklace is a bit heavy on him — he seems to like it. I feel a little uncomfortable — I feel I'd like to have the necklace myself. But it would be too small to go over my head. The necklace breaks as Elie is touching it and pulling on the beads. The long stone beads fall to the ground with some of the heishi but most of the heishi remain on the string. I take the string with the remaining beads and place it on the bench next to Carla. Then I begin to pick up the stones and heishi on the floor. I have six or seven beads in my hand and Elie finds another one. The stones are blue and brown with dark shades within. Some are smooth and some rough, they feel cold. Some seem old and others newer. They have holes for stringing. I'm reminded of the necklaces Polynesian men wear — small beads interspersed with larger ones though the necklace doesn't look Polynesian. It's not a Hopi necklace. Wondering where the stones came from. Some seem very old.

Strephon asks me about restringing them. I have some nylon thread and a needle and begin to place the heishi from the old string onto the new one. I'm wondering how I will rearrange the stones as I don't remember what the old order was. Strephon asks something about whether I can create a new order and what principle I will use. I talk about symmetry and aesthetics and he asks if there's another way I can order it. I feel a longing to know the old order and I feel uncertain about how to rearrange the stones. I'm wishing I could remember the old order. Feeling it would be easier to create a new order if I'd been able to understand the significance of the old order. Strephon says the challenge for me is to create a new order and also asks if I can put the beads out of order. I can though it feels uncomfortable. I close my eyes and arrange them randomly, they don't look good, they're at angles to each other, it looks chaotic, not pretty. Then Strephon asks me to arrange them. I arrange them symmetrically with the longest stone bead in the centre. The only bead I remember from the original was a blue bead on the outer left and I place it there. Strephon asks me if I can place it in the middle. I do but it doesn't feel or look right so I put it back. I still feel uncomfortable (feeling localized in my solar plexus).

Strephon asks how Carla feels — what she thinks of the necklace. She's smiling at me telling me it's just a necklace, that my wanting to put it back in its original order has to do with my moon in Virgo, that it's okay the way it is, that it's one of my lessons.

Strephon asks if I can accept the new order. I'm still feeling uncomfortable but I feel I have to accept it as I don't seem to be able to find the old order. This is the reality of the situation though it's still hard for me to let go of my longing to know what the old order was. Feel it's my responsibility to put the necklace back together and wishing I could have put it back the way it had been. I hold the necklace for a while. Strephon asks me about putting it on. It's too small for me and I know it's for Elie. I'm still feeling some discomfort and energy in my solar plexus. Strephon suggests that I rub my solar plexus. I take my crystal and make a circular motion over the area with it in my hand. Some of the energy is released and I feel more comfortable though still with a sense of wistfulness about the original order.

I put the necklace on Elie — he seems rather indifferent about it all. Carla's amused by the dilemma and is still smiling.

Strephon asks if I have enough humbleness to accept it — I say 'yes' though a part of me still hasn't let go of the desire of knowing and restringing the old order of the beads and the feeling that I would have liked to have understood the significance. I'm more comfortable with it than I was and ask about the necklace changing to the hunting scene.

The stones change into stained glass type plastic decals of various aspects of hunting scenes with hunter on horse with rifle and hunting dog. I don't like them. Strephon has me ask Carla about them. She says it's because I'm still searching for the key, for the old order.

At one point when I'm rearranging them the necklace is in one corner and they're on the table and I try to pick them up to get rid of them but they're stuck to the table. Strephon says something about my not liking the necklace and I say I like it a lot better than these plastic decals. The necklace seems a lot more appealing to me after seeing what it can turn into when I don't accept the new order and keep searching for the original pattern. I take the beaded necklace in my hand and feel I want to hold it and sit with it so that I can accept it and feel more comfortable with it.

Dreamwork Entry
— Symbol Immersion

Instructions

— After writing your dream down choose a major symbol in your dream. Much comes from the unconscious forcing us into the problem of choice. We let the dreams come. But then which symbol or symbols do we choose to emphasize? And what is the context for our choices? These are some possibilities:

  — Choose the symbol with the greatest energy for you.
  — Choose the symbol with the greatest meaning or healing.
  — Choose the symbol most foreign to you or most fearful.
  — Let your feelings or spontaneous intuition choose the symbol.
  — Whatever you do, choose, choose and keep choosing. The journey does not go forward without choices.

— Close your eyes, relax into a meditative state, letting go of outside anxieties and opening up within yourself a clear blank space. If working with a guide she or he does the same thing. Make sure throughout this experience that you will not be interrupted.

— Now let your dream symbol be there very much alive for you. Focus in on its details. Feel it. Get involved. Have it be alive in itself, in its essentialness.

— The one thing you do not do is let your symbol evolve or regress. Stay with it as it is and let it unfold, expand, grow fuller, be more its functionality, its essence. Do not shift your focus to new symbols as you might do in a dream re-entry. You remain focused and drink the symbol to its dregs. The goal is to have the symbol come alive by exhausting it. When you have done this you will know to stop. You will feel some sort of resolution.

— It is helpful to describe your process, as it is happening, out loud to someone or into the tape recorder. You might even type or write out your experience as it is happening. In all events, write up your experience as soon as it has happened, if possible.

— Some people experience the expansion of the symbol as a flow of descriptive qualities, insights, feelings, etc. which seem to come from it. Others may see the experience and interact with it directly. There may even be some dialogue.

— Try not to evaluate your experience as it is happening. That part of yourself takes the observer role and remembers while another part focuses and may interact.

— After your experience write it down and evaluate. How does this symbol experience contrast with what happened in your dream? What came through for you in your symbol immersion? What central feeling, insight or essence came through?

— Do you feel a sense of awe and meaning? Many people do. Somehow the energy of the unconscious is evoked and we feel more than what we normally consider ourselves to be. This is the life source. We work with our unconscious to enliven and transform our being.

— If doing symbol immersion in a group, participants are asked *not* to analyze the other people's experiences, including the dream sharer. Even asking questions may violate the mood and be an intrusion. What people can do is share their own experience of the symbol. When in a group I always ask everyone to go into a meditative state and have their own experience. This prevents people observing or analyzing. This context applies to any dream group experience.

— Symbol immersion and other unconscious process techniques may be used with myths as well as stories to help involvement in the material.

— Can you feel the difference between having a lecturer standing up in front of an audience and telling them what a myth means versus taking people through experiencing the myth for themselves? One approach is rational. The other is personal, evocative and evolving. No expert can tell me how to experience my own unconscious. We need practitioners far more than we need experts in this life.

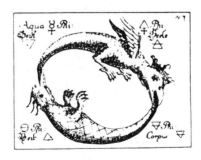

The Nature of Amplification

We start with some basic definitions and contrasts:

Amplification is **symbol inherency**. What is the symbol in itself? What is its own inherent functionality? In probing towards inherency we are working for objectivity as much as possible.

Association is **symbol linking** through memory, knowledge, beliefs and attitudes. The linking is not an inherent characterization of the symbol but an imposition onto it. Association is a highly personalized and subjective action.

The amplified characteristics of a symbol are what make the symbol exist.

Associated characteristics are not necessary to the life of the symbol.

In amplification we have the formula: symbol : referent : symbol : referent : symbol : referent. We keep returning to the symbol.

In association we have the formula: symbol : referent : referent : referent : referent. We keep working away from the symbol.

In amplification we stay with the one symbol, discovering its essential characteristics and plunging into the core.

In association we start with one symbol and leap to another and another and another.

Symbol amplification generally brings out the collective unconscious, the realm of the archetypes which underlie all existence, inner and outer.

Symbol association usually unearths the personal unconscious wherein our specific life material is stored and activated.

Amplification seeks the qualities and relations within the symbol.

Association imposes an outside system onto the symbol.

Bringing to light the inherent qualities in mythic figures and situations is amplification.

Linking mythic figures and situations to dream figures and situations is association. This is association and not amplification, as is commonly misunderstood in Jungian circles. Jung himself does not seem to make a sufficient distinction on this point.

The Stages of Amplification

The archetype manifests in a continuum as channel, energy, function, image, feeling, functional specificity and concept.
    In amplification we started at the conceptual level.

— What are the various inherent qualities of the symbol?
    In doing so we may refer to what the image represents in *the outer*. The dream centre seems to take as its language the language of image as it is experienced in the contemporary culture of the dreamer and in the universal natural language of symbol built up over the centuries.
— We ask, how does this symbol function in the outer? What are its necessary characteristics?
    We are first generalizing the nature of the symbol, broadening it so to speak, in order to include many possibilities.

Then we move to how the symbol may be characterized in the dream itself.

— What are the characteristics of this symbol in your dream. What is the effect of these images being together? How does this symbol function in the dream?
— We might ask also, what are the feeling qualities of this symbol?

By now we have generated a large number of possible characteristics which may be bewildering. It might even seem that the symbol can mean almost anything. And this may in fact be true, depending on the nature of the particular symbol. With all symbols there are levels of meaning. In this approach we do not try to fixate at any one level.

We now bring into play the principle of 'reduction to essence.'

— Out of all these characteristics what quality or essence might bring it all together?
— What for you are the outstanding qualities?
— Which qualities have the greatest energy?

Note that we have not yet brought in symbol association.

In order to distinguish between possible characteristics we may ask for personal associations.

Which of the general characteristics do you have specific associations to?

This brings into play the personal unconscious, which is not to say that symbols represent mostly the personal unconscious. Hopefully, a balance between the personal and the collective unconscious develops. We see in dream groups how individuals have tendencies in either direction. We have before us the cosmic versus the mundane dreamers!

Another way to get to the core qualities of the symbol is through question asking in order to keep peeling away the symbol's qualities until one arrives at the absolute base quality. This can also be done through symbol immersion, an unconscious process technique described elsewhere.

Thus we have finally arrived at what may be called the symbol's archetypal base.

Dreamwork Example — Amplification and Association

The following is a fairly clear example of amplification with association using the methods described here. There is awareness as to how the object functions in outer reality, a compiling of general characteristics and some reference to culture and myth.

There is also the application of the characteristics to personality and to outer life situations. This is based on the hypothesis that dream symbols reflect personality dynamics, which may or may not be valid. This dreamworker also brings in personal associations to help him 'sort through' the general characteristics.

He also moves to how the symbol operates in the dream and the possible meanings derived from this.

Dream Title: The Javelin Thrower   *Date: April 15, 1979 (Easter)*

On a long field, I am gaming with others, Ken Hans among them. He is talking too much, as usual. Also there is Anto (he teaches me to pronounce the last syllable — 'to'), a Jewish fellow. Ken and I are throwing javelins that resemble thick knitting needles, of various lengths, some rather bent. Anto, who is on the field to run, with somebody else (Dean?), asks that I watch out for him — not to hurl a javelin in his direction as he runs. I agree not to, but ask him, 'Didn't I hear you speaking on the radio? An interviewer was asking you about education in Jerusalem, schools for children that are providing special, advanced education.' Anto apparently knows about the education programme, but wasn't the one on the radio.

Ken and I throw javelins, poorly, and I note that Anto has already run down the field, almost to its end. My javelin goes very short of him, for which I am thankful, because I don't want him to notice, after I promised to look after him. I won't throw another javelin with him downfield. We go pick up the javelin and walk back. After the second throw, Anto brings one back for us — mine — and I walk to retrieve Ken's, which was almost lost and badly bent, misshapen. I straighten it, removing kinks in it, but Ken doesn't want to use it again. He has a long one he wants to throw now.

Comments

The javelin is the symbol with the most clarity in this dream. It is not one I am familiar with; I regard it as a possible symbol because it carries connotations and diverse implications. It's a bed of suggestions, at least loosely linked, which is my notion of symbol. Its implications, though I sense they share unifying elements, are nonetheless vague. This corresponds with Jung's idea of symbol, as I understand it, in his introduction to *Man and His Symbols*.

Dream Tasks: Amplifying the Dream

The javelin, in 'outer reality', is a sort of ritualistic tool, a presentation of the hunter's spear, used for games in which men demonstrate their prowess in community gatherings. Thus, for the community it serves a ritual depicting the vigour and strengths of the community, perhaps in competition with other communities.

As a spear, which I think needs consideration also, it is a tool for gathering food and facing foes — defensively and offensively (i.e., for protection as well as expansion, conquest). Its bearers are strong — the men who are the hunters, the warriors, the 'braves'.

The javelin and spear are inherently masculine. They thrust, and the thrust can be creative — reaping food.

Elements inherent in the javelin are speed, direction, and sharpness. It cuts through the air swiftly, with a whistling.

In myths and rituals the javelin and spear are often the weapons used in sacrifices. *The Golden Bough* notes its use in the mystical ceremonies celebrating the death of *Attis*, where the consecrated spear slays the bull whose blood washes away the stings of the participants who are baptized in it. In various 'Scape Goat' rituals it is also a consecrated tool for sacrificing. John, in the New Testament, notes the spear that pierced Jesus, whose body bled blood and water.

Biblically, the javelin and spear represent warfare. The Psalms use *spear* as a metaphor, or symbol, for war. Saul twice hurled a javelin at David, intending to pin him to the wall. David dodged both times, and it was understood that Yahweh was with David and not with Saul. Phinehas, a grandson of Aaron, slayed with a spear a sinning Israelite and his concubine, thus mitigating Yahweh's wrath, saving Israel from further plague. For this act, Yahweh extended his covenant of peace to Phinehas, and an everlasting priesthood — to him and his 'seed'. This suggests the sacrifice again.

In the western world, it seems, the javelin is notable as a war weapon and as a part of sacrifices, the tool bringing death to the selected victim and life to the believers. It can be regarded, then, as the expedient effecting the climax of the mystery of sacrifice.

Psychological dynamics include ideas of thrusting and aggression.

Personal associations — Important to me has been the observation of a friend that Sagittarians have the elements of the arrow — direction (single, unswerving directionality), pointedness, sureness. Thus, she concluded, they can be single-minded, capable of devotion, much concentration on specific goals; drawbacks are that they are less likely to be easy-going and casual. It describes me to a tee: all or nothing, like an arrow once released. Positive points are acuteness, discerningness, sometimes necessary, and generally good for certain sorts of accomplishments, requiring discipline. The javelin calls back to me all these associations.

Expressing my intentness, I even straighten a bent javelin — the superlative of all these qualities is implied!

In the dream, the javelin also mirrors knitting needles, tools for constructing fabric with thread — 'knitting', in all of its senses. This is singular, not present in myth.

I'm inclined to regard the javelin in connection with knitting and the centaur's arrow, since those have been internalized. The mythical elements lend power, even excitement, in the javelin as symbol, but not much more, it seems.

Relating the dream to the outer world, I would say it shows me practising my skills, testing my powers. In my life, skill and knowledge are the sources of power, and I am preoccupied, concern over my skills, or lack of them. Being with a student links the dream to my professional activities. I could be trying my skills as a teacher. This makes sense; I rarely stop thinking about them and feeling guilty when I don't make more of an effort to improve them.

Hurling the javelin at Anto suggests clumsiness and absence of concentration. In the dream, my dream ego feels embarrassed.

Dreamwork Entry – Amplifying Your Dream

— After writing your dream down choose a major symbol from your dream and re-describe it even more fully in terms of the dream than you have before. Focus in on the detail perhaps, or re-write your description with more feeling tone and even attention to such qualities as colour and action.

— Then take the outer entity which corresponds to your dream symbol and describe all its major qualities and characteristics. Then add the level of functionality or how the symbol acts and relates to its environment.

— Now take your dream symbol and describe its specific qualities and characteristics in the dream. What is the context within which it operates? How does it function in the dream? What is its feeling level? What actions and feelings does it evoke from others in the dream, including your dream ego? What is your waking ego's reaction to this symbol? How does this contrast with reactions within the dream?

— It quickly becomes apparent in employing many symbols that they each have a wealth of inherent and primary characteristics. After we have sought out and listed the primary characteristics of a dream symbol, what then? How do we select, or give importance to, the symbol's characteristics to be emphasized? The assumption is that not all the general characteristics of a symbol are equally evocative or meaningful in a given dream. We select and in selection try to make sense of the totality by focusing in on what seems most central. Here are eight bases for selecting symbol characteristics.

— Selection through applying the principle of contrasts. Which characteristics of the symbol seem to be being emphasized by being in contrast with other characteristics or symbols in the dream?

— Selection through applying the principle of similarities. Which characteristics of the symbol seem to be being emphasized by having a marked similarity with other symbols or characteristics in the dream?

— Selection through the symbol itself exaggerating or highlighting one or more characteristics. The dream plane has ten propellers instead of the normal two in outer reality.

— Selection based on certain inherent characteristics receiving emphasis through how the dream ego does or does not interact with the symbol. The dream ego peels the orange and eats it rather than planting it in the ground.

— Selection based on the interactions of other symbols with the chosen symbol. The man is shooting ducks at close range.

— Selection is based on what characteristics change or are different when the same general symbol appears in more than one dream. The plane had only two propellers instead of eight in a subsequent dream.

— Selection of symbol characteristics can be based on personal associations. A house in a dream which among other things has a theatre in it can have this theatre characteristic emphasized if the dreamer was or is an actress.

— Selection of certain characteristics can be based on outside factors such as the dreamer's feeling reactions to certain characteristics. Thus a strong positive or negative feeling reaction to a certain characteristic would emphasize that characteristic. One might also choose characteristics based on certain values or current life themes. The fact that my dead father is alive again in my dream makes me want to work with the fact of new life in the death.

Selection is in itself a necessary methodology for consciousness. We all select from all of the life stimuli coming to us. What we select, and the context within which this is based, may well crucially determine at what level of meaning we live our lives.

Having developed and selected the characteristics of your dream symbol the next step is to organize the characteristics in some multi-faceted coherent whole. In doing this, write a full description of your symbol's characteristics with key questions which arise from this. Note that there are two basic levels of question asking in regard to symbols.

One is asking the question using the symbol's images, such as, how would a plane with ten propellers be different from a plane with two? Two is asking the question more conceptually, such as follows, how do you in your life right now over-exaggerate things?

— Finally what specific tasks or projects can you create and act on to manifest the symbol's qualities? Manifestation is everything. The archetype sends us the new potential in the form of a symbol but it is always up to us to manifest that potential in outer reality.

— After amplification and association you may want to do a *symbol immersion* and see what happens for you.

— You might also *dialogue* with the symbol and ask it which of the possible characteristics seem most relevant? Or would the symbol itself add any characteristics?

— Dream re-entry can also be used to have your symbol interact more fully, or in new ways, with other dream symbols.

— Or use *symbol evolvement*, my term for a method discovered by Jung in which the dreamer focuses on the symbol in active imagination and watches to see what happens to it.

These last unconscious process techniques are quite dynamic and are described later in great detail. The unconscious process techniques mark the real departure of the Jungian-Senoi approach from interpretative techniques.

The Test

It is not so much whether our amplification of the symbol makes sense to us or not as it is whether what we have discovered from the symbol works in reality.

Reality is the testing ground for all ideas.

It is so easy for the ego to fool itself through its own interpretations of symbols. Since dreams are symbolic it is easy for the ego to find what it wants to in the dream. But how much harder is it to really objectify the dream's potentials? We have learned how to begin to do this through the procedures for amplification. This is the stage of internal objectification.

But we have also an objectification process of testing one's insights in outer reality. This is the stage of external objectification. If your description of the symbol's potential is 'true' do something which tests this in outer reality. If your dreams seem to be saying that you should pursue a certain course in life, do it and see what happens. If reality goes against you, you are probably way off in your ability to objectify your dreams. If you are off in your approach it will also probably show up in future dreams. This is why we must develop the commitment to writing down every dream we remember no matter what we think or feel about it. The ego is definitely needed to carry out the journey process. But always be cautious about your own ego's bias. The ego is a fallible organ and subject to demanding its own needs, even when this goes against the needs of the total psyche, or even when this goes against reality itself.

If you feel certain about something, question what your ego is secretly demanding.

Certainty is the greatest bias, the final block to objectivity.

Thus the completing stage in the amplification process is to carry out specific tasks which test your description of the symbol's meaning, and then to reflect upon the results of such tasks.

We add a *warning*, however.

— Do not mistake inner dream reality for outer concrete reality.

— Do not literally follow your dreams in the outer.

True, certain dreams can predict future events or at best indicate the potentials for future events. But dreams can themselves be projections of inner dynamics into the dream mirror. Dreams have been used to justify every paranoia and glory under the sun, moon and stars.

— Do not literally act out your dreams in the outer unless it seems appropriate to the outer situation.

Remember also that using the unconscious process techniques described in this manual can help you work out many emotional situations on an inner level. Through the powers of the imagination you are freed from identification with outer reality. But this does not mean that you space out and disappear into the abysses of the unconscious, leaving the everyday world behind. In fact, the reverse. We disidentify from the outer in order to have greater clarity and flexibility for dealing with the outer.

A warning is only a caution. Nothing can stop anyone from doing anything except the laws of reality, inner and outer.

The Stages of Amplification Summarized

1. Select a symbol with major intensity or energy.
2. List many of the possible inherent characteristics of the symbol.
3. Develop the symbol's characteristics using the eight principles of selection: contrasts, similarities, exaggeration, relation to dream ego, interactions with other dream symbols, changes in other dreams, personal associations, and outside factors such as feelings and values.
4. Organize the symbol's characteristics into a coherent whole and adding key questions.
5. Test the objectivity of your amplification by doing tasks which test this and then reflecting on the consequences. Further dreams may also shed light on your process.

Certain other procedures can also be used to add or test your amplification description:

1. Do a dialogue with the symbol asking it what it means, etc.
2. Do a symbol immersion to get the unconscious to fountain out characteristics.
3. Do a symbol evolvement to experience where the symbol is going or what happens next.
4. Do a dream re-entry in which you allow the symbol to interact more fully with other symbols in the dream.

Metaphorical Processing

Is a dream anything more than a dream?

Does the symbolism of a dream reflect internal dynamics of the psyche or is it merely a spontaneous symbol experience in itself?

Is the dream solely a symbolic manifestation of the creative imagination of the psyche? In what sense does it *not* represent internal states specifically?

Is it true that sometimes in dreams we have external people and situations reflected? Or that we have interior personality behaviour dramatically exposed? It would be more reasonable to suggest that our 'metaphorical mind' is processing life conditions using symbols rather than concepts. Concepts are usually what the more conscious side of the personality, the ego, uses in its processing.

There are many dream situations in which there seems to be little or no reference to outer things. What do we do with these?

We can make an assumption, as the depth and psychoanalytic psychologists do, that these are more disguised symbols for personality dynamics and life situations.

If so, then why doesn't the dream source speak more clearly? Either the

dream source is quite clear and we are the ones who cannot read the symbols or the dream source is deliberately masking material we would resist if exposed to it directly. Traditionally the Freudian assumption of resistance comes in here in which the person is assumed to be hiding direct sexual or murderous impulses.

We have found to the contrary in Institute dream groups that people have and share dreams in which they are shitting, having sex, and killing people. It's all perfectly natural in the dream world.

There is Jung's famous question asked of Freud at one of the early psychoanalytic conferences:

'But, Herr Professor Freud, what if one should dream of an erect penis, what then?'

With this the whole edifice of the Freudian theory fell into ruin for many people. For the Freudians believed that the unconscious disguised things through symbolism. Sexual drive would be masked and one would dream of erect tall buildings instead of erect penises. Thus phallic symbols become sexy and the ordinary penis not sexy at all.

Jung asked, 'Why doesn't the unconscious mean exactly what it says in dreams?'

Yet he himself felt compelled to go to other symbol systems, such as to myth and alchemy, to get at the meaning of symbols.

One of the levels of questioning applied to dreams at the Jungian-Senoi Institute is to ask 'How does this dream reflect certain attitudes or dynamics within myself?'

It was assumed by us that the dream naturally did mirror internal mental states and that the unconscious was giving us the dream so that we could make more conscious unconscious processes.

This dynamic may well be true but it is only an assumption.

It might well be that we are simply using *the dream as metaphor* to process dynamics of our unconscious or situations in our life. In other words, we may be taking a symbolic structure, the dream, and fitting it to a specific situation.

The results are often quite meaningful when we ask, to give and example, 'How does this dream reflect what is going on in my relationship right now?'

With this question we can obtain useful insight but we cannot say absolutely that the dream came to us because the unconscious wanted to make conscious how we relate to people.

The same dream as metaphor can usually be applied to a number of external and internal situations with meaningful results. In other words, we can never go wrong with a dream!

The danger may be more in the assumption that the dream has one and only one level of possible meaning and that our job is to ferret this out like a detective. People have lived their lives under this assumption. What have they missed?

At the Institute we take a broader view of dreamwork. Yes, there may be only one level which 'clicks' with a person, as Jung would say. But this might be dogmatizing the dream. Why not explore a number of possible levels? Why not open up one's consciousness instead of closing it down?

Focus is not achieved at the insight level but at the choice level.

The method is to broaden insight so as to offer the widest number of possibilities for choice. After getting clear on the alternatives, after using the dream as a metaphor applied to more than one situation, then choose the most valuable context to develop further.

To take a dramatic example – I have a dream in which I have died and know I am dead. Yet I wake up from the dream fully alive but shocked and afraid. Does the dream mean I am going to die soon? Does it mean there is life after life? Does it mean I am being shocked by my unconscious into changing my life-style? Does it mean that it is now time to deal with my own fears of dying and the ageing process? Does it mean that my personality ego is getting disidentified from itself? Does it mean there is a new level of consciousness happening? Does it mean I have had an out of the body experience?

There are more possible questions. Obviously people have dreams in which they are dead but wake up not dead. What is going on?

What if I dreamed I was dead one night and I was dead? It might be the most vivid dream of my life – death! And how would I ever know that I was dead if I was not dead?

Perhaps in a 'one's own death' dream one has been dead in life and is only now on the verge of recognizing it?

The dream as metaphor? Metaphorical processing? Which, if not all, of the proceeding questions are relevant to the dream and the life of the dreamer who dreamed it?

The response, perhaps, is that we do not need to know which is the appropriate question or the right answer. We apply the dream as metaphor working with possibilities. Out of this application we re-experience the dream within the actual context of life, and out of that experience comes the meaning.

We choose the context we want to work in. We may choose the one we are most drawn to. And for holistic balance we may choose the context we are least drawn to or even repelled by. We may choose to try out a number of different contexts.

And we still have the issue, what is it exactly the dream is trying to get us to face? Some people feel they know. Some people work with a moral, discriminating quality, while others seem to emphasize more an openness to all possibilities.

The dream as metaphor? Dreamwork as metaphorical processing?

Your life as metaphor? What is your life for? What does your life symbolize? What does your life reflect, if anything, of an underlying reality?

Perhaps only you can know? Perhaps it is up to you alone to choose the context?

And by what you choose shall you become manifest!

Dreamwork Entry – Metaphorical Processing

This technique can be used with any dream but usually a simple, concise dream works best. Although one person used a long dream of hers and went through it step by step writing up the dream's dynamics as personal references to what had gone on in her childhood for her.

— After writing down your dream objectify the dream by becoming clear on the dream's internal dynamics.

— Re-write the dream generalizing it somewhat and making its imagery and structure clearer. You may not need to do this step if the dream seems relatively clear.

— Next choose two different or even opposed contexts within which to process the dream as metaphor. Here are some suggestions to which you may want to add ones of your own.

- What does this dream say about my sexual relationships?
- How does this dream illustrate my attitudes towards money?
- What aspects of my own childhood is this dream bringing up for me?
- What sort of parent-child problems are being exposed here?
- In what sense is this dream about my own need for healing? What are the healing symbols in this dream?
- How does this dream reflect how I do or do not make choices?
- What future possibilities in my life is this dream possibly predicting?
- In what way does this dream reflect the political events coming in the next decade?
- How does this dream reflect certain internal dynamics in my personality?

It is hard, is it not?, to choose more than one context for the dream. After all, the ego already has its opinion, its context, and the ego is always right.

This technique has been successfully used in training others in dreamwork. Participants were all given a dream in common to take on as their own dream.

They were asked to re-enter the dream meditatively and let their feelings and images flow. Many reported profound, 'as if it were my own dream' experiences.
What does metaphorical processing do to the 'right interpretation clicks' theory?

— Yet we still have the possibility that certain contexts evoke more meaning than others. So after you have explored two different contexts choose, if you can, the one which seems more right for you and try to explain why. Check out with a friend who knows you well about how he or she would evaluate the two contexts you have chosen. They might suggest still a different context.

— Another way to do metaphorical processing is to develop the *levels of dreamwork* such as follows,

  • What is the nature of this dream in itself?
  • What does this dream say about my present personality dynamics?
  • What does this dream reflect about my past, inner and outer?
  • What does this dream indicate as potentials for future living, inner and outer?
  • What does this dream evoke concerning issues in my life right now?
  • What attitudes and feelings are reflected in this dream?
  • What does this dream indicate about my ego, inner and outer?
  • What of the spirit world may be reflected in this dream?
  • What of transcendent and ultimate questions is presented in this dream?

Choose from the above questions or develop them all. These are many of the levels of meaning possible in working with a dream. What other levels might you add? It is almost always important to develop more than one level of a dream.

— After you have responded to the above you might design specific outer-oriented tasks to do in order to test out the metaphorical insight you have gained.
— Concrete reality is the great metaphor for spirit!

The Nature of Bringing Resolution

Bringing resolution to the dream state has evolved as a major aspect of the Jungian-Senoi approach.

In working with dreams and with people's problems and psyches in the therapeutic process it was found that these situations were full of conflicts, problems, potentials for new life and an ego, or choice-maker, ill-equipped in attitude or skill for dealing adequately and creatively with these natural life dilemmas.

What was to be done?

It was not enough to bring out what the conflicts and potentials were. This would often produce greater anxiety and feelings of inability than before. For insight in and of itself does not necessarily compel action. Action arises from a commitment to manifesting 'truth' as it becomes known.

Nor was it satisfying to fixate on solutions or answers to these problems from the outside. Taking positions on things would not really help since these 'solutions' did not often arise internally from the problems themselves.

Nothing less than transformation was needed. But how was it to be effected? This much became clear.

Whatever solutions there were must arise internally from within the source of the difficulties. For a unity cannot be forced from the outside.

And that in order to effect solutions the art of bringing resolution must come into play.

The Nature of Resolution

Resolution is the bringing to completion, to closure, to a natural integrative ending what has been developing but left hanging or in fixed conflict.

When resolution is evoked the total situation moves forward to a goal. One thing becomes another. Blocks are removed and the whole process flows and recombines itself. A centre is formed which unifies opposites and creates an evolving third point out of these opposites.

The art of bringing resolution is the way to evoke transformation and produce meaning.

Bringing resolution is one of the central practices of the meditative life.

Not only within dreams but within life and within each day lives the need to bring resolution to a myriad of conflicts and potentials which have developed.

At the end of each day do I review what has happened, see what has been left hanging, and evoke resolution so that I can enter sleep, the belly of the new, cleared and open?

The dying review their lives, including the unlived or unresolved life, in order to bring resolution to the resolution occurring in the physical.

Each day everyone mulls over innumerable things that have already been lived. This is the mind trying to effect resolution.

Great ceremonies, rites of passage and supreme crises are there to effect resolution.

Without resolution the old life hangs on, preventing new life from being born.

There is nothing more pathetic than something which refuses to die when its time has come.

The art of resolution means *sacrifice* as well as transformation. Certain things must be ended before new things can develop. For every 'yes' which is said a 'no' must echo down the halls of eternity. And what is eternity but the past? For the future comes at us limited by what can be actualized in the now.

Thus in working with dreams, and not merely dreaming the dream or even analyzing it, we work towards resolving the conflicts and potentials within these dreams. And then upon that foundation we take the dreamwork experience to the outer and work on resolving aspects of our personalities and life situations to which the dream and the dreamwork seem to relate.

We learn also in the art of bringing resolution the nature of a developing consciousness. We participate actively in the conscious creation of new life, and such an act is an act of meaning.

The Twelve Stages of Bringing Resolution

As seen in this metaphysical diagram the art of bringing resolution can be

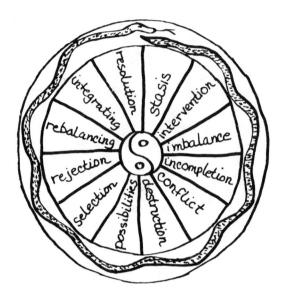

divided into *twelve stages*. For simplicity's sake you can take as an example the process of a physical wound and its healing. Or you can apply the resolving of a relationship to the diagram.

All things are from time to time in balance. When this balance begins to last too long it produces *stasis* or inhibition of the life flow. An *intervention* occurs ending stasis and producing *imbalance* or one-sidedness. A lack of certain elements is experienced causing *incompletion* which gives rise to *conflict*. Things are split apart, some become hidden, some are too obvious. This condition then creates the *destroying* of certain things previously necessary to the state of being. The void formed out of such a destruction produces a vacuum which attracts new *possibilities*. These new possibilities, when combined with the old which remains, threaten to clog or overwhelm the situation, thus making necessary a process of *selection* and *rejection*. That which is needed to create a new balance must be brought into play. All else is excluded as superfluous and inhibitory. Selection and rejection go on until a *balancing* of all the essentials occurs, creating thereby a centre and a harmonious interrelating of all the parts which is called *integration*. Finally, the *resolution* occurs in which the conflict is restored into a new unity. This new unity is the resolution. The whole process has been one of *transformation* in which one thing becomes another. The original condition in stasis has undergone the transformational process and a new, more full and meaningful condition has come into being.

A Simpler Version of the Transformation Cycle

A simpler version of the transformation cycle is as follows:

— Things exist in an *original unity*. All is merged into one harmonious whole.

— *Differentiation of opposites* begins to occur via *conflicts* developing between the various parts.

— *Imbalance* occurs in which certain opposites are exalted or given much of the available energy. This evokes compensation, or the tendency to rebalance opposites with equal amounts of energy.

— An *enantiodromic cycle* is set in motion in which energy keeps flowing from one opposite to the other in a seesaw effect.

— The danger exists of going into one opposite and *fixating* there as a way of solving the conflict.

— If this danger is resisted by the ego, and a *balanced tension* is maintained between the opposites, then transformation can occur.

— Maintaining the tension between the opposites allows a *unity* to develop between them which brings *resolution* to the conflict.

— A new *harmony* exists which has both *unity* and *differentiation of opposites*. This is the *transformation* of the old into the new.

Examples of the Transformation Cycle

Now what does this mean on an everyday level?

In the dreamwork example of guided symbol immersion the original unity of the beaded necklace was broken literally in the dream. In the symbol immersion the dreamer's task was to put the necklace back together and to deal with to whom did it belong, herself or her son? There was also the conflict of the old traditional ways of doing things versus the new ways of doing things. The transformation and resolution is in putting the necklace back together, and in giving it to her son and in not having it turn into plastic because she is still trying to hold onto the old order. There is still tension and differentiation. But a new harmonizing of the various parts has also occurred.

As another example, the transformation cycle might be applied to a common problem in relationships as follows. One of a pair is attracted to a third party. This creates tension in the original relationship and the old unity is destroyed. The person affected may choose to go with the new attraction and thus go into the new opposite. Once this is being lived out ambivalence, or the swinging from one lover to another, may occur. To choose to go with either one and deny the other at this point would be fixating in one opposite and not integrating all the energies evoked.

If tension is maintained and the qualities of both relationships accepted, then a new unity can occur within the affected individuals. Transformation occurs when the tension is resolved through integration.

The person may choose to stay with the original relationship partner but now both of them have been changed through dealing with the new relationship. The new energy evoked, hopefully, has been integrated into their relationship.

Or the choice may be to end the old relationship because a new unity does not evolve out of the shattered old unity. The person may choose not to relate to either but seek a totally new relationship which embodies more opposites than either one did before. There are many possibilities.

The 'new ethic' here is to consciously go with the transformation cycle and not fixate in any one opposite by denying and repressing a whole aspect of life. We are not saying, either, that everything which is evoked in us is best lived out in the outer. At some level, inner or outer, what is evoked in life needs acknowledgement and acceptance in order to be integrated and transformed.

Thus, as we see here, transformation is the process and resolution is the outcome, producing a new state of being. Thus, endings, the 'little deaths', can be seen as transitions and transformations and not merely drop-offs into the abyss. Resolution prepares us by making us ready for the new. To hang on, to look back, during the crucial points is to evoke disaster. The refusal to sacrifice, to let go, means that we let fate, whose ferocity is far greater than our own, create the death for us. Such a death is often a disaster from which no recovery may be possible. Transformation does not occur and the re-birth, for which death is the necessary preparation, cannot manifest.

Not only a new state of being but the production of meaning is the result of the transformational, bringing-resolution process.

Meaning

Meaning is the experience of relation between things. In bringing resolution the old is related to the new, death becomes the evoker of new life, choice copes with fate to produce destiny, and the wound and its healing are brought into a new unity.

With such a process we may well ask what is the relation of suffering to meaning? *Creative suffering* is the acceptance of the necessary pain involved in conflicts and letting go. Chosen purposeful suffering grounds one, makes one's life worthwhile. It is necessary counterbalance to real joy. *Joy* is the infallible evidence for the presence of transformation. We have made the sacrifice and a new, more fuller reality leaps into being.

The Affair as Waking Dream

The affair is a special instance of the waking dream. Many people who record their dreams regularly find that in the dreams they may be having attractions to or sex with partners other than their chosen outer partner. When archetypal sexual energy intrudes on the outer life, the person may have an affair in the outer. He or she experiences a waking dream.

What is going on? A merely polygamous nature expressing itself? Is the conscious outer life of a committed monogamous relationship primarily a situation of two horses hitched to a somewhat stable wagon? Who doesn't want to run free into the wilds? But ah! The consequences.

A waking dream occurs when we are overcome by strong archetypal material which breaks through into the outer. The presence of the waking dream may mean that we are unable or unwilling to contain, for processing, certain vital life experiences within the realm of the inner. Or it may be necessary as part of the inner life journey to go with archetypal material emerging into the outer life. If we deal with our unconscious forces mainly by repressing them, our life will be a continual waking dream in which nothing we do is truly our own but is governed by unconscious forces. Repression creates indentification with certain contents of the unconscious and projection of other, usually opposite, contents onto outer persons and situations.

There is no absolute protection against the waking dream. We are not all that in control of our lives. But there is one general principle and method which can provide, if not security, at least a ground of being out of which to act and journey forward.

That method and principle is to accept and process whatever comes up in life.

Do I really accept reality as it is or do I resist it? Do I attempt to control the other person or situation or do I attempt to blend, structure and integrate with whatever or whoever is there?

An affair is not an affair merely. It is an intervention of the Other. Powerful forces are at work for some purpose and have come to the fore. This may be seen and felt as the end of the world or the end of the relationship. But it need not be so. What energy is being evoked by this intervention into what has been my somewhat stable and controlled life? And what is the intervention's purpose and how can I grow from it?

To react against the event for long, to resist it absolutely, is to magnify its proportions and to drive us into life-contracting defensiveness. An affair is only an affair, or is it?

Substitute, for the word affair, a major sickness or a death and you have the same intervention of the Other, the waking dream.

First, acceptance of the actual forces at work is required. 'Let's sit down and deal with this. Let's get to our feelings, our attributes, let's get to the root of this thing and accept it.'

Thus, communication is best developed and maintained among all parties involved. Yes, the third parties also. Too often the middle person is played off against the other. If two men are interested in the same woman, they may need to communicate and exchange energies with each other instead of making her the sole battleground. Why get her to fight your life battles for you? The same is true for two women interested in one man.

With as full a communication established as possible, the next steps are to explore and express all the energies evoked. Why am I doing this anyway? What does this person evoke for me? What is off in my present relationship that this would even happen? What in me is bursting out that I would be letting this develop? What can I do to integrate this energy on an inner level? What must be expressed in the outer? What is the quality of my choice-making in this situation? How am I dealing with fear as well as sexuality?

A key point is not to let the new energy get locked into an outer circumstance. Try to avoid being too dramatic. And seek support in processing the energies involved. An affair is usually not the end of a marriage or relationship unless you let it be. An affair is a waking dream needing processing.

What exactly are the energies involved? What are the qualities of each person? What is the archetypal base? What is the play of masculine and feminine in this situation? What parental, dependency stuff is being challenged? What excess of psychic energy is breaking out? What is the spiritual factor? What basic values are being challenged or formulated? How is this situation a death I must deal with? What is the new life possible from this event? How does this event challenge me to deal with suffering better? How can I integrate this and grow into a more complete person?

Have we made the point? The affair is archetypal energy on the move. It is a stirring for new unity. It is the need to evoke new energy for life vitality. It is the challenge to deal with our unconscious forces more fully.

It is a chance to increase out total acceptance of the life journey and get on with it.

What the Self most needs is what is most required of us. And always and ultimately, every affair is an affair with ourselves. We are all alone in this life. The only relationship there really is, is the relationship with oneself. The others? They may be partners, companions along the way. I learn from them. They evoke me and I evoke them. But what is evoked is always within. Find it there within your own soul and you will be truly free to relate to others.

Direct Re-entry into the Dream State

A Central Method

One of the central methods I have developed in doing dreamwork groups since 1972 is that of direct intervention into the dream state.

Essentially, this means re-entering or re-doing the dream in some form with the intention of bringing resolution to certain situations and elements in the dream. This re-entry or revision is done in the waking state usually by entering into a semi-trance condition, re-experiencing the dream, putting the intention for seeking resolution into it, and letting go and seeing how the imagery and dialogue develop.

This process is often deeply moving and may be accompanied by the expression of much intense emotion and feeling. But this need not be the case to be effective. Simply going through the process of re-dreaming produces meaning, a felt change and possibly a change in the patterns deep within the unconscious.

This is working archetypally below and beyond the conscious level.

The approach can also be used while dreaming as in the case of waking from a nightmare and immediately falling back asleep with the intention to get back into the dream, seeing what happens, and wait for or bring it to resolution.

The method of direct intervention differs from what orthodox Jungians do. Their position would be that you do not tamper with the dream and the unconscious. If you just let the unconscious unfold, these people would say, healing will naturally take place. I for one would like to see direct and specific evidence that this *laissez-faire* approach works with dreams or anything else for that matter.

The dream is not a dogma which is not to be tampered with because it is considered a sacred object from God, the Unconscious. As with anything else, we need to lend consciousness to the 'primal state' and evoke transformation.

Intervening in the Unconscious

Jung's example of the man who dreamed of climbing a mountain and stepping out into space was dealt with by Jung using his considerable interpretive powers. Jung told the man that if he was not extremely careful in his mountain climbing he would kill himself. The man laughed, went mountain climbing, and literally was seen to step off into space, killing himself and his companion. If this man had been open to it, the new approach would have been to guide him in re-entering the dream, experiencing it in full symbolically, bringing it to resolution, either in the 'mountain death' or in 'clinging to life,' and then deriving meaning and choice-making from the total experience. Possibly transformation could have occurred. For what is fully experienced symbolically does not necessarily have to be lived out in the outer.

This sort of approach of course raises issues. Taking account of another person's process, on what basis do we intervene? There is danger of intervention too soon or too late. When is the time of ripeness? The first stages of dream re-entry are more concerned with expanding the dream or opening up possibilities. Once that is done we can then seek the natural resolution inherent in the dream state.

This is of course a *spiritual* or *transpersonal* process. For the healing, the way, the direction, the resolution, does seem to come out of a mystery uncontrolled by our intentions. But it then becomes a question for each of us as to how much we are willing to let go to the process.

And is our commitment and capacity for transformation great enough to include the worst terror or evil?

The History of the Method

The history of the development of the method started in 1972 when I was assigned to be one of the dream elders for a daily Senoi dream session working with psychotic teenagers at St. George Homes Inc., a residential, innovative treatment centre in Berkeley, founded by Dorothea Romankiw.

Through dream sharing we were able to obtain much inner material. But it soon became apparent that our teenagers did not have enough ego to become conscious of the dynamics reflected in their dreams. Moreover they often had frightening and chaotic dreams which, if left alone, made them feel as bad or worse than when they started. The dreams reflected the mental states they were in much more often than they compensated for them.

And I have also found in working with 'normal' adults that most of their dreams also are full of conflict, un-harmony and un-resolution.

What was to be done?

What if healing symbols were introduced into the dreamwork projects. The dramatic moment came when an extremely psychotic boy, who habitually lacerated himself severly among other things, started painting his 'monsters' as he called them. I instructed the art therapist to paint golden circles around his figures and in the future he would paint his monsters within the golden circle. The golden circle is a classic symbol for wholeness and protection from demons. Dream intervention, rather than just expression and interpretation, had been launched.

The idea of a daily dream session had been started by Dorothea Romankiw and developed further at St. George by Dr. Albert Belante following his reading of Kilton Stewart's classic paper on Senoi dreamwork. Many staff have contributed to the Senoi dream session at St. George. Among these Steve Ledyard contributed the basic dream pouch ritual taken in part from Native American practices. I was mainly responsible for the development of Jungian amplification, ritual, meditation and relating the symbols to personality dynamics as well as the ongoing of a full dream task programme working in art, drama, and special school projects. The task idea comes as much from Dorothea Romankiw as from Senoi tradition and is one of the basics for her whole approach to the treatment of the severely disturbed.

In 1976 I left St. George Homes to devote my full time to developing dreamwork, using it in therapy, and teaching it to the general public. At this time I coined the term, 'Jungian-Senoi Dreamwork' to emphasize a difference and a further development from St. George.

In doing dream groups in Berkeley I was struck by the amount of passivity and un-resolved conflicts in the so-called normal adult's dream. I found little difference between the dreams of psychotic teenagers at St. George and the adults with which I was now working. Something more was needed.

It was not possible to train the average adult in extensive dream-change while dreaming, which was supposedly the Senoi tradition. In the Senoi culture the children were reported to have been trained from birth to change their dreams towards resolution while dreaming. And there was even question as to whether Kilton Stewart's paper was fiction or not.

It became clear that most dreams presented conflict and not resolution. In early 1977, then, I discovered the method of guided re-entry into the dream state and I took my first person back into the dream to re-experience it and to allow it to come to resolution. This was an immediate and introvertedly frightening experience at first. But it worked. People lost all sense of the external world in the dream state and dreams moved to resolutions in ways which were totally unexpected and often quite moving to the persons involved.

Since then I have further developed this and other methods, some discovered here at the Institute and others being refinements of already existing methods. The focus has always been the total development of dreamwork and not narrowing down on only a few methods or an approach. Whatever works is real, has been the focus of the Institute's activities. Many of the refinements and ideas have come from dreamwork participants too numerous to mention.

Outside of my extensive reading in Jung and other Jungians I have read little in the way of books on dreams. I have preferred to re-approach the dream as original experience and go from there. In the process I have also found where Jung as an original explorer may have missed things.

Jung's contribution, as I understand it, was to develop the method of active imagination. He sometimes had his people do 'carrying the dream forward' by starting where the dream leaves off and imagining what might come next. This is an effective method, but Jung did not have anyone re-enter and re-work the dream as far as I know.

There is no desire at the Institute to popularize dreamwork by pandering to anyone's collective fancies. The culture is in many ways, in my estimation, dying. The voices we listen to at the Institute come from those searching for realness, people capable of manifesting a spiritual quest and not exploiting dreams or anything else for their own egocentric purposes. There are many such individuals everywhere asserting themselves through various psychological and spiritual disciplines. May the numbers and influence of those who would be real to the very depths of their souls increase in great number. The wave of the future must not be engulfed by the dark and death-dealing waves of the past.

The Age of Resolution

We need an age in which the battles are also seen as inward, and in which the skills and commitments for bringing resolution, no matter what the conflicts, are acknowledged and practised as an integral part of the individual's and the collective culture's journey into the possible future. If all nations, as well as groups, couples and individuals adopted as their 'First Principle' the bringing of resolution to all conflicts, this world would take a giant evolutionary step forward.

The Unresolved Dream

One of the characteristics of most remembered dreams is that they are full of unresolved situations and conflicts. A conversation is only begun. The dreamer is sent on an errand but never arrives at his destination. The dreamer is at the door of a house but does not enter. The dreamer is being attacked but awakes before the ordeal has completed itself. The treasure is found, the baby is born, but nobody seems to know exactly what to do.

And so it goes. Look at your own dreams and see if this is not so? Issues are raised but seldom creatively dealt with in dreams.

The Art of Resolution

Do we end each day having brought resolution, at least in part, to whatever has come up during the day?

No. Usually we wake the next morning full of what happened the previous day hanging there still unresolved, and thus a weight preventing us from being fully present in the new day. Or how many relationships really reach resolution? Whenever we dream of a former lover or marriage partner what do we do with the dream? Is it possible that the Self is presenting such a dream so that we may bring resolution to a relationship which only exists now in inner reality?

Why basically are most dreams unresolved?

A mystery. But the approach becomes clear.

Fundamental to the art of dreamwork is the bringing of resolution to conflicts, issues, situations and so forth raised in dream states.

Dreaming about something does not usually bring resolution in itself. We must evoke resolution. This is the art of healing.

Once in a while there will be a dream which seems whole, complete in itself and with whatever it presents resolved. Like in drama, each act has been played in full, and we are left with a sense of completeness. We have relative certainty. We know what we must do.

So we take our cue from such a dream and seek resolution also for those other dreams which seem unresolved.

In bringing resolution there is always a danger of the ego's forcing a rational solution onto the experience. This is the danger of effecting a false resolution which closes off possibilities. There is a time for waiting and a time for evoking completion, a time for tension and imbalance and a time for direct closure. We must learn the difference between truly waiting for ripeness and resisting totally the process. Yes, we open ourselves and let it happen. But what is the point at which we know we must choose with everything we have and tip the scales decisively towards wholeness?

The practice of bringing resolution in dreamwork, becomes also the practice of bringing resolution to one's everyday life, as well as to one's ultimate quest.

In describing the approach these stages seem central:

The Stages of Bringing Resolution to Dream States

A dream is remembered and in looking at it certain issues are revealed needing resolution. It also often seems apparent that such a dream reflects internal or external dynamics needing resolution in a person's life. If we go to bed anxious we are likely to have an anxiety dream, otherwise termed a nightmare or that which we wake ourselves up from in fear.

— After perceiving the conflict the ego then directs its attention to resolving the conflict.
— It develops the major possibilities inherent in the dream.
— The ego then seeks resolution by evoking the resolving, integrating, transforming power of the central archetype of the Self.
— The ego and the larger psyche then usually experience a resolution. The ego brings this experience to consciousness and takes measures to implement the resolution, the healing, the insights, in everyday reality. If this last stage happens then the ego experiences confirmation of the whole experience. Also perhaps further issues are raised needing work and resolution. This is natural to the creative process.

What follows is a brief description of a number of methods for bringing resolution to dream states. In the next sections we will be describing some of the methods in detail and working with them.

Primary Methods for Bringing Resolution to Dream States

Guided Re-entry into the Dream State
The dreamer immerses him or herself back into the dream using re-visualizing of the dream and letting go to new imagery and sometimes dialogue. The intention of bringing resolution is also usually taken into the dream. The dream events are described to a guide who also is in a meditative state with eyes closed and who asks questions and makes suggestions for activity as things proceed.

Self Re-entry into the Dream State

The dreamer immerses him or herself in the dream. Through re-visualizing it and letting go to the imagery and possibly dialogue. The intention for resolution is also present. There is no guide. The results are written down afterwards.

Re-writing the Dream

Elements needing change or resolution, including what the dream ego is doing or not doing, are analyzed and creative, meaningful resolutions chosen. The dream is then re-written imaginatively within the context of the changes desired.

Carrying the Dream Forward

The dream state is re-entered imaginatively at its remembered end using re-visualization. New imagery, feeling, dialogue, etc. are allowed to flow spontaneously until a point where resolution feels like it has occurred. The method is excellent for dreams only partially remembered, or which seem unresolved or where ending due to abrupt waking up happened.

Method of the Four Quadrants

We use artwork to draw the dream in three acts. The action is clearly seen with its progression. The fourth quadrant is for drawing a spontaneous resolution to the 'dream drama.'

Carrying the Dream Backward

This is similar to carrying the dream forward. Only we use symbol regression to take things back to prior states. This is useful for dreams which seem to start abruptly and for such questions as 'How did it happen?' or 'How did my dream ego get into *that* situation?'

Symbol Immersion

Symbol immersion deals with one symbol while dream re-entry deals with the many symbols in a dream. Sometimes with a really developed symbol immersion all the other nuances and dynamics of the dream will seem to constellate around the one symbol and the whole thing will reach resolution. It is as if within each symbol as one plunges deeper the archetype itself is revealed at the core with its tendency to unite opposites.

Change is More Possible in the Inner Life than in the Outer Life

A fundamental premise: It is usually far more possible to bring resolution to a conflict expressed in dream life than to the same conflict as expressed in the outer. In outer life it is often easier than in the inner life to discover what needs resolution but harder to change the outer reality and bring resolution.

Dream life is the natural arena for dealing with the dynamics of life, inner and outer, and how they affect us. In the symbolic world of dreams we have a level of flexibility within which to try things out generally lacking in the outer world. We have also in the inner life a greater potential for resolution. Certain conflicts in the outer which do not have much potential for resolution will appear in the dream world and become resolved, either spontaneously or by our intervention. Whether in the inner or in the outer life it is the lack of resolution which hangs us up.

What happens in us is more important than what happens in the outer. It may well be that we live an outer life to evoke inner realities which need transformation. An outer reality is here today and disappears over the brink tomorrow. But its inner component, its 'soul', may stay with us forever. Where is your childhood? Is it out there? Is it dead? Does it not still live in you, an eternal reality?

Dreamwork Entry
— Discovering What Needs Resolution

In this dreamwork you will not be actively bringing resolution to your dream state. You will be expanding the dream by focusing on what needs resolution and highlighting it. This process in itself will probably create some meaning for you. And it may set the stage for further development or resolution in future dreams and dreamwork.

This method is an exercise in developing the tension and waiting to see what can happen.

— After writing down your dream list all the conflicts you can perceive in it. Describe them in some detail, even elaborating on what you have written in the original dream.

— Now choose a central conflict or two and redescribe it in as many ways as possible. What you are to do in part is to generalize the issue, to take the issue out of its specific dream context.

— Relate this issue back to the dream and to dynamics in your inner and outer life.

— Now describe any resolutions you perceived in the dream itself. Then describe these in a number of ways and generalize the main resolutions.

— How might these resolutions relate or not relate to the conflicts already described?

— How do these issues and resolutions relate to your outer life and personality?

— Perhaps you might choose to incubate a dream dealing with one of your issues needing resolution?

Self Re-entry into the Dream State

Re-entry into the dream state can have a number of purposes:

— To evoke or bring resolution to some aspect of the dream.
— To re-experience the dream in itself and see where it goes, if anywhere, or just see what it feels like.
— To change archetypal patterns reflected in the dream symbolism. By re-experiencing the dream symbols and letting them evolve or come to resolution we may be unlocking a fixated archetypal pattern and thus freeing psychic energy to flow more freely.

The above purposes are common also to the method of Guided Re-entry into the Dream State. But in this case the dreamer him or herself re-enters the dream solo without a guide. This has proven effective for many people in re-experiencing more fully, and bringing resolution to their dreams. The guided re-entry is different in that the guide intervenes and affects the course of development and resolution within the dream. This can have positive and negative effects. Sometimes using a skilled guide can be a support to the dreamer's letting go more.

Whether what we call 're-entering the dream' is really entering the original dream or not probably in not knowable or of serious consequence. We do

know that people often feel like they are back in the dream and they lose all sense of outer reality and time. Also, they often have profound and emotional experiences.

Re-entering the dream state means that a person closes his or her eyes, clears the internal space and visualizes a dream scene as originally remembered. In addition the person may enact an intention in regard to the dream imagery and see what develops. The process is also one of letting go and seeing what happens.

The following example of Self Re-entry into the Dream State involves working with the first dream in this way. The second and third dreams recapitulate the theme started in the first dream, but each time the theme is brought closer and closer to resolution.

Dream Title: Permission to Use the Road — 1978

I was walking down a road with my mother and needed to get her to an inn before nightfall. However, road workmen would not let me through even though the road was clear. I asked permission and they said 'yes' if I would not touch any of their equipment.

Strephon's Comments
This dreamer was new to dream session. We did not go into her outer life of the previous day or into her thoughts and feelings about her mother or the workmen. We took a major issue or theme in the dream and dealt with that as the following dreamwork shows.

Dream Task
Re-enter the dream again in your imagination but this time do not ask permission to use the road. Tell them you need to go through, and that you are going through, and see what happens.

The Dream Re-entry
The dreamer did as suggested in the task. The workmen did not stop her. They let her pass and she went to the inn with her mother.

Evaluation
She felt good about the experience and realized that if she asserted herself it would not necessarily mean that others would oppose her. It felt better as an adult to assert her equality and 'right to the road'.

The following two dreams came in subsequent weeks in the order they are given here. One of this dreamer's ongoing tasks became to watch her dreams around this issue of assertiveness and intend and re-work the dreams toward greater assertion. These new dreams are confirming dreams in their function in that they indicate that she was succeeding in her task, and that the unconscious liked this emphasis in her dreamwork.

Dream Title: Overcoming Objections — 1978

I was back in Paris walking down this street to get to my destination. But the street came to an end. This did not stop me as I went into a house despite objections of people there, and climbed the stairs and went on my journey.

Comments
This was a significant change for the dreamer in that her new assertiveness appears naturally in a dream state. This is what I call a *confirming dream,* a dream in which the 'dream source' likes what the dreamer is doing with her dreams or outer life and confirms it with a similar inner scene on the theme.

Dream Title: The Wall with the Open Door — 1978

I was back in my hometown in France riding my bicycle. In this narrow street two cars are blocking it. I went right through without even stopping or asking. Next I came to a solid wall of rocks. There seemed no way to get through. Then there was a door in the wall which slid easily. I walked through with my dog Perrot on a leash.

It opened out into levels of a beautiful landscape. On one of the levels was a small cottage that a priest lived in. I was to be his secretary with many responsibilities. I wasn't sure whether I had the strength or whether the responsibilities would wipe me out.

Comments
A dramatic breakthrough. This time the dreamer will not be deterred in her journey. She asserts herself. Then she comes to an 'ultimate roadblock'. She can no longer go on of her own free will. There must be a response from the other side, the Mystery. But she has proven that she wants to move on, so now the healing response can come. A door in the wall opens to a beautiful landscape. She goes on foot and meets a spiritual figure and her task of many responsibilities. But also there is a 'dip' back into her old problem. She is not sure she has the strength, or can assert herself enough to accept her spiritual responsibilities. At this time she had stopped her leading of meditation groups because she felt herself inadequate, though others did not think so.

The major dream task was to paint the scene in order to make it extremely vivid, and to write in her journal about whether she had the strength or not, or what it would take to serve and meet her spiritual responsibilities. She also had to face her Catholic roots as well as her Eastern meditation experience. The priest turned out to look somewhat like her Eastern guru.

In the outer life she decided not to make Thanksgiving dinner for her family after doing so for 25 years and instead they all had pot luck with no hassles. And she also decided, based on this and other dreams, to begin again the process of teaching meditation.

Two dreamwork principles I have formulated are:
— As in the dream so in life.
— To change your life change your dreams.

These both apply to this woman's dreams and dreamwork experience. Over the months of our working together she had other profound individual spiritual experiences. Quite simply, dreamwork is soulwork. Dreamwork can be the most profound guiding force in a person's life since we dream nightly and dreams come from such a deep and moving source.

Dreamwork Example — Self Re-entry into Dream State

Strephon's Comments
This example of another person's self re-entry into her dream is given here to present a full illustration of what the experience is like. We note that she is making conscious certain dynamics in herself, not by analyzing or interpreting her dream, but by using unconscious process techniques, dialogue and dream re-entry. Thus, her insight is achieved emotionally rather than rationally. The material speaks for itself.

Dream: The Seals — 24 January 1979
Some seals are being transported in a truck. Two small ones are frozen and will be thawed out later — two larger ones are under anaesthesia. They are hooked up to lights on the back door of the truck and one light is out, so I suspect that at least one of the seals is dead, and I don't know if the other one will make it. I open the door and look in. A woman with me suggests that if one is dead, it should be taken out. Should I take them out and really see what the situation is? No, I don't feel ready to deal with it — also I might disturb the situation and make it worse. I'd rather just get the seals where they're going. I close the door.

Dialogue
Seals, who are you?
We are your hurt feelings. You leave us frozen or asleep.
Where are you from?
We are from present life. We want you to know that when you take care of everyone else you ignore us to the point that we are very ill.
What would you like me to do?
Take us out and look at us. Separate the living from the dead.

Dream Self Re-entry

I open the ambulance door and look at the seals. I take out the larger one — it's heavy and hard to carry — and take it over to a bed of clean white sand. The sun is warm. It's covered with shit — has been sitting in its own shit for a long time. I wash it from a nearby stream, wrap it in a fluffy white blanket and leave it to go and get the other one. The other is in worse shape. As I take it out of its cubicle, it is shuddering. It is very sick and frightened, and bites my arm hard. I have to give it a shot of tranquillizer. It becomes limp and I carry it over to the bed of sand. I put it in the stream and wash it — its shit smells sick and foul. I wrap it in a blanket and lay it beside its friend. Now I go back to the ambulance to clean out the seal's cubicles. I start with the larger one's and scrub it out thoroughly with soapy water. I stop and reach into a little compartment above the cubicles and get out a bottle — it's healing lotion. Not time to use it yet. I put it on top of the truck. Now I scrub out the smaller seal's cubicle and rinse them both well with a hose. I spread some of the lotion on the cubicle walls — no, I shouldn't do that yet — I need to dry them first. I take a fresh white towel and dry the cubicles. Now I spread the lotion on the walls. I leave the door open so that the sun and air can get in. I go back up to the seals and spread lotion on them, too. The larger needs it only on her face and chest. The smaller needs it all over. I massage him to bring him back to consciousness and life. I carry them one at a time down to the ambulance and put them in their clean cubicles. I cut a window in the door for the larger and a little square air hole for the smaller. I drive them to my home. The larger stays with me in the kitchen, the smaller I put to bed, and I care for him until he recovers. I'm starting to get tired of having seals around all the time underfoot, so I move them to the backyard. They have a little round swimming pool there. This still isn't ideal because I have to keep bringing them fish all the time. They need to be able to take care of themselves. I don't want to just desert them and have them gone forever, so I move to a house near the sea. Here they can take care of themselves in the ocean, but come to visit once in a while. I like this arrangement very much.

Dialogue
Seals, how would you like me to handle my feelings differently?
Watch them, and when they are hurt in any way, stand up for them, protect them. Don't always give to everybody else at their (our) expense and don't let other people injure them (us).

Dreamwork Entry — Self Re-entry

— After writing down your dream look for the key issues in the dream and state them in the form of descriptive questions using the imagery of the dream whenever possible. You are looking primarily for conflicts and situations which seem unresolved. You are also looking for actions and dialogues which are only begun in the dream and which might be valuable for continuing and bringing to resolution.

— After developing the above, choose which issues and aspects of the dream you need most to deal with, and have also the strength to deal with. Write this down as an intention for when you re-enter the dream.

— As preparation for the self re-entry make sure you are alone in a place where you will not be interrupted or distracted by anything. No-one is to interrupt your solitude in person, by phone or in any other way! You should allow yourself an hour, sometimes less, sometimes more.

— Having formulated your intention for re-entering the dream you now choose the most relevant place to re-enter the dream. This may not be at the beginning of the dream. You will not necessarily be involved in the whole dream but only certain scenes.

— Have your journal ready to write down the results. You might also want to describe into a tape recorder your re-entry experience as it is happening.

— In either a lying down or a sitting position close your eyes and clear your mental space of external reality, somewhat as follows. Note that it is easier to fall asleep, by going completely unconscious, when lying down rather than sitting up.

'With your eyes closed let a place empty inside of you. It is your central area that you are clearing out, so it is simply empty of anything. Any distractions, any thoughts or anxieties from external reality, let these slide by, without invading your central space. Let, also, any internal feelings, images, anxieties fall aside so your central space is clear. Let your breathing be regular and let go

to it. Let its energy clear out your central space with its rhythmic flow.

'Now that your space is empty and you are relaxed let the scene from your dream re-appear in that space. Focus in on the details and describe them to yourself. Let the dream figures be there. When it seems right let the action of the dream begin again, remembering the intention you have for this dream. Perhaps your dream ego or other characters will act differently or develop their actions more? Who knows? You are letting go. You are not fixed on your intention. You are letting go to it and seeing what happens.

'What is happening now in your dream? Let go to the images and let them move and develop. Your intention is only part of the process. The dream itself is now alive for you as you let things happen.'

— And so on. Let the dream continue until a natural resolution develops or you choose to stop the process because that is all you want to or can handle.

— After your experience write it down in your dreamwork journal so you have it and can process it. You need do nothing further. For you have contributed energy back to your unconscious and affected the patterns there which produced your dream in the first place. But you can also continue the dreamwork and do any of the following.

— Become aware of the dynamics and issues raised in your dream re-entry in the same way you have with the original dream.

— Make yourself really aware of the feelings and emotions aroused by your re-entry. Anxiety? Joy? Fear? Certainty? Resolve? Etc.?

— What outer life tasks might you do to actualize the insights and values gained from your dream re-entry?

— What personality dynamics and attitudes need changing based on this dreamwork?

— And what kind of acknowledgement of source can you make as a result of this dreamwork? Gratitude is a returned blessing for being shaken and then blessed.

Guided Re-entry into the Dream State

The guided re-entry is generally the same as the self dream re-entry. But the two techniques may differ in the following ways.

With a guide the dream re-entry is partly directed by the guide who works sensitively to aid development and resolution. Too directing a guide can intrude on the dreamer's own process. Such a guide may interject subjective material of his or her own.

The state for a guide to be in is one of open receptivity without an overly particular point of view. The overall point of view that is helpful is that of seeking involvement in and resolution to dream states.

Re-entry into the dream state is similar to psycho-drama except that dream re-entry deals with dynamics on an introverted rather than 'acted out' level. The patterns are internal anyway so the massive energy of psycho-drama may not be necessary to changing internal patterns.

Bringing resolution is the other key aspect of the approach. Psycho-drama and visualization experiences may have as their emphasis the re-enactment of the material, whether dream or trauma, without trying trying to change it in any way. The focus of bringing resolution emphasizes evoking a healing centre. New feeling and imagery develop which is experienced as resolving or completing the original material.

So the dream re-entry guide is sensitive and supportive, never forcing anything, yet not just listening and reflecting either. Sometimes a slim edge of consciousness is needed which predisposes the experience towards healing and meaning.

The guide is also tuned into the unconscious, effecting perhaps a psychic bonding with the dreamer so that the suggestions which come arrive from their mutual collective unconscious. Whatever is really happening, we know that both guide and dreamer find themselves in a state of awareness and action almost totally different from what happens in the external world. Thus the guide from a more objective viewpoint within their mutual inner world may be able to intuit and suggest a direction to go in re-experiencing the dream. The dreamer is told at the beginning that he or she, of course, has free choice and does not have to do anything in the re-entry that seems too scary or inappropriate. This cannot be emphasized enough. The re-dreamer must keep in touch with the power of choice and let go to the healing process in the unconscious. The guide is only a supporter, not a determiner of the process. It is only rarely that I have felt it necessary to take a strong point of view to get someone through something to a new place. But it is only my openness to letting whatever wants to happen happen which gives me the freedom to take a position once in a while. And even then I will be off if I am not listening carefully to what may be going on in the other person.

Possible Harmful Effects in Using the Method

Re-entry into the dream state can be a powerful experience which could possibly have harmful as well as healing effects. Examples of harmful effects are:

— Leaving the person stuck in an emotional conflict which the re-experiencing of the dream got them back into. The way out is to keep working for some healing resolution.

— Taking a position for or against some situation in the dream since this closes down the symbol rather than opens it up to the possibilities. People tend to take positions regarding a symbol by identifying with one of the opposites in the symbol. For example, one has a dream of oneself dying, the tendency would be to see such a symbolic event as terrible, to see death as the end. Whereas the other opposite possibility would be to see the death of oneself as a prelude to rebirth. What are the positive and negative aspects of experiencing yourself dying in this dream?

We fixate on one possibility regarding a symbol by identifying with one of its inherent opposites. But the creative primary way to deal with opposites in a symbol is through choice rather than identification. Thus in a dream re-entry, open up the possibilities rather than close them off by taking a position. There are choices to be made within the re-entry. And there is possibility of resolution. Resolution is *not* the fixating on an opposite.

Resolution is evoking a unity which brings the opposites together.
— Another harmful effect is the guide's projecting unsolved problems into the other person's situation. This dumping of one's psyche creates confusion and extra psychic burdens. Archetypally, when the guide projects the wounded or sick part of him or herself the guide also identifies with the healer archetype, thus rejecting the wounded side of him or herself.

There are no healers, only a healing power which can be evoked within oneself. Anyone who calls him or herself a healer is probably identified with the archetype of wounded-healer and therefore inflated. Such a person is in danger of ceasing to be human by identifying with the archetypes. This is, of course, the great danger of calling anyone doctor, as is so prevalent in this culture. If the doctor identifies with the role, woe to his or her personal life!

The Main Issue

There are other dangers I am sure, but the main issue seems to be whether anyone can be severely damaged or not by any psychological technique.

In terms of dream re-entry and other techniques for working with the unconscious, if things get too overwhelming a person's own natural resistances will probably come up as a protection.

The techniques described in this book are in some ways the revelation of therapeutic secrets. Will they be misused?

Of course they will, but that is the nature of communicating openly in a 'free' society. I have to assume that more people will benefit from this information than will be hurt by it. And those who are drawn to the approach will perhaps want to come to the Institute for training. Only so much can be conveyed through a book. The Jungian-Senoi Institute backs up this approach with its training programme.

Doing a Guided Re-entry

The setting for doing a guided re-entry into the dream state is either working individually or in the dream group.

Working individually can be done between close friends or in a therapuetic or teaching situation. The choice in working with dreams is sometimes between using some of the more consciously orientated techniques versus using unconscious process methods. If the person is on the rational side too often, working directly with the unconscious is indicated. The Jungian-Senoi approach puts much more emphasis on unconscious techniques than the orthodox Jungians or most dreamwork approaches. We attempt to balance the dreamwork to include both conscious and unconscious processes.

Guided Re-entry in the Dream Group

In a dream group setting everyone is asked to close their eyes and get into a meditative mood of alert emptiness. Each person, by letting go to their own images, will have an individual experience of the dream. Thus one person's dream becomes effectively every person's dream. The dreamwork guide then asks questions and gives suggestions to the dream sharer. The sequence could go something like this:

— At what point would you like to re-enter your dream?

— Would you describe to us the scene in detail?

— What would you like to have changed in the dream?

— Now would you let the scene materialize just as you dreamed it but also letting go, without censoring, to new things developing. Also, you are free to make whatever choices you wish to make.

— Why did you make that choice? What if you did the opposite or another choice?

— What is happening now? Yes, continue to describe to us what is happening.

— If you feel inadequate or too afraid you may bring in a helper or a healing symbol. Who would you like to bring into your dream now? Do it and see what happens.

— Why don't you let the dream complete itself? What would you like to do about the blocks?

— Does it feel now like things have come to resolution or found a resting place? If so, then what gesture or action would you like to do with your dream beings before you see the scene for the last time for a while, and knowing that it will always be there as a resource to re-visit when you choose? Good, do it and slowly come back to this reality and open your eyes and look around.

After such an experience, which can take from twenty minutes to two hours, people are in a deeply introverted and numinous state. All sense of linear time has vanished and the dream has become every person's dream who hears it. The dream guide then calls for any who would like to share to give their own experience of the dream re-entry, but without analyzing it or interpreting what the dreamer's experience was. In training people the Guided Dream Re-entry is used as a demonstration. Then the group is asked to do a Self Re-entry meditatively with their own dreams and later share the results.

An Example of a Guided Re-entry

Perhaps the most numinous example I have experienced so far of using Guided Dream Re-entry is in this next experience. A woman reported the following dream, which she had had a number of times in the past as a recurrent dream.

'I dreamed I miscarried and I was in the operating room for a D and C. The doctor started working in me before the anaesthetic had taken effect. I was in terrific panic and pain and woke up.'

Comment:

A number of years ago, when she was seventeen, this dreamer had become pregnant while away at college. She felt unable to tell her father or mother because of her father's judgmentalness and she also felt unable to tell any of the girls in the dorm because they never discussed sex. She·told the psychiatrist at the student health service who arranged for an illegal abortion in New York City. But three days later before she was to go for her appointment she had a miscarriage and received a D and C, or scraping of the uterus. The doctor was extremely judgmental and chauvinistic. He made remarks about her sexual morality and seemed to be intentionally rough in his operating on her. At the present time this dreamer is active sexually but has not had a menstrual period for two years since becoming ill from using an IUD. The doctors at present can find nothing wrong with her.

Recurrent dreams are to be considered as major dreams reflecting fundamental patterns in the dreamer's psyche, patterns which are somehow 'locked in' and not capable of flow or change. Obviously the original trauma and all the feelings and issues surrounding this woman's feminine principle, from the sexual, through the mother, all the way up to the highest spiritual questions, are involved. They are all 'locked together' preventing the natural functioning of the vital instincts. Healing is needed. The method chosen here was the Guided Dream Re-entry which lasted two hours and left us both released and exhausted.

The Guided Re-entry

We both decided that the best place to re-enter the dream would be at the beginning of the traumatic experience, of which the dream shared was only a segment. This is valid because dreams seem to reflect clusters of energy or patterns within the psyche. Thus, we can not only carry dreams forward in active imagination but we can take dreams backward (symbol regression) to arrive at prior content, and with the final goal being the evocation of the total pattern and its transformation.

Stage 1:

The dreamer re-lived finding out that she is pregnant and calling her former lover long distance to try and get him to be with her and support her through the experience. And then his refusal and her walking the streets feeling completely unsupported and alone and in panic. The sense of isolation, the seeking help from strangers and the decision to get an abortion.

Stage 2:

The dreamer then, as in the original experience, begins feeling the pains in her stomach, the nausea, her getting to her bed in the dormitory and lying down, feeling her body getting hotter and hotter and not knowing what to do. Then realizing she is in panic lying on her bed and in a large pool of blood.

With Guided Re-entry, of course, the participant has the chance to make choices which were not made in the original experience. I suggested at this point that she could have a friend come into the room and support her. The dreamer then chose her outer life woman therapist to be by her bedside and then burst into tears. This was the dramatic moment, the fulcrum point towards possible healing. For why else the tears if not the feeling of profound redemption, of being supported and cared for in a way that had never happened in the original experience? I also was crying, feeling the natural empathy of being a caring man and one who has been helped myself in the midst of great personal suffering.

So the inner blockage had been broken wide open by the possibility of healing and now the dreamer tells her therapist friend how alone she is and how she didn't choose for the baby to die. When it seemed appropriate I suggested that she dialogue with the spirit of the baby who was not to live. This conversation also was quite moving and redemptive. She expressed that she was sorry that she had conceived the baby and that it had to die. The guilt of having been destructive was melting in the acknowledging of exactly what she did, and that she wished the spirit of the baby well wherever it was. Obviously, this stage was one of dialogue, of expressing the appropriate feelings with all the energies, beings or spirits involved. Her therapist was 'the spirit of healing' and the miscarried baby 'the spirit of suffering', of new life that had died, had even needed to die before its time. The energies and ultimate concerns were being freed, accepted and transformed.

Stage 3:

But what still needed to be faced was the most traumatic point of the original experience as reflected in the current dream. The dreamer was now asked if she was ready to go into the operating room and go through the trauma again. She said she was scared but ready. So I had her describe the scene. I asked her if she wanted to have a helping figure there but she said no, she wanted to go through the experience alone. So I questioned her on what she could do differently, such as being more assertive. She agreed with this and we began the descent into the experience. She again felt all the panic, coldness, the pain, the doctor's biting attitude, but this time she asserted herself and had him not go so quickly. She did not feel like fighting with him and I cried as she described the procedure she was once again living through. What we notice here is that it did not seem appropriate to change or mitigate the original experience. It must again be lived through just as it happened so that the total acceptance of the trauma, rather than defensively resisting it, occurs.

Stage 4:

The time had come for *resolution*, one of the key functions of the healing process and of all dreamwork. In the operating room the dreamer had felt herself quite disorientated from having been given tranquillizers and anaesthesia. In other words she had had her consciousness function impaired, preventing her from integrating the experience as it was happening. And it is our unintegrated experiences which block future experiences from flowing creatively.

So this final scene takes us back to her room where she removes pieces of metal she feels in her womb and applies healing salves to her cuts. The resolution had come. Through the Guided Re-entry she was enabled to relive a previously traumatic major life experience, yet this time with the support and consciousness necessary to process and integrate the material.

Later that night after this experience the man who had first made the dreamer pregnant called from out of town, not having seen her for six months. During the following week the dreamer had to be assertive in dealing with the man, which she did at a new decisive level. Such 'explosions of synchronicity' often accompany profound dreamwork experiences as if the third or intermediary reality had been evoked by the work. *Synchronicity* is meaningful coincidence between inner and outer events and is one of the few direct evidences for the existence of a 'God-Source'. In this case the dreamer being challenged to deal with the man at a new level was exactly what she needed to ground the whole experience in concrete reality. It also seemed to be confirmation of work well done at an essentially spiritual level.

The Principles Underlying Direct Dream Re-entry

1. *That one of the primary functions of dreams is to effect resolution within the psyche of all life experiences.* Internalized experiences which are left unresolved block the life flow of the psyche, at least in the areas affected by the original trauma. If the above is true it follows that dreamwork methods should be directed towards bringing resolution to archetypal or psychic energies evoked. This principle is also true for a meditative life in which one seeks to bring resolution through meditation at the end of the day to most, if not all, the energies evoked during that day. Not to do so creates anxiety, or unresolved energy, which carries over and blocks full participation in the next day. Thus dreamwork would seem essential for effecting resolution and being fully present in reality.

2. *That people are able to go back into the dream state, or inner reality, from the waking state, or outer reality.* And that this faculty, when developed, allows for processing inner experiences with maximum insight, intentionality and consciousness. In fact, this method is more effective, perhaps, than attempting to affect the dream state while dreaming (lucid dreaming). This is because

more intentionality and choice are possible. The re-entered dream can be shared with others, and it is more within conscious control.

3. *That one of the major goals in working with dreams is to bridge the gap between inner and outer realities by evoking and manifesting a 'third reality' which underlies the two.* Direct dream intervention does this by bringing inner and outer material together.

4. *That the inner world as reflected in dreams and other directly intuited experiences is prior to outer reality.* That it is within the inner world that the *potentials* for change, meaning and growth lie. And that it is the outer world which is the chief arena for *manifesting* and concretizing the potentials of the psyche. Neither world is superior to the other but they have separate functions. It may well be, however, that the *'third reality'* is best defined as the 'reality of potential' and that the inner reality is the arena of the manifesting of inner personality potentials. How best to describe the total process is still fluid.

5. *That the methods of actualization involve one in direct primary experiences of dreams and of life, and that the methods of interpretation distance one from direct experiences of the dream or of life.* Paradoxically both *distancing* and *involvement* are needed in order to serve the total process. I have intentionally emphasized actualization in an attempt to bring balance to the whole interpretive approach to dreams now prevalent in our culture.

The method as described here could represent somewhat of a major development in working with dreams and the healing process in the unconscious. What could be more dramatic and powerful than directly effecting and transforming major patterns in the psyche through Dream Re-entry?

Dreamwork Entry
— Guided Re-entry

Please follow the basic procedures as described in the chapter, 'Dreamwork Entry — Self Re-entry into the Dream State'. The guide and the dreamer should both be familiar with this chapter by virtue of having worked with it themselves.

A guided re-entry is useful when,

— the dreamer has difficulty doing active imagination.
— the dreamer is afraid of some of the dream's content and needs support.
— the dreamer feels blocked with regard to the dream's contents and need for resolution and needs a skilful sensitive guide to help get him or her through it.
— the dreamer needs to let go more to the flow. Having a guide who can intervene when necessary can be a support in letting go.
— the dreamer can benefit from another point of view interacting with her or his own.

The dreamwork guide should be someone who is in a supportive relationship with the dreamer and a person actively working with his or her own dreams.

The following is relevant to the guide's role in the guided re-entry.

— Become clear with the dreamer on his or her issues and intentions for the dream re-entry. Do not try and put across your point of view. This is not your dream. Your role is to help the flow from the unconscious get going and transform itself.
— Refer to the basic instructions in the self re-entry section and say the meditative procedure for both of you. The guide is to immerse into the same meditative state as the dreamer.
— The guide is to open him or herself up to his or her own unconscious sources. Listen for the right suggestions to give the dreamer as the dream re-entry progresses. Do not give many suggestions. See the dream re-entry

yourself. Have your own experience with it. Know that you might do things differently in your own unconscious.

— In making suggestions be aware of the opposites. If the dreamer seems blocked suggest an opposite or a new element. Listen for it. Always give the dreamer choice to take the suggestion or not. 'You have a choice here. Would you like to do the following?'

— At some point the dreamer will usually feel a resolution occurring or at least a stopping place wherein the available energy has been pretty well used up. If resolution or ending does not seem to be occurring you might suggest, 'Does it feel like things are coming to a conclusion for now?' or 'What resolution can be made at this point?'

— After slowly and quietly coming out of the meditative state you might both share some of what you have experienced. Do not interpret but you may want to suggest simple questions to focus with.

— Again, what has happened and what can be distilled to be put into dream tasks?

Carrying the Dream Forward

What is a dream?

Again this basic question and discovery.

Is the remembered dream only a segment of a continuous stream of images going all the time in the unconscious? Jung has said we may be dreaming twenty-four hours a day, only our focus of consciousness is on the outer so much that we do not recognize this.

Is the unconscious continually processing stuff happening within our personalities and outer lives? Is the organizing, evaluating mechanism more in the unconscious, perhaps within the central Self, than in the conscious side of things where the ego resides? It would be amazing if we had such a centre at work below the level of consciousness. Certainly dreams when worked with do suggest an entity far more knowledgeable and wise than our conscious selves at work in our psyches.

Dream sleep research indicates we have three to five major periods of vivid dreaming a night, called Rapid Eye Movement (REM) sleep. Physiological activity is highest then than in any other part of our twenty-four hour day. Men get erections and women moisten. It is also true that people may recall dreams from non-REM states of sleep. Thus we could say that while something is going on all the time in the unconscious, there are major periods of mystical-integrative experience in which the organism is at its most heightened and impassioned activity. And what about those who do not become aware of this activity? To miss totally the vital periods of our day can be a great loss indeed.

Do the dream-sleep researchers even work with their own dreams? How many dreamwork guides develop their own dreams in dreamwork?

We are quite possibly on the verge of a major revolution in consciousness. Awareness of our totality, yes, but also the realization that we can no longer neglect those periods of the day-night when we are in our most intensified physical, mental and spiritual activity.

The method of carrying the dream forward was discovered by Jung and there are examples in his books of his analysands carrying their symbols, visions and dreams forward.

Another term I use for this process is 'symbol evolvement' because I am trying to show that there is an inherent evolving potential within symbols which can be evoked. However, the term 'symbol evolvement' is reserved for working with a single dream symbol while the term 'dream re-entry' is used for evoking the imaginal flow of many symbols in a dream.

If, as Jung says, we are dreaming twenty-four hours a day, does carrying the dream forward mean that we are able to re-enter the unconscious and get the next segment of the dream? Who knows? It is my intuition that the unconscious does not only manifest itself in linear form (Journey archetype). It manifests also from basic entities, archetypes and complexes, which 'spark' manifestations when evoked. This is a symbol evolvement in which we evoke the latent potential within the archetypes. And we may also evoke the manifest potential into consciousness.

When I re-enter my dream imaginatively at the end and let the dream continue, observing where things go, would this be the same dream as if I had stayed asleep and dreamed longer?

We can perhaps never know. What we do learn is that people often report a degree of involvement and authenticity about the new dream.

Things are further complicated by the fact that the imaginative process may still be different from the dream process.

Usually artistic work is more rational, more bounded in by aesthetic and cultural conventions than are dreamwork productions.

Guided Fantasy and Dreamwork Compared

Today we have all sorts of healers, growth leaders, therapists, etc. doing *guided fantasy.* Guided fantasy, in which a leader suggests certain imaginary situations and the experiencer fills in the scene with his or her own images, is still different from dreamwork. Guided fantasy can be very moving but it is still rational. The unconscious is still having logical structures imposed upon it.

Unconscious process dreamwork techniques are more directly linked with the unconscious as it really is in each individual. The manifesting structures and evolvement come from the Self within, not from some ego saying 'fantasize this!'

Is guided fantasy dominating the unconscious rather than listening to it?

In the Jungian-Senoi Institute approach we certainly choose to evoke the unconscious. But we do it consistent with the spontaneous product of the unconscious, the dream itself.

The rationalists think they are now going to work with the unconscious by governing it and telling it which symbols to manifest.

All rationalists are probably by nature afraid of the unconscious. If they let the deeper psyche give forth of its own material, as in dreams, they will have to be recognizing a force superior in many ways to their own rationalism. Psychosynthesis is a case in point of imposing a system onto the unconscious instead of listening to what it has to say in itself. Its people work with guided fantasy but they relegate dreams to a minor position in working with the unconscious.

When to Use the Methods

The method of carrying the dream forward is used when we have woken ourselves up, or have been woken up, and we feel our dream has not reached completion. We may either fall asleep again and try to continue the dream, or we may re-enter the dream meditatively and carry the dream forward.

We may also do carrying the dream backward or symbol regression. The remembered dream may seem to start abruptly. What if we let ourselves immerse into the dream at its beginning and go backward to what went before? Symbol regression may be intercepting the stream of consciousness and taking the symbol back closer to its core.

The value of symbol regression or symbol evolvement is to bring more totality to the particular dream experience. It also expands the manifestation of the symbol, thereby allowing more possibility for meaning. And it can increase the imaginative-creative functions of the psyche.

Note that a particular issue involves whether it is more fulfilling to bring resolution by direct re-entry into the dream state or by carrying the dream forward or backward. Our experience as of this time is to prefer re-entering the original dream and staying with its dynamics rather than moving into vastly new material as may occur in carrying the dream forward or dream evolvement.

Dreamwork Entry
— Dream Evolvement

— This technique can be done either as a guided re-entry or as a self re-entry into the dream state. See other sections on dream re-entry for background.

— Either the dream re-entry may be done forward or backward depending on choice and your sense of the dream's need for completeness.

— After writing your dream down re-enter your dream at the beginning and let the images flow backwards. What went before? Where was a particular character? What was the previous scene and the one before that?

— Now you may choose to carry your dream forward. Go through the remembered dream next and as you come to the end, what seems to develop? Let these images, feelings, dialogues, etc., flow until they come to a natural stopping place for resolution.

— Write your total experience down to preserve it, then evaluate. How are the new parts connected to the remembered dream? What are the commom themes through it all? What sort of developmental direction is there? What is the meaning of the total experience for you?

— What will you do with the insights?

Working with Nightmares

A *nightmare* is any dream from which we wake ourselves up in fear. The reason so few people have dreams in which they actually die may be that they usually wake themselves up before this can happen. It is important to realize that your *dream ego,* the image of yourself in the dream, can be different from your *waking ego,* that part of yourself which makes choices in outer life and which remembers the dream. What if during a nightmare the remembering, waking ego keeps you asleep even while you are being shot or falling?

The lesson is clear. Deal with your fear. Try to keep yourself asleep and see what happens next. Let that wave come over you. Let the car crash. Dream reality has different laws than waking reality.

Keeping ourselves in the dream situation no matter what and seeing what happens will give us a greater capacity for dealing with fearful experiences. When people remain in a fearful dream, it often comes to resolution in some major or startling way. When I allowed myself to be shot recently in a dream without giving in to the fear, the bullets came and I experienced a brilliant white light. It was beautiful. It was tremendous. I had dealt with fear at a new level.

Another way of dealing with nightmares is, again, to keep yourself in the dream past the fear point but to also turn and confront the adversary, fight or relate in a friendly way to that which you feel would destroy you and see what happens.

One dreamer, in desperation, finally turned on her pursuer, a terrible witchlike figure, and asked for help. Immediately her adversary changed and became friendly. But how often in life do we let this happen to us? By running from our adversaries we give them double power, our own and theirs. By confronting adversaries we balance our own power with theirs and sometimes get their power as well.

These two methods — letting happen what we most fear and confronting what we most fear — can be learned while dreaming, usually by taking into the sleep state the intention to change our dreaming. For instance, fall asleep repeating to yourself 'I will not wake up no matter how fearful the dream, I will face whatever attacks me in the dream and not run.'

For those occasions when intentional dreaming does not work, we have devised methods for dream change which may be done from the waking state.

Using the method of direct dream re-entry, we remember the nightmare or other dream, objectify the issues around what scared us enough in the dream to wake us up. Then we re-enter the dream in a meditative state, this time facing and allowing the situation to develop without waking up. This is often scary but produces a sense of accomplishment and insight as to why we had the dream. The procedure is to first decide how you would like the dream to be different, consistent with the dream's dynamics. But keep in mind that changing all unhappy dreams into happy ones is not the goal. As in dreams, so in life. We do not pretend that darkness does not exist, but we face the dark side of life and deal with it courageously.

So choose what you would like to face in your dream. Then close your eyes and see the dream scene again. Focus in on the details. Then let things develop in the way they did in the dream, only this time, instead of waking yourself up, deal with the situation directly. This process requires being both courageously active and letting go to the dream's own processes. Often there will be some resolution. For example, in one person's dream re-entry, what was at first a strange and bloody mess becomes an embryo of new birth.

I have used this method successfully with many people as a guided re-entry, but self-re-entry into the dream state can be done on your own. In the guided re-entry, I take the person back into their fearful dream and support them while they deal with it. In self-re-entry, however, you must decide how much you can deal with by yourself. Stop when you feel you have gone far enough. The experience can be overwhelming. And if it becomes too much to handle, why not seek competent help?

Another perhaps easier method to use in the waking state is rewriting the dream. First determine what the issues are for you in the dream. Were you blocked or ineffective or paralyzed or running away in fear? Then why not rewrite your dream as a story but with your dream ego more decisive and aware? Instead of letting the child drown or the car crash, take charge and see what happens. Let new imagery come to you as you interact more effectively in this new version of your dream.

What you are doing with this kind of dreamwork is opening up possibilities for action other than just those which occurred in your original dream. Original dreams often present us with the way we habitually act in a situation. We are shown this so we may evaluate our dream behaviour and change it. We assume this because the new, more creative behaviour will often show up in future dreams as well as in outer life. The unconscious, or dream source, shows its appreciation by sending us a confirming dream. And, likewise, the dream source points out our negatavistic behaviour by putting us into nightmarish situations.

Perhaps the lesson here is that dreamwork can be the arena within, in which we rehearse and transform our lives. Using the methods described here we can continue the dreamwork process in the waking state. By transforming our usual patterns we can not only change outer circumstances, but how we deal with them as well.

Nightmare — The Action of God? — An Example

Nightmare! In the dream the normal boundaries of reality ceased to exist. I thought I was in a science fiction film. I was being manipulated by adversaries, my environment and the film. It was citified, walls breaking apart, the void of absolute darkness crashing in on me. I found myself in a terrible struggle to get out of it. There was no way out. I was helpless to do anything about it. Finally I had to wake myself up.

Yes, there was no escape in the dream. I felt overwhelmed. I could not cope with the situation. My only flight was into waking reality. But what if in waking reality I had a psychotic break and the normal boundaries of waking reality came crashing in on me? Where could I go? Where could I escape into then? Perhaps the space-out, the mental break, is escaping outer reality into dream reality?

I was deeply challenged by this dream, of course. Why I had this dream was uncertain. That I had this dream was extremely certain. My struggle in the dream reality and getting back into the waking reality felt amazingly real.

In dream group, the leader took me back into the dream in a guided dream re-entry. This time I re-experienced the dream as a tremendous void of absolute darkness crashing in on me. Images came of an enormous ship ploughing over me and adversaries putting ropes around my neck and pulling me hopelessly. When the dream leader suggested I let a healing image come into the scene, a pale white liquid lake, perfectly round, appeared like a hole in the thick darkness. And up from the centre of this lake seemed to spout a tower of the same luminescent white liquid light. And that was as far as I could go with the dream. I was deeply moved and even shaken up.

As a child I can remember having bouts with the unconscious in which the bounds of normal reality began to reverberate and disintegrate, producing extreme fear for my ego who felt its choice-making ability helplessly limited. As an adult I have also had some of these bouts and have had to learn to endure them and evoke healing at the same time through ritual and repeating healing sayings.

So now a similar situation has happened in the dream state.

One dream task question asked of me by a member of the group was 'Could I not have prayed for help in the dream rather than have struggled?'

This shocked me, for I consider myself a deeply spiritual person who has become devoted to spiritual sources and have felt their effect many times over in my life.

When put to it, when put to the ultimate struggle of my ego being confronted by superior forces, why did I not call on some saving power? Perhaps this was a new level to which my spiritual commitment had not yet reached?

Or was it even that my struggle was itself a spiritual act and that God was my Adversary rather than my Saviour? I know I appreciated the struggle I had gone through. Perhaps God needed my struggle as a contrast to His-Her overwhelming forces.

Was this nightmare struggle a challenge to my God concept? If God is my Saviour, why did He-She not save me from these enormous forces? Is God only a Saviour when evoked? The ego *in extremis* is being overwhelmed by God and therefore has to evoke God against Him-Herself.

Why is it that the ego must ultimately save itself?

Or is it possible that God is not a Saviour, that this is an immature God concept, a throwback from childhood with God being the Great Parent in the sky?

Is my God in effect the Great Adversary? What was that force which had the power to almost overwhelm my ego? It had also to be God.

Do I in fact gain more from struggling with God than from being saved by God?

This makes the spiritual life so much more difficult. God might not even exist. He-She might even be beyond existence as we know it.

What is the ego's role then?

I know I exist because of the immensity of my ego's struggle with the forces of The Other. I affirm my existence in that struggle. I know God exists as that which I struggle with. So struggle is a necessary affirmation of the existence of God.

But, as the member of the dream group asked, was it the appropriate choice to have struggled? Perhaps I should not have done it all myself and instead evoked God through prayer to save me?

I am stubborn. I find it a great contradiction and paradox to risk God overwhelming me by my ceasing to struggle in preserving myself. Would prayer be giving up the ego's prerogative to save itself by allowing the forces to overwhelm it?

If the ego did not struggle, its other choice would be to allow the forces to overwhelm it. It could want, even demand, that God save the ego from Him-Herself.

But what if God did not respond, did not even have the power to respond? What then? The ego would be overwhelmed, would it not? The forces of God would come crashing in and the ego would cease to exist, no longer even a metaphor for the struggle which is God and Person creating history together?

What then?

Does anyone out there have meaningful responses to all of this?

I do not seem to know ultimately whether what I did in the original dream itself of absolute struggle with the forces was appropriate, was the most meaningful way to respond to the situation.

I do know that doing dreamwork, doing the guided dream re-entry, in which I again experienced that struggle, but this time experiencing also a centrum of light, within the void, gives me two alternate experiences around the issue of dealing with God's adversarial forces. I choose to use the word 'God' as the source of power and purpose which was challenging my very existence as ego. Having two contrasting experiences creates alternatives, a new breath of freedom which I did not seem to have before. I not only struggled in the dream. I have now struggled with the issues and I go into future life and dreaming better prepared to deal with whatever comes my way.

The question now nags at me, what if I had simply let go, let God overwhelm me without even praying or wanting salvation? What then? Would this not be the ultimate letting go, the ultimate purification of ego? Perhaps I as ego would be saved, perhaps annihilated? Perhaps it would be an irresponsible act for the ego not to maintain itself?

Respond to that one if you can.

I was put to the test. Did I fail or succeed? What is the most meaningful position?

I await further mystery. How will I act?

A Nightmare Transformed — Will Over Fear

The following dreamwork episode continues the themes raised in dealing with the previously described nightmare. But this time a new step along the journey has occurred. This time, through a dream-sleep re-entry I as ego was able to face the adversarial forces without fighting them or evoking a saviour factor. This next nightmare occurred about two months after the previous one and left me feeling quite excited and vital.

The Dream
I'm in this house and there is something scary to confront. I don't want to do it and am all alone. I'm quite afraid. I wake up.

Dream Re-entry
I fall back asleep doing a dream re-entry. This time I make myself enter the bathroom where the source of my fears seems to be. I do not want to enter. I am afraid, so afraid that the flow of images stops. But through sheer will I make myself enter the bathroom ready for anything. I think of taking my machette and thrashing around with it if I am attacked. But I decide against

this because I want to confront my fear by willing myself to stay with the situation no matter what. I am wondering about using Aikido to blend with the situation. The main point is that I will myself to go in and endure no matter what comes at me. I am ready to face that which could overwhelm me and exist with it rather than try to defeat it.

As I enter the bathroom I am quite frightened but I don't let this stop me.

I have one goal. To enter that bathroom fully and face what is there. Whatever it is seems to be around behind the door. I think of getting in a safe place but I know I have to get in the bathtub to really see it and to prevent my own escape.

When I do, there seems to be a hulking luminescent figure there. It does not attack me but changes into a dwarf-like figure, long arms, roundish head, like Yoda. We face each other. I have stayed with the situation. No attack comes. I realize also that in the bathtub I have protected my backside. My fear goes away when I experience what is there behind the door, and has been there so many years going back to childhood. What has been there behind every door and scary place is fear itself and my inability to fully deal with it.

This is the first time in a dream state that I have completely faced fear and it has not been able to dominate my will. There was something there behind the door. But I, as dream ego, no longer let fear dominate me. I went into the worst fear possible, fear itself.

When the facing of what was behind that door was complete, I woke up.

This started as a conscious dream re-entry into the first dream, but as I was doing it I fell asleep because, after it was over, I woke up to write this all down. Did I even dream the dream re-entry? I do not think so, because I remember it took a new and tremendous effort of will to make myself go fully into that bathroom.

As I have been writing this, I have the vague impression of an older helping woman with me now. But the original act of will was entirely my own. No one else could possibly do it for me. I resisted myself and must myself overcome to face whatever there was to face.

Dialogue with the Figure Behind the Door

Yoda figure, who are you?

I am your alter ego. I am your shadow. I am everything. I am nothing.

Yes, what is the significance of this event?

You have written it up well. You have confronted God and liked it. God did not and could not save you here. You had to confront the fear absolutely alone and that is exactly what you did. It is humorous really. To fight with your own ego, to become your own worst adversary. And when you had settled that, I was there, certainly you had something to fear as long as you were afraid. There was something there, me or some nameless other, but also your fear was there. Then you made your will superior to your fear by experiencing your fear fully, but not yielding to it. Do you understand?

Yes, fundamentally I do. Thank you very much.

You are most certainly welcome.

Evaluation

Of course I am immensely excited by this. I think of a fairly recent dream in which the normal bounds of reality were crashing in on me into a chaotic darkness and I woke up in great fear, feeling I could not handle it. Then in dream session I was guided back into the dream and was asked if I could let a healing symbol come. In the pitch darkness a spout of light appeared out of a perfectly round mandala city. A healing centre was evoked, but I still had my ego and its fears to deal with. I accept the healing of the mandala symbol coming. For it said to me that while absolute darkness was absolute in itself, it was not everything. There was also, when evoked, its opposite, absolute light, or focus in the midst of total diffuseness. But I still have my ego to deal with. Only the ego feels fear, and therefore only the ego could deal with fear. It could not be ultimately saved, except possibly by itself! The will would have to become stronger than the fear, not by denying the fear but by feeling it fully and being present with it without being dissolved by it.

Now this all could seem quite philosophical. For what does this have to do with everyday living? Within every situation the ego lives the everyday life. But how it lives and what potentials it realizes and does not realize depend on its own nature.

Thus my dream and my dreamwork re-entry have been the arena for developing my ego more fully so that when it interacts with the rest of life it will not be afraid. And what is it to really enter life unafraid? What great potential for new life there is in not withdrawing from adversarial situations. A whole new level of manifesting reality is possible. Thus one of the major personality accomplishments is the mastering of fear. I am, I hope, another step along the way. How will I now face each new danger, each new adversity, inner and outer?

With some to use fear courageously.

With others to still work to evoke a healing factor in the midst of great darkness.

And in all situations to assert the primacy of will over fear so that I myself may be open to the greatest potential in each moment, a potential which includes both the light and the dark, the nightmare as well as the gloriously beautiful dream.

Dreamwork Entry
— Working with Nightmares

— First, of course, record your dream, even if you do not want to.

— Next, you might choose to write all the feelings you are experiencing immediately as a result of the dream.

— Or, immediately after recording your dream, you may choose to re-enter the dream and deal further with the adversarial forces, thus:

  — either visualize the dream again and keep your dream ego in the situation past the point at which you woke yourself up, and see what happens.

  — or visualize the dream again and do or evoke some healing action. Befriend or dialogue with the adversary and find out what it wants. You might also re-enter the dream, taking with you some healing symbol such as a lit candle or a protector-guide, and let the dream continue.

— If you choose not to re-enter the dream on your own, you may want to ask someone you trust to guide you into it again and continue with it and seek resolution. Caution may be needed by all parties involved.

— You may also choose to simply rewrite the dream consciously, embodying more courage, relation, healing, and working towards resolution.

— Caution — do not create superficial resolutions. Feel the conflict and then *allow* resolution. If the dream does not resolve, but remains in tension, that may be necessary also. Tension is the necessary preparation for resolution.

For Your Journal

— What is unresolved in your original nightmare? What are some possible causes of this?

— What would be some meaningful resolutions to the issues raises in your nightmare?

— If you did a dream re-entry, what new things developed for you? What resolutions came about? What was still left in tension?

— How does this nightmare relate to other nightmares you have had?

— What situations or choice-patterns in the outer might be evoking this nightmare?

— What new choices and changes in behaviour will you attempt coming out of working with this dream?

— What does this dream and dreamwork have to say to you about your ego, God-source, and the way life really is?

— Create an intention you will attempt in future dream behaviour should you have a nightmare or adversarial dream again.

Incubating Your Dream

What is dream incubation?

Why might we even choose to incubate or evoke a dream from our dream source on a specific subject?

Dream incubation is the evoking of a dream as a response to some question or concern we present to our dream source.

Dream incubation is not necessarily getting an answer through a dream to a specific question. Dreams are symbolic, are loaded with potentials for possibility. A dream is always a question and never an answer. Dream incubation can evoke a meaningful, even extraordinary, response to a concern we present to our transcendent selves as we fall asleep. But we are still left with the ego's task of how to relate to the dream which comes.

How do I know the dream I had following my incubation request is really related to my request?

Perhaps we do not know absolutely but we can work with the dream as if it

is a direct response and use it to create meaning for our lives.

And, as in the example which follows, often the dream imagery will correspond to the incubation request. We ask for a gift and in the dream literally we receive a gift. The kind of gift and what it means is still left up to us to discover.

From a hypnosis point of view such a dream is a result of programming the mind through self-hypnosis. It is true that any outside input into our inner world does have its effect. But self-hypnosis cannot explain why or how incubated dreams seem particularly related to an individual's journey. Something is at work in the psyche which sparks of soul. The psyche is simply not a slave which can be totally manipulated. Hypnosis hypnotizes the hypnotist, not the psyche.

For anyone working regularly with their dreams the question may well arise, why seek to incubate a dream? If I follow my dreams won't I be dealing with my problems anyway?

In a sense every dream we have is incubated at some level, however unconsciously. For dreams do seem to respond directly to what we are dealing with in life and in ourselves. The method of dream incubation just makes this process more conscious and directed.

One goal of the individuation-wholeness process is to be so in tune with one's own centre that the appropriate dream at the appropriate time is always coming to one.

Yet who is there among us all who is so in tune that he or she does not on occasion need to ask for a healing dream?

It seems clear that dream incubation is especially appropriate for when a person really feels stuck on a problem or when the person is passing through a major occasion for new life direction such as on a birthday or at the New Year.

Some Central Dream Incubation Questions

The following questions can be useful in developing your dream incubation experience.

— What am I to ask for?
— Who or what part of myself does the asking?
— In what way can I ask that will get a response?
— Who or what responds?
— What exactly is the response?
— Is anything which happens a response?
— Is the response true or false? Are these categories even relevant?
— How does the response relate to my original question?
— What will I do about the response?
— What commitment or intention have I formulated as to how I will respond to the response no matter what it is?

— In what sense is no response still a response?

— In formulating my question am I really asking the right or central question?

— What question in terms of my life is the response really a response to?

— Am I doing dream incubation to create 'spiritual power' rather than meaning and direction in life? If yes, what will I do about this?

— What question is the dream I receive a response to?

Using Dream Incubation — The Stages

Many people, including writers and scientists, have reported receiving creative ideas and discoveries through the dream or visionary state. This is usually preceded by a period of intense immersion in the particular problem or subject.

In incubating a dream at one basic level we immerse ourselves in the problem by thinking about it and letting go to all its possibilities. Then in entering sleep we stay with the problem, repeating it to ourselves, or focus it more in a question which we repeat as we fall asleep. As we relate to our dreams more fully this level of incubation can be almost a nightly occurrence.

At a fuller level of dream incubation we might thoroughly go into the problem or situation considering all possibilities. But we will also be working with ourselves in a letting go process.

— Do I really want to know an answer to what I am facing?

— Am I willing to follow a direction different from that which I may want?

— Am I willing to still make my choice based on all the possibilities, with the dream as only one of the possibilities?

As part of the process one may do journalwork or enter into meditation. Some acknowledgement of source other than oneself is also important. Perhaps this is done in the form of a ritual, prayer or the creation of a symbol. Included also is a sense of affirmation and a willingness to sacrifice that which stands in the way of the deepest possible direction.

One of the greatest life agonies may be in that moment before we choose a new direction coming to us from deep sources and full of what we would have to sacrifice to attain the new value. In this profound sense one dream can be the destiny dream for a whole lifetime.

Thus the fervency or passion by which one makes the request to the dream source determines the response one gets. There must be a concentration of energy and feeling, an openness to personal need, character traits of sincerity and integrity and a receptivity to what comes in the night. Look also for synchronistic events to happen in the outer as part of the response.

After the request is made write down anything which comes into consciousness the next morning, whether it is a dream or not. Do not reject any dream, dream fragment or other thought. And in one sense, do not expect results. We do not control the night. We are given the night to let go in and what happens is not our choice and only partly our making. Perhaps it will take several days of dream incubating to get a response. Or if we do not feel we are getting a response, that, too, has its significance.

Dreamwork is the next stage in working with the dream which comes.

— How is the dream a response to my incubated question? How is it not a response?
— What is the question to which this dream is a response?

Perhaps it will be necessary to expand the dream's dynamics through dialogue or any of the dreamwork methods.

And finally there is the level of asking, what choices and directions do I create out of this total experience?

Dreamwork in Relation to Other Oracular Experiences

Working with the *I Ching,* tarot, psychic readings, astrology, etc., to gain further perspective on a problem can be very meaningful. Dream incubation is similar to these but can have also the added value of being specific to the individual since it comes directly out of his or her own depths. In non-dream-oriented methods for gaining perspective often an interpreter is needed. With dream incubation an outside viewpoint may or may not be helpful. It is my intuition that if an outside person is needed in dream incubation, especially after dreamwork skills have been learned, then the dream incubation has failed or turned an oblique corner. The dream which comes can be so vivid and direct that the dreamer knows deeply and at a feeling level what has been the response to his or her request.

And always the *caution.* Do not throw your own choice-making or consciousness to the winds and say, 'The dream told me what to do.' A dream is always a possibility and never a certainty. The dream is there to help you create meaning in your own life. We co-create together.

Dream Incubation — Dreamwork Example

Strephon's Introduction
The following incubated dream of one of the students in Institute training is significant both as an incubated dream response and because of the nature of the response, indicating, at least to me, that there is a source at work other than the dreamer's own consciousness.

Note that in the dreamer's preparation, which was done in meditation, she asks for a gift for the women she is to work with and instead in the dream wants and receives the gift for herself. The unconscious knows what it is doing! The figure in the amethyst crystal is the one who says the crystal is to belong to the dreamer. In other words the gift does not come from the outside or even from the dream ego's wanting it. The gift comes from her own spiritual feminine deep within herself. The spiritual masculine, in the form of the Buddha, is not even the one to acknowledge the gift as belonging to the dreamer. What is essential, of course, is that the dreamer in the dream wants the gift of the spiritual centre for herself. For it is only out of her own centre that she can truly give to anyone else. And with the spiritual feminine is the traditional symbol for the woman's spiritual masculine, the bird. It is significant also that the dreamer offers an exchange of work in order to have the crystal as her own. In terms of the outer, herbs and crystals are symbols in her spiritual practice.

The dreamer was able to use this dream and other dreams to develop more security within herself about her own resources for working with other people. She is also intensely involved in developing dream incubation as part of her meditative practice.

How would you respond to the issues? Was she practising dream control? Was she creating her own universe? Or was she focusing on a need and letting go to the possibility for a response out of Mystery, a response at once universal and uniquely tailored to her own individuation journey?

Dreamwork Example — The Amethyst Crystal — June 10, 1979

Dream Incubation Preparation.
I am planning to hold the first meeting of a women's group the next evening and ask for a gift for the women to come through in my dream.

The Dream.
I'm in a bead store and find a beautiful amethyst crystal. I'm very drawn to it and pick it up. It has a crack in it and when I look through the crack I see a tiny Buddha sitting on a rug and to the side, a figure standing. The woman in the store tells me the figure is Nicole. I say, 'Oh, his student' and then look at it intently. She tells me that it speaks to people differently and as she's telling me this, the figure looks at me and says, 'it's yours, ' smiling at me. Then I turn

the crystal around and ask if it's for me or for my husband as I've been thinking of giving him a crystal. At first the figures seem to have disappeared and then I see them again. Nicole seems to have a bird on her hand. I get the sense the crystal is for me — I really want it and ask the woman if I can trade for it. I'll make some beaded leather things for the store. I leave and walk home — over a hill. I meet some friends and invite them over to the house. I show them my leather herb pouch and the crystal. We talk about it and someone remembers having looked at it before.

Dreamwork Entry
— Incubation

Instructions

— List in your journal the major issues in your life right now.
— Choose from this list one central issue and construct a specific or overall question which epitomizes this issue.
— List the various positions and choices which are possible solutions to your problem question.
— Which way would you like the problem resolved?
— Which way would be the most meaningful resolution for all concerned?
— Now write a short statement or evocation which puts your issue-question in the form of a direct request for a dream on the subject from the dream source. Put this some special place like under your pillow.
— Just before sleep meditate on your issue and on your request for a dream about it. Perhaps you have a personal altar or symbol which represents the centre for you. Address your request to that centre, repeating it a number of times in meditation and as you fall asleep.

— Maintain, if possible, peripheral consciousness while asleep about your issue and the fact that you are dreaming. Prime yourself also to awaken right at the end of your dream and write it down.

— Upon awakening write your dream down and/or anything which comes into your head. If the dream seems incomplete try to fall asleep and dream the dream onward by re-entering the dream and seeing its events again.

— When you can, do whatever dreamwork is appropriate with your dream. Remember it is important to compare your original request with the actual dream you receive.

— If you do not receive or remember a dream, continue for three nights. If you still do not receive a dream then make your choices anyway and record the dreams which come after your choice. They may bear directly on your choice one way or another. You might also create an imaginary dream as the response to your incubation question. It may be significant.

— Finally take your dream to outer life by making appropriate choices and see what dreams come as a result.

We dream to become awake to life.

Lucid Dreaming

What is Lucid Dreaming?

In general, people have reported the following as sometimes being characteristic of lucid dreaming:

— While asleep and dreaming, the person realizes he or she is dreaming.
— Again, while dreaming, the person is aware of dreaming and makes certain choices to alter the dream state, such as deciding to fly or to change a negative scene into a positive one.
— The dream is experienced as tremendously vivid with intensity of colour and detail. In addition, there may be heightened or fantastical imagery.
— While dreaming, one also experiences heightened bodily sensations such as energy flows and sexual orgasms.

The Issue of Control

With lucid dreaming the issue is one of control:

— To what extent can the conscious side of our personality control or influence the dream state?
— To what extent would it be valuable for the conscious side to influence or change the dream state while dreaming?
— What is the effect, or is it desirable, for the ego, or conscious side, to dictate, according to its own rules, needs and wants, what the dream source is to present in dreaming?
— What is the effect, or is it desirable, to just let dreams happen from dream source without any attempt on the part of the ego to evoke or influence dream contents?
— In effect, the question is not, 'Can I influence or control my dreams?' but 'Who is to control or produce the dream state?' The conscious side or the

unconscious side of the personality? Or is the most desirable or healing state that of mutual regulation of the dream source?

— The issue of control is a major one in dreamwork. But it is also a central issue in terms of how one lives life. How much do I seek to control, structure, influence, dominate, eliminate, make happen what occurs in my life?

— How much do I seek to let go to, open myself to, follow the guidance of, be blown about and even terrorized by what happens in my life?

In terms of dreamwork, there are degrees of exercising control over the dream state.

— One may merely let the dreams happen and record them, influencing or changing the original dreaming experience only in the act of remembering and recording the dream.

— One may not only record dreams but seek also to interpret, analyze, and come to definite conclusions about what they mean, as is typical in traditional Jungian analysis.

— One may record dreams and do unconscious-process techniques in re-experiencing and reworking the dream state after the original dreaming experience. This is a typical Jungian-Senoi approach.

— One may seek to influence or evoke a certain kind of dream by using the method of dream incubation. This is also typical of the Jungian-Senoi approach. The influence of the conscious side of the personality is confined to evoking a dream on a chosen subject; but the ego does not try to control the contents of the dream which comes.

— One may seek to produce more and more dreams in which one is aware that one is dreaming. One may also seek to control the contents of the dream while dreaming. This is the approach of lucid dreamers. This is not typical of the Jungian-Senoi approach because we do not give primacy to the ego in the process of working with the unconscious.

— One may seek to eliminate or transform regular imagistic dreaming into a state no different from waking consciousness. In this heightened state of consciousness, the dreaming consciousness and the waking consciousness are similar and are described in terms of pure energy states such as great light. This method is typical of certain Tibetan, Yogic, and Islamic systems of meditation.

In the Jungian-Senoi position, we do not want to eliminate the rich imagery of dreams, because for us dreams as they come from the unconscious are a rich source in themselves for transforming one's everyday life and personality. We work with consciousness to process energies rather than control them.

There is no way of knowing absolutely which response to the question of how much to control the dream state is best. We do not yet know enough about working with dreams and the dream source. The decision as to where to place one's emphasis becomes a matter of choice and values.

On the everday level the issue of dream control can show itself in statements such as the following: 'I've developed the ability to control my dreams so that when I don't like what is happening in a dream, I can change it to what I want.' Certain questions arise from this statement. Is the person trying to transform negative dream energy which would be depressing? Or is he escaping his and life's darkness by changing everything into pleasant experiences? In more symbolic terms, do we reject darkness by going to the light? Or do we transform darkness by bringing the light to the darkness? Do I stay outside the cave in the sunshine, or do I take a light with me and enter the cave to explore and reveal what is hidden in the darkness? Or do I, without even taking a light, plunge into the utter darkness of the cave and see what happens?

Dealing with Conflict and Power in Daily Life

Another everyday question concerning dreamwork can be stated as follows. When faced with conflictual situations in dream life and in outer life, do I tend to withdraw, become passive or get overwhelmed? Or do I evoke healing and transformation in the midst of conflict?

We can deal with conflict by using the Senoi aspect of the Jungian-Senoi approach. Thus, when we are being attacked by an adversary in a dream, we can choose to confront that adversary and transform the conflictual situation into one of relationship. One person was being chased by a terrible witch until, finally, in utter desperation in her dream she turned and said, 'Hey, I need your help.' In the dream her adversary changed in that moment and she received help. In the Jungian-Senoi approach we do dream re-entries to deal with adversarial situations. This method trains people to be more active in meeting conflict in dream life and in outer life. The goal is not to control the dream state but to deal with it more effectively. We do not seek to eliminate adversaries but to establish relationships with them and utilize their energy. Darkness, evil, conflict, whatever one chooses to call it, can teach us in ways that light, good and harmony cannot. Our thirst is for integration, not the enhancement of one opposite to the avoidance of the other.

Whether we call the issue one of control, or of power, or of the ego and self co-operating together, in using effective dreamwork methods we must not only choose but also have a context within which we choose. What are my values in terms of spiritual and psychological power? Do I avoid it or embrace it for wholeness? Or do I seek power for my own enhancement and self, imagining that I am, after all, the centre of my own universe?

To do battle with the unconscious is one thing. But to seek to rule or dominate it has its consequences. When I seek to control, how am I in fact being controlled?

What goes out one door will surely come in at another!

Dreamwork Entry —Lucid Dreaming

— First, determine your values, reasons, and intentions for producing lucid dreaming.
— List the dangers in terms of your own ego-inflation, or self-importance, which might take you over in your attempt to produce lucid dreaming.
— Formulate one simple action or signal which, when it occurs in a dream, will let you know that you are dreaming. You might choose a dream symbol such as your hands to focus on while dreaming. Or every time you see a mirror in a dream, that will clue you in that you are dreaming. Keep a record of your successes and failures.
— When you have been able to signal yourself once in a while that you are dreaming, then introduce the element of choice. As soon as you realize you are dreaming, make a choice in terms of the dream landscape you are in. Start flying or open a door or produce something. Afterwards record the

whole dream and note what part your conscious intentionality played in it.

— The next phase is choosing what to do with your ability to choose and create while dreaming. You can manipulate the dream state in various ways for the experience in itself. For example, you can choose to fly or to leave your body and explore another city. However, you may need to be able to process whatever comes up for you. You do not have unlimited choice. If you choose to leave your body, you may experience difficulty getting back into it. If you explore another city, who knows what you will find there? So become aware of your values and possible consequences. The Senoi people's context for lucid or intentional dreaming was to complete dream experiences and bring back into waking reality some meaningful gift, such as a song or new idea. Thus, a Senoi dreamer might defeat an adversary and demand a gift or complete a dream love experience and demand a gift.

— Record your process and its importance to you. Evaluate what meaning the experience has in terms of the rest of your life.

— When a lucid dream happens spontaneously or is induced by you, an excellent method to use with it is following the Dream Ego because it may have a lot to do with your own consciousness and choice-making.

— Also, examine spontaneous lucid dreams for any common images which might be recognized in future dreams as signals that you are becoming conscious within the dream state.

Transpersonal Dreamwork

In essence, *transpersonal dreamwork* means using dreams to relate to source experiences other than those directly created by the ego or conscious choice-making side of the personality. Transpersonal source experiences can come from within the psyche and personality, such as from the dream source, or, in Jungian terms, from the Self. Source phenomena can also come from without

and be experienced as psychic phenomena and transcendent realities.

I see the transpersonal as primarily the study of the manifestation of the future. It seeks solutions to present problems, not in what already exists, but in what is as yet unknown. Thus it presupposes a source at the core of and yet beyond present realities. As a psychology, the transpersonal emphasizes not only human potential, what a person is, but also the transformation of personality based on the 'never-before-manifested.' It is a bridge from the present into the future and acknowledges that history is not just a reaction to the past (causation) but a creation out of the yet unknown potentials (synchronicity). Its commitment is to manifest those potentials in present reality.

Thus, we work with the supposition that dreams are one of the primary mediums for expressing energies which go beyond ego-bound strivings and survival needs. Not that dreams neglect these very human levels to which we are all subject. A difference between a merely personalized approach to dreams and a transpersonal approach is the key word, dialogue. We find that in working with dreams our personal attitudes, foibles, etc, are often in contrast or even in conflict with deeper levels in dreams which seem to want responses from us.

Something is at work in the dream state which we seek to actualize in dreamwork experiences. What that something is remains always a mystery perhaps, but a mystery which moves us and can achieve great specificity even in a dream's symbolism. And there are other 'evidences' for a source outside ourselves at work in dreams. These include synchronicity (meaningful coincidence) and confirming dreams.

Any dream can, from what we have described so far, be worked with as a transpersonal dream. Thus, any dream seems to have material in it which has not been directly a part of the ego's consciousness and is, therefore, a product of a source other than ego. Dreamwork itself can be seen as what the ego does with a dream and can thus be a further creation of transpersonal experience in that a relation has been established through dreamwork, between the ego and non-ego sources.

But we can also make a further transpersonal distinction in terms of dreams by seeking and focusing on those dreams or symbols within dreams which carry for us a more universal and, therefore, partly transcendent energy. Often, the experiencing of these symbols is accompanied by feelings of awe, or fear of the tremendum. Such symbols might include any of the primary archetypal manifestations, such as dream landscapes of vastness, climbing mountains or plunging into dark abysses. Thus, transpersonal does not mean experiencing only the light and bright. Hell's imagery is as much transpersonal as Heaven's. God is everywhere and nowhere visible.

Dreamwork Example: Exploring the Spiritual Feminine

The following are four examples of using dreamwork to enhance one's spiritual life. This dreamer is concerned about developing her own relation to centre in life and is not able to identify with any one religion or approach. For her the spiritual life has to be on an individual dimension. She has explored different forms of religious thought and practice. We see here in her dreams her own unconscious producing out of itself the spiritual symbols and necessities which are particularly relevant to her own life. These spiritual dream figures have come to her in a number of dreams over the last three years. She has researched her dreams to bring the symbols together and then carried out dialogues with each of her spiritual figures to get to the essence of who they are and what they have to say to her. They are not easy on her but they are very compassionate in dishing out the truth.

   We also see here that she has made clear the relation of her dream ego to the spiritual figures. The dream ego, as the representative for the waking ego, choice-making function, is quite necessary to the total picture. For without a choice-maker and consciousness carrier present there would be no relation to deity, or Source. And without relation, how can there be manifestation? We see in the dreamworker's comments exactly what the complete experience means to her.

Dream — The Ceremony — August 1976

I dreamed we were having a ceremony at the treatment centre at which I was working. I was to be the medicine man/woman in the circle. I was to wear a long woollen blanket, hold a peace pipe in my mouth and have a large high black hat which I have seen Native American men wear. I went to prepare for the ceremony and was excited, honoured and nervous about being given such a powerful role. Before the ceremony started, Strephon said he made something special for me that I should wear. It was a beautiful embryo-shaped jade necklace surrounded by translucent glass with gold specks in the jade and the glass, and the edge was a gold edge thick like lead. I was pleased and told Strephon but I was confused about what part he had made. I asked if he had put the gold specks in or combined the glass and jade. He said. 'No, not that.'

Dream Ego's Relation to Her
The dream ego is the medicine man/woman or is at least wearing her costume in the ceremony.

Dialogue
Me — What do you have to tell me?
She — I am the costume you need to learn to wear. It is very masculine but has changed in your recent dreams as you get more in touch with your own feminine. You were also given the jade necklace as your own personal power which must be cultivated and grow. It is all there within you.

Comments
I was given this dream the night before I was to lead a three-day mountain journey with adults. The quality of the trip was to be introspective and spiritually oriented. I began to relate to the medicine woman figure during the journey because I felt a wisdom greater than my own was needed. Later that summer I guided a group through a Native American Indian sacred area and felt that in order to deepen the process for all of us I would call on the spirit of the medicine woman again. This time I consciously chose a special blanket to wear and had a jade-like stone I found at the ocean. Evoking the wisdom and power of the medicine woman through the dream objects moved me into a deeper place than I might otherwise have reached. I still continue to evoke the wisdom and power of this figure when I feel my ego limiting my power negatively.

Second Dream — The Indian Woman — October 1976

I had to descend down a long hill with narrow steep steps in order to go back up another street to get to work. On the last part of the steps there was an Eskimo or Mexican Indian woman sitting on a sled with a little baby. I had only a few inches in which to pass by. When I tried to pass them, the baby started falling off the sled. The Indian woman caught her and told me I could pass because she would hold onto the baby.

Dream Ego's Relation
The Indian woman is both an obstacle by being on the steps and an aid by helping the dream ego continue her descent.

Dialogue
Me — What do you have to tell me?
She — You have gone on a steep descent into your soul and are often fearful about your journey. I am here in your path to remind you of my existence and also that I am holding your child for you. I will protect it so it doesn't get hurt or destroyed during your journey.

Comments

I had this dream when I was living separately from my husband and in a state of much inner turmoil. It was a time of intense introspection about my life choices and of looking deeply into my psyche to better understand my motivations for separation. This dream reflected the difficulty of the descent and my fear of what I might lose. The Indian woman coming to me at this point in my life confirmed that there was a core strength that would protect me during my descent into myself.

Third Dream — The Malagas — February 1977

I was in a room with a Mexican woman in her thirties wearing a bright blue robe eating rice and vegetables. Someone told me she was a Mexican shaman. A friend brought me into another room where there were several women with blue robes. They were also 'malagas' or ''malagras,' which they told me was the Spanish word for medicine woman, and were from different villages in Mexico. As I left the room, the first 'malaga' told me that I had to learn how to focus my energy better. I was also given a special blue robe by a friend and told I had to do something to make it my own. I said I would put gold trimming around the edge of it.

Dream Ego's Relation

She gives me specific advice and I am given a shaman robe to wear that she is also wearing.

Dialogue

Me — What do you have to tell me?

She — I have already told you to learn to focus your energy and you are still in need of doing that better. You seem to have made more specific choices for yourself in life, and that helps to focus, but on a daily level you are still undisciplined. Meditation would help you as it has helped you before. It slows you down, focuses you on your central issues and eliminates that needless chatter in your mind.

Comments

I do not know Spanish but found out that 'malagra' means miracle. To me there is a close tie between miracles and what shamans do, so once again the dream goes beyond our conscious knowledge. I had been working on being more disciplined in the outer and was emphasizing it to myself as a masculine trait I needed to acquire. But it is the feminine wisdom which tells me to focus and then I am given a robe of my own. I feel my healing side is being confirmed during a time of dealing with my own wounds. I am given the cloak of the healing woman and also encouragement to make it more my own.

Fourth Dream — Thousands of Eagles — May 1979

I am on a beach where there is a ritual going on and people are taking off their clothes. Then thousands of huge eagles fly down in V-shape formations. The sky is filled with them. I leave with my daughter and others to wait in a mountain house to see what the eagles will do. Nothing happens so we go back down on the beach. The eagles are still landing by the thousands and their power and numbers are frightening. On another area of the beach are lines of people sending positive healing energy to the eagles. They aren't sure the eagles are violent or afraid but know they need calming energy. There is a young Indian woman who is leading the healing group.

Dream Ego's Relation
The dream ego feels frightened by the eagles' power and is glad the Indian woman is there to bring healing energy.

Dialogue
Me —   What do you have to tell me?
She —   I know the power of the eagles is overwhelming you and you are frightened by their possible malevolent intent, but we do not know anything except that they are all gathering together. Their power and numbers are awesome and at this point we can only bring positive energy to them. I am here mainly as a vehicle so that the collective can be directed. You have to make your own peace with these eagles but I urge you not to do it alone, but to join our power.

Comments

This healer, like the Indian woman on the sled, offers me support and guidance in the face of outer difficulties. Except this time the difficulties are a collective issue and not just my individual struggle. I have also worked with the symbol of the eagle in art and with amplification. Synchronistically several months later I chose from over 100 choices of symbols in a group ceremony and I picked the eagle to work with in clay.

Summary

As a therapist and dreamwork leader I am obviously working on evoking the healing element within me for myself and for others. Thus I have found these dreams to be very inspirational. On a conscious level I had been exploring more easily my darker sides but often felt hesitant about allowing too much of my spiritual or lighter side out. I had seen too many people get inflated in their role as healer and consequently shied away from that side. I feel these dreams have not only been there for me as a balance and support when I was exploring my own darkness but as confirmation in exploring the spiritual feminine within me.

Dreamwork Entry — Transpersonal Dreamwork

In terms of living a more meaningful life, the use of dreams for a transpersonal perspective might involve any of the following:

— Establishing an ongoing relationship to one's dreams which involves regular dreamwork in which the ego makes more and more choices in terms of the greatest potential and meaning revealed in dreams and dreamwork.

— Focusing on major dream symbols and dreams which seem to have transcendent aspects and evoke awe. Such symbolism may be similar to or different from the spiritual symbols dominant in a culture.

— Being especially aware of dream elements which may involve psychic happenings, such as special knowledge or predicting possibilities for the future.

— Weaving together elements of personal, spiritual practice based on converting transpersonal dream symbolism into art objects, prayers, meditations and actions. One may also contribute to a community's spiritual practices using elements from dreams, such as rituals, chants and wisdom sayings.

— Working with the *great dream*, a dream, because of its especially vivid symbolism, relevance to one's destiny and sense of resolution, we know comes to inspire us in making a major transition in our lives.

— Incubating a dream around a central life concern with a prior commitment to follow, to the best of one's ability, the direction indicated by the dream which results.

Procedure
Process a dream using any of the above contexts. You may want to use a variety of techniques to fully develop the context.

Evaluation
Meditate on your spiritual or transpersonal experience and what dreamwork has contributed to it. Then, formulate out of it some life principles which, when followed, will give added meaning to your life.

Using Dream Wisdom

When we look at the Bible or almost any religion's literature we can surmise that the ideas and statements could have been originally written by individual

human beings like you and me. Or perhaps these religious writers were extraordinary spiritual figures who indeed did have direct revelations from deity? But even if this is so, does it follow that we ourselves cannot tune into the same sources and find revelations?

The experiences of participants doing Jungian-Senoi dreamwork show that the revelatory function is very much alive in many people. Sometimes spiritual statements appear directly in dreams, often more paradoxical than those in traditional religions.

— Where do those statements come from?
— What does it mean that an ordinary everyday person has spiritual wisdom revealed in dreams?

Is this person to go out and proclaim a new religion? Certainly this is highly unlikely. But wisdom statements can be lived in the personal life rather than preached to others. This is the everyday, grounding level.

Another level of dream wisdom comes directly out of dreamwork experiences, such as in doing a dialogue with a dream figure.

We all have life principles and attitudes by which we try to live our lives. One's own compilation of personal dream wisdom can become part of the bedrock of principles upon which to live one's life.

What is important is meditating on one's dream wisdom statements, letting the possible meanings emerge, and then letting those meanings form a context within which to evaluate how one is living a certain part of one's life.

When I received the statement in a dream that 'One must not consider one's healing dreams nightmares', I was faced with these possible meanings:

— that I was afraid of my healing dreams, those dreams which showed me new possiblities for choice and transformation.
— that I need no longer fear my nightmares but face them, including the fear they produced, and see what healing could be evoked by them.

The result was that I did more fully re-orient my own consciousness towards dealing with that which made me afraid, inner and outer.

Dream wisdom statements come to everyone who works with their dreams regularly in the Jungian-Senoi approach. In this sense each of us has a spiritual source and a spiritual book which expresses that source. We do not then have to be completely dependent on outside spiritual experiences and wisdom. These external sources, such as traditional religions, texts, East or West, can add a valuable leavening to our lives. But what the dream source and dreamwork approach does is make our relation to source and spiritual wisdom individual and unique. As part of this process the dream source will often take traditional religious images and wisdom and modify them uniquely for the individual. One person from a Christian background was having a controversy with someone over a passage in the Bible. In the dream she referred to the Bible as the final authority but the dreamer said, 'Let's ask Jesus about it', which he did. Thus, unlike traditional Christianity, he went right to the source.

Suggestions for Working with Dream Wisdom

— Keep a couple of pages at the back of your journal to write your dream widsom as it comes to you.
— Go through a dream and see how many wisdom statements you can write from the material.
— Put your dream wisdom on cards which you choose one statement from to meditate on each day. Repeat the statement over and over to yourself and observe the effect.
— Put dream wisdom on posters and illustrate with art.

The Wisdom of Dreams

The following are statements remembered directly from dreams.

— 'It's serious business deciding what you are going to do with the rest of your eternity.'
— 'Pull your ego together.'
— 'You are a spark of the infinite God glowing in the darkness.'
— 'I am to get close to the vortex, the raging whirlwinds of fire, and tame them by bringing the opposites together.'
— 'In order to leave you must build the door you came through.'
— 'Structure it and let it go completely.'
— 'You choose things because you want them. I choose things for the suffering they bring and the sacrifices they demand.'
— 'It is only at the centre we hear things.'
— 'You have to crouch low and kick off into darkness.'
— 'Be sure and include descriptions and exercises for the dark side, not necessarily horrible stuff, but definitely ordinary stuff.'
— 'I want you to be able to swim on the desert and walk on the water.'
— 'It doesn't look like my garbage.'

Researching Dreams

For Jung, connecting a whole series of dreams together was a necessary method in understanding dreams. In fact, he went so far to say that a single dream could not usually be understood alone (CW 16:322).

The Jungian-Senoi position used here is that there is no one way for working with dreams. What we do try to do is open up issues in order to consider many points of view from which to choose. Thus we can work with single dreams or with series of dreams and derive values.

Some Values for Connecting Symbols from Dreams

When we follow a symbol cluster or theme as it appears in different dreams over several months or years, we can see how the symbol seems to be changing or developing. This can give confirmation to our growth process.

After my parents died, one or both parents would appear in subsequent dreams. A number of times I revisited the family apartment and it became bigger, more spacious and beautiful. Part of this series with my parents involved finally receiving gifts from my father. He had been a well-known poet and editor, Oscar Williams, but I had not been encouraged or supported in

developing writing myself. Finally in a dream my father presents me with a small library of his books. This dream was an affirmation to me that I was receiving at last the family heritage and could now feel a rootedness which would help sustain me as I myself entered the arena of the world. In a later dream at the apartment I receive this time from my father a very special large red book which is to be my book. We do not know the title or what is in it, but its significance was that now what I was to give to the world, and to myself, was there in potential and could be developed. Other dreams involved various events such as having a funeral service for my father and expressing profound grief. The last major dream in the series was of my father, now a very old shrivelled up man in his nineties, dying in my arms. What a wonderful dream and integrating of the Father energy!

Currently, a major recurrent symbol for me is my former analyst and spiritual teacher of ten years. I had resigned from her organization under negative circumstances with, I felt, extreme judgementalness on her part. Since then, she has appeared in my dreams as a spiritual leader who has not been supportive, certainly consistent with her position in outer life. But as I have been in touch with my own spiritual power, and the ability to manifest it in the world, her figure in my dreams has changed and become more supportive. Most recently in a New Year's dream she and I are actively working together for the first time on an important dreamwork paper for the Jungians.

The value I gain from actualizing the dream symbols which most seem to recur in my dreams is that I gradually deal with and integrate their energy. As this happens the symbols themsleves change and become more positive and supportive, indicating that I myself am more and more able to express in my own life the energy they constellate. This is in turn confirmed by new dreams. I also feel that I am working with my own unconscious, and not against it. This is because of the give and take based on my integrative actions and the 'symbol exchange' which the unconscious contributes in return as confirmation.

— Another value for working with recurrent symbols is to discover, develop and balance out your own unique dream landscape.

What symbols occur most frequently for you? Then that is where your most psychic energy is constellated, where your greatest problems are, where you are likely to be most one-sided, and where perhaps your greatest gifts are. One person dreams of relationship a lot. It is as if she had chosen to express herself in life through relationships. But, as she found out in working with this dynamic, she was putting too much energy into relationships and very little into that essential part of herself which could not be expressed through relation to someone else. There is now a shift in some of her dream content which shows her journeying and doing things alone.

— Researching dreams for the dominant dream landscape can possibly be used for vocational counselling. In developing one's work productivity it is best to be in an area in which one's psychic energy most expresses itself.

As examples, one young woman was frequently dreaming of nature and ecological landscapes, so she is now active in the ecology movement. Someone else who was always very relational in her dreams is studying to be a therapist.

— Another value is discovering which archetypes are dominant in your pysche.

Repeat symbols and themes on a personal, unconscious level seem to indicate one's dominant personality problems which need solving. On a collective unconscious level, repeat symbols and themes seem to indicate which archetypes are dominant and how they are dominant in the psyche. These may indicate one's natural direction in life.

A father problem will show up in dreams both in the image of the personal father and in dream figures functioning as the father. Gradually most of the parental dynamics constellated in childhood will be revealed through following the symbols.

On a collective unconscious, purely archetypal level, one can research which major archetypes seem to be dominating the psyche and how they do this. Some people seem to have very few symbols of a directly spiritual nature, such as mandalas, gifts, treasures or traditional religious symbolism. This could indicate that the Self, or central archetype, is not very active. This same person could have many dreams of a devouring feminine or monster figures. The dominant archetypes need to be made clear and in the dreamwork steps taken to evoke other archetypes to balance them out. This does not mean we go against the dominant archetype. We may even develop its significance further, while at the same time evoking its opposite.

— Still another value in working with repeat symbols and themes is to develop also the relation or lack of relation of the dream ego to the repeating symbols.

At one end of the spectrum is the dream ego which is either being attacked by the symbol or merely observes it, or is not even in the dream. At the more positive end is the dream ego which is in active and direct interaction with the dream symbol. Is the dream ego always stopping when it comes up against obstructions in the dreams? We then do dream re-entries and re-writing of the dreams to train the dream ego and the outer waking ego to become more active and involved when confronted with the archetypal life energies reflected in the symbols. Thus one person began to change from having dreams in which she was confronted by terrible wounds but could do nothing about them, to being able to interact with the woundedness and engage in a healing process. This was after extensive dreamwork on the part of the dreamer.

Someone else followed his dream ego in dreams over several months. He found that at the beginning the dream ego was typically starting out to go places or complete a task but never quite make it. Later dreams showed his dream ego able to start out and arrive somewhere consistent with original intentions. Also his dream ego progressed in becoming more in tune with the universal laws or energies which showed themselves in the dreams.

— Another value is to see how dream series parallel outer life events.

In this variation on the method a person consciously looks for and remembers the dreams on birthdays and special days like Christmas and New Year's. These are what I call 'dreams of destiny.' On such major days certain archetypical energies are more evoked and active. The collective breaks through the personal unconscious and we are, for the moment, pulled out of our identification with our everyday lives into a more mythic and universal perspective.

In the dreamwork done with such dreams one looks for major themes and directions which can last the whole year, from birthday to birthday, for instance. My dreams of destiny have often had major significance, even predicting the future course of events and what I must do about them. The year before I left my spiritual community of ten years I had a dream in which I was choosing certain beautiful antiques from my spiritual leader's house which was being sold. This dream occurred on my birthday and in it I wanted a cut glass mirror which I was able to obtain when I fell back asleep and redreamed the dream. When I shared this dream with my analyst and spiritual leader, she questioned why I was taking the antiques for myself and not for her organization. I knew then that she would never really support my own direction, and that whatever I did would have to be completely on my own. A year later outer events had developed in such a way that I was forced to resign and go out completely on my own. This destiny dream was and is a major support to me through terrifying times of developing my own relation to source. I continue to usually have significant major dreams at major destiny times.

— Following recurrent dream symbols can indicate the effect our specific dreamwork is having on the symbols.

If we actively confront our adversaries in doing self re-entries into our adversary dreams, we will probably reach the point where in the dreams themselves we are confronting adversaries. We may also begin to have fewer adversary dreams and more helping dreams. Developing more assertiveness on the part of the dream ego and more resolution in terms of the whole dream are two of the major experiences which seem to occur through ongoing dreamwork. What seems to be happening is that we use the dreams and dreamwork arena to do the major pattern changing within the psyche. Then, as the inner pattern changes, the outer behaviour will change. These changes in both inner and outer will be reflected in future dreams containing the same symbols and themes. The primary arena is the inner life which is far more fluid and full of possibility than the outer world. Changes in the outer then confirm and ground the inner processes in concrete manifestation, the real test that the changes are solid and not of spirit only.

— Still another value in researching dominant symbols and themes is to discover and develop one's personal myth.

To live life without knowing the myth by which one lives is to live unconsciously. We have that choice. No one can give it to us or take it away. But whether conscious or not, we cannot live without our myth. How much better is it to know that myth by which we are choosing to live. Dreams seen in series can make our underlying mythic reality abundantly clear. It is how the archetypes, the universal energies, manifest through us which determines our own uniqueness. We can live at the surface of things or we can take the plunge and discover our underlying reality and what is needed to manifest it and bring it to wholeness. Dreams and dreamwork are passageways to this undergirding reality of the soul. Following and working with one's dominant symbols and themes would seem essential to the development of full being.

The Internal Dynamics of Dreams Seen in Series

A basic aspect of this approach to dreamwork is to objectify the dream itself through delineating its internal dynamics. This can also be done with dream series. These are some of the possible categories.

— Following the same exact symbol of *place* or *person*. For example, the same person reappearing in several dreams or all my dreams of my childhood house.

— Following the same *action* or *function*. I may put together all my sex dreams, violence dreams, wisdom dreams, or defecating dreams, and so on.

— Following the same *feeling* or *attitude*. I may look into all my terror dreams or protest dreams and the like. I may discover from this which feelings, emotions and attitudes seem to be dominant in my psyche by virtue of their repeating themselves the most in my dreams.

— I may categorize on the basis of which symbols are *surrealistic, bizarre* and distorted versus those symbols which seem nearly exact replicas of external everyday reality. Notice I do not attempt to explain why. I merely get clear on what is happening in my dreams.

— I may categorize dream symbols on the basis of *symbol clusters*. Examples would be taking various symbols of spiritual teachers or feminine figures, positive and negative. But who is to say when a symbol is positive or negative in itself? Within a dream the dream ego may react to a dream negatively or positively but when we look at the symbol in itself, who knows? Probably all symbols are paradoxical, they contain the opposites of positive and negative. This is why we separate out what the dream ego's reactions are to a symbol and question and bring up the other side.

— Still we may categorize using *positive* and *negative*. The dream ego can be the basis for this evaluation or the waking ego. We may also evaluate in terms of the total dream in itself. Is this symbol creative or destructive in terms of the other dream symbols? It may be quite revealing to ask what are my most positive dream symbols over the past year and my most negative?

A Word of Caution

Be careful that you do not get caught in over-analyzing your dreams, as this is the rational function in which the ego uses logic to try and keep its dominance over the total psyche. One can also get very picky and lost in detail, the sensation function.

The essential choice in studying dream symbols and themes is to choose which series and which ways of categorizing will have the most meaning for you. You cannot do them all and you cannot be perfect. You cannot dominate the unconscious and the creative process with logic and rationalism. But you can use the thinking function to sort things out and make your way through the thousands of symbols produced yearly by your unconscious. Thus, to someone who is actively remembering and working with their dreams, methods for organizing and choosing will become necessary. Finding out one's dominant symbols and themes will help in this sorting-out process.

Process Techniques for Dealing with Dream Series

The unconscious process techniques help us to get below the rational functions to where the free, rooted energy of the psyche flows. Thus we may not only discover our symbol series but also devise ongoing techniques for working with the series. We may choose to do any of the following,

— *Paint* or put into *clay* a repeat symbol whenever it comes up. The effect is vivid and dramatic even though we may not know, or need to know for the moment, what the symbol constellates or means.

— We may have a *dialogue* with a certain figure whenever he or she appears in a dream. Dialogue often offers 'sudden insight' and demonstrates our renewed interest in a symbol.

— We may use *metaphorical processing* by taking an ongoing symbol and applying it, or paralleling it, to certain personality dynamics or life situations. In my flying dreams how do they show my tendency to avoid reality? And so on.

— We may *re-write* certain dreams right after we have dreamed them. Thus, one person changed her 'being chased' dreams by re-writing each dream with her dream ego confronting rather than running away from the adversary.

— We may do a *re-entry* and bring to resolution a certain kind of dream, such as relationship dreams which come up unresolved.

Weaving the Dreamwork Tapestry

We have demonstrated the value of working with a series of dreams and discovering how certain symbols change and develop. Yes, it takes being organized, but so does life at a certain point take being organized. We simply can't remain reactive to things or avoid forever that choice-making which chooses priorities in life and sacrifices the rest.

In this life we can choose to live at the surface of things and face the consequences. The ego hangs on tenuously at best when its fabric of existence is constructed mainly out of itself. What about the larger psyche? What about the totality? Dreams, and especially a series of dreams, show the soul at work. One could do well to create the tapestry, the continuity of one's life, on ongoing and ever more meaningful dreamwork.

Dreamwork Entry
— Researching Dreams

Determine your goals in using this method and make sure they are reasonably accomplishable. It is important, of course, not to take on too big a project and then not finish it and have nothing.

— What are the goals or values you are seeking? Make a statement of these. Review the values in the previous section or formulate your own.
— Next outline the methods you will use to accomplish these goals. Include the specifics of time commitments each day, each week, for the year, etc. And include also how you will do the researching. The following are some of the key methods.

Note: A *dream symbol* is an image or action with energy. This may include any dream figure, object or action. A *dream theme* may be any constellation of images which represent a certain category, mood, feeling or action.

— Choose *one type of dream* such as journey dreams, spiritual dreams or sex dreams and read them as a unit, looking for chronological development and change. Out of this you may want to formulate dreamwork tasks to further change the symbols in current or future dreams.

— Choose *one symbol* that you know repeats and bring all the dreams together of this symbol. Describe all the characteristics of the symbol from the various dreams. Look for a full spectrum of archetypal manifestation and for a sequence of change in the symbol. You may also want to see if this sequence parallels changes in your outer life and personality. Again, what dreamwork tasks would formulate to actualize or affect this symbol?

— Choose a symbol which reappears in your dreams and devise a dreamwork method you will do each time with it. You might wish to paint the symbol or have a dialogue with it. You might do a symbol immersion each time or write a poem. There are many more task possibilities. The point to this approach is *doing process* with the symbol rather than analyzing it. After you have a series you may understand better what is going on.

— Keep a *symbol book* of your dreams. The book is indexed and you put in order descriptions of dream symbols with the dates of the dreams. When compiled you can see which symbols repeat and their nature.

— You create more support for the work if you can organize a day or weekend of interested friends working on their dreams together. The day is paced with periods of silent introversion to work on dreams and times or sharing on what is being discovered. Such a weekend at the middle and end of the year is helpful.

The Choice

This is a difficult subject.

Ultimately we are each totally alone in our decisions. What we choose is what we become.

Thus it is vitally important, as part of the consciousness process, to develop a *context for choosing.*

— How do I know I am making the most valuable or meaningful choice?

— Which part of me, or how much of my totality, is making the choice?

— How have I made choices in the past?

— How do I know the information coming at me is of reality?

— And in dreamwork, and working with the unconscious in general, who or what speaks? From which part of the total psyche does each voice come?

— And when do I know I have enough information to make an appropriate and valid choice?

— How do I process the information, some of it often contradictory?

— And who or what is the final authority for making my choices?

The Ego-Self Axis

In dreamwork we open ourselves to all sorts of new information. We go to our sources for help because the information we can gather from outer reality is not sufficient to deal with outer reality.

We need a greater perspective. We need to get free of our outer reality, to get disidentified from it, in order to deal with it.

Dreams and dreamwork are full of symbolic comments on the way things are, really are, inner and outer. But how do we decipher the symbols? How do we become clearer? How do we come to exactitude so we can make our choices?

Yes, the ego or choice-maker is learning that it does not want to only take its own point of view in the matter.

The ego is the choice-maker, not the integrative function for the whole psyche.

For integration and transformation the central archtype of the Self is needed.

But the Self does not choose. It only reveals and integrates what is chosen.

The ego, as director of the psychic energy available to it, chooses how a potential gets manifested in reality.

Thus the Self and the ego together are the integrative function.

Jesus discovered a fundamental psyche law which comes to us as follows:

'Whoever tries to save his or her life will lose it. But whoever loses his or her life will find it.'

Re-said in psychological terms closer to the literal meaning of the original Greek text:

'If the ego tries to build walls around the psyche it will strangle it. But if the ego breaks down the walls around the psyche it will have life abundantly.'

And re-said in dreamwork terms:

'If the ego blocks itself off from the unconscious, and its dreams and primary intuitions, then the ego will strangle itself and the unconscious. If, on the other hand, the ego opens up channels between itself and the unconscious through working actively with dreams, intuitions and feelings, then life will flow abundantly.'

And so the ego chooses.

It learns how to say "yes" to one thing and "no" to all the alternatives which conflict with that chosen choice.

It learns how to consider and consciously take the consequences for what it chooses.

It learns how to 'open itself up to freedom', to consider the many and sometimes contradictory alternatives before making the choice.

The ego learns to consider its own needs as choice-maker but not to choose egocentrically or totally and finally for itself.

The ego has much to learn in this process.

It learns how to maintain the tension of ambivalence long enough for the alternatives to become clear.

Yet it learns also the necessity to act at the precise moment when the time is ripe, when the full potential is 'at the crest' or the moment for maximum manifestation is lost.

This matter of ego and choice is one central reason why we have formulated the dreamwork technique, 'following the dream ego'.

The Moment of Choice

And so we come now to the moment of choice which only the ego can make.

Perhaps it is scared or weak. Perhaps it has tried to jump the gun or has tried to wait forever. Or perhaps it has sought some exterior authority to make the choice for it.

A reality: *No one can make our choices for us. The consequences we must take ourselves.*

The dreamwork has been an opening-up process. The dreamwork has greatly increased the measure of freedom within which the ego can choose by revealing potentials and unconscious predispositions to choice.

But the dream and the dreamwork does not say which choice to make. Only the ego can do that by choosing.

But how to choose? What is the process by which we can most creatively choose? Here are some procedures.

— Enlarge as much as you can your awareness of the possibilities for choice.

— Evaluate which of these you would most and least like to choose personally and why.

— Free your ego of its own subjectivity by considering fully what it itself wants and how this is similar to or different from what the Self, or more total centre wants.

— But what does the Self want? How can we know? In developing awareness of the alternatives seek also that which might integrate the most into a totality. Or go for the greatest essence. Or that which brings greatest resolution to the totality. Or that which most unifies inner and outer. Or that which has the ring of certainty. Ultimately for you, what is the most meaningful context within which to make your choices? Only *you* can decide.

— Choice defines who you are. Ambivalence leaves you wishy-washy, a weak and contradictory person. The only way to become a definite person is to make the strongest and the most meaningful choices you are capable of making.

— Remember that in dreamwork there are many voices. Thus when we do dialogues with figures in dreams, which figures do we dialogue with and what if there are different points of view? There *are* different points of view.

— There are no certainties in life because the Absolute is unknowable. Yet nothing is relative in the act of choice.

— *Choice is the one absolute.*

The principles of 'considering totality' and 'finding the integrative centre' are the two principles I find most useful for dealing with the many and often contradictory voices for life.

— And now *the choice,* the choosing of one alternative and not another. And is not the greatest agony and joy when I am faced with more than one valuable choice?

Finally in my imperfection I choose and take the consequences.

Do I really say a 'yes' that is a 'no' to all else? Am I decisive? Do I make the choice with as much of my being as I can know at that point of time? Am I passionate? Have I become fully involved? What have I intentionally sacrificed so what I have chosen may become a reality? From what centre within myself and in life have I finally made my choice?

— And after the choice *the consequences.* How am I fully accepting and dealing with what follows? How is what is now happening different from what I had expected? Am I fully dealing with what comes, or going unconscious or rebelling?

A choice that does not deal with consequences is a choice half-made.

The consequences, and their acceptance, are the preparation for the next choice. And how does my next choice build on what has gone before?

— And finally *the confirmation*. How has there been confirmation or reaction to my choice?

In dreamwork often there will be a confirming dream, a dream which replays the choice-making process, lending additional insight and possibility to it. This can be an awesome moment, experiencing as we do, some comment, some awareness by the 'other' about what we are doing. We may also experience synchronicity, outer coincidence with inner happening, as part of the confirming process.

— And no choice is *irredeemable?* Or is this not true? What about the choice which denies the consciousness process itself?

If we say we can never know, we will never know.

If we deny consciousness we destroy that by which we can become conscious.

The irredeemable choice.

One choice is all it takes. The right choice at the right time will do far more to move mountains than faith can ever do.

[Written as a Dark Friday meditation, Easter Weekend, April, 1979.]

Dreamwork Entry
— Creating Choice

Instructions

— Follow your dream ego through the dream and list the choices it does and does not make. This can be done in two separate parallel columns.

— Then describe for yourself the context within which you seemed to make your choices in the dream. What were the attitudes and values by which you made your choices?

— If it seems relevant, analyze in the same way how anyone else in the dream is making choices.

— Re-look at your dream and your dreamwork for choice work that could be more valuable than occurred in the dream. Re-write that section making the new choices.

— From all this dreamwork take the choice-making and decide how you will apply it to outer life situations. Make a list or plan of how you will choose in the outer. Be aware of consequences. List some possible consequences. It is realistic to be aware of possibilities, but we never know until we choose.

— At a later date, after you have carried through on your outer choices, return to this dreamwork and add an evaluation of the choices and consequences which resulted from it.

The farmer plants the seed in order to reap the harvest. Not merely to break new ground or flee from the seed which is about to grow.

The Jungian-Senoi Dream Session

It is time. The four participants and the dreamwork leader have been sitting quietly in a circle on cushions. Meditative music has been playing very softly as people arrive in silence. Transition is being accomplished from the exterior world of intense energy, problems and demands to this more interior setting where the soul, the inner being can more easily be heard.

The room has a number of sacred objects. There is a place as part of their circle where the dream session candle is kept, as well as the bell for ending their time together. There are the baskets of stones, shells and driftwood which are part of the ceremony for dream sharing. The first ritual is to light the candle with perhaps a few words said about what this may affirm this week.

After the lighting of the candle a short meditation is read by the leader. This night it comes from Jung's writings.

A new member is joining the group. He has brought his dream journal and is quietly waiting. The leader breaks the silence by suggesting that they each go around the circle, starting with herself, and say as much of their names as they feel for. And then a few words about why dreamwork may be important to them or what they want from the experience.

One person says she follows her dreams so she will not waste the night, which is a third of her life. Another is interested in her relationship dreams. Her former friend had got much out of the group. Someone else has been practising meditation for years and come to an impasse and hopes that working with his dreams will help. The new person has been dreaming a lot lately, he says, and is curious about what may be going on. He is already in regular therapy but they don't really work with his dreams. The leader, herself, has just had a new kind of dream she doesn't think she has ever had before. She is curious about working with it in the dream group for leaders since she does not share her dreams here.

Having a new member to the group is always an exciting thing. A new wealth of dreams comes into the situation as well as a person who may choose to make ongoing dreamwork part of his or her own life direction.

Before people have arrived the leader has spent fifteen minutes in her own meditation, knowing that she cannot be fully a vehicle for working with others unless she herself is prepared and has made the transition. At the end of the dream session she will again spend fifteen minutes in meditation or journal work dealing with what has been evoked. The evening itself lasts for two and one-half hours, which allows each participant to have around one-half hour of time to deal with the dream and dreamwork fully.

The leader explains the nature of the evening briefly to the new member, explaining that meditation and simple ritual are used as ways of deepening and honouring the process of working with dreams. It is as if the centre must be affirmed to deal with dreams at their full level of potential. For ritual itself is another form of symbolic process, like dreamwork, for working with the unconscious.

The first part of dream session, the leader expains, is for people to share the dreamwork they did during the week, which came out of last week's sharing and task suggestions.

One person finally did that dialogue with her dead father originating out of a dream task suggested six weeks ago. Despite her fears she felt herself ready now. She had cried and received a new sense of affirmation from the father she never really had. In the silence she read the dialogue. Another person thought about his own dream during the week but had not done specific dream tasks with it. In dialogue with the leader he realized that more had been happening than he had suspected. A woman in the group shared how she had re-entered her relationship dream and really acted more assertively with her former lover. And in the outer she reported on a decision to minimize contact with him so she would no longer be caught in ambivalent feelings. The leader suggested then an ongoing task to seek to bring to resolution any relationship dreams about her former lover which came up in the future.

The time for task-sharing has ended. Now the leader explains the ritual for sharing the new dream. The baskets of wood, stone or shell are passed around the circle and each person chooses one object which has significance. The ritual, the leader explains, is based in part on the native American tradition of carrying power objects in a medicine pouch. In this ceremony an empty basket is then passed and each member puts a ritual object in the basket, saying perhaps a word as to its meaning for the individual. The leader then takes the five objects and places them in the dream pouch and places the dream pouch in the centre. When a person is ready to share a dream they take the pouch and hold it as they share.

Thus spirit finds its place in substance and ritual action frees one from the literalness of the mundane world.

The dreams are shared, one dream or one evening's dreams per participant. The fabric of the evening is being woven. Each person with a unique dream landscape and yet much in common with others.

'It is fascinating to see how he handles nightmares differently from how I handle them ...' 'Her dream ego looks as weak as mine ...' 'I was tremendously moved by this dream. The moon was getting brighter and brighter. I felt like I was viewing a new phase in the world's history ...' 'In what sense,' the dreamwork leader responds, 'is this a new phase in your own history?' 'Why don't you list in your journal all the ways this can be an extraordinary year for you? Just let it flow. Go way out on it ...'

Dream session continues. Someone incubated a dream but could not see how the dream connected up with her original question to her dream source. The leader then gives her six ways of possibly making the connection to work with during the week. Someone else still fairly new to the group begins commenting on the other person's dreams and is stopped by the leader.

'How would you put your intuitions into a question, into a suggestion for a task to do? Who knows what the dream is really all about? I am sure the dream represents something for each of us. Do you begin to see the difference between suggesting tasks and telling the other person what you think the dream means?'

The tapestry of the evening grows. The new person wanted to know more about remembering dreams. He wondered also if his dreams were predicting the future. The leader chose to take him through a guided re-entry in order to break through an impasse in the dream. The new participant was amazed with what came out. 'Is that really all in a dream?' he asked. 'Well, is it?' responded the leader.

It is essential to honour time by ending on time. The unconscious forces must not be allowed, usually, to run on. And so the leader warns gently the last dream-sharer that there is only fifteen minutes left.

At the end of the time the objects are taken from the dream pouch by the leader and placed in the basket to be passed around again so each participant can take back his or her object. These they return to the original baskets. A circle of hands is formed. The leader suggests that each visualize some healing symbol in the centre to carry into the week. The candle is blown out, taking the light inside, and the bell is rung ending the dream session for that week.

People leave quietly and those whose fees are due pay for a month's worth of sessions.

When the participants are gone there is quiet. The wind noises its way softly through the trees and the leader sits listening to the thoughts rushing into her head. She lets them happen, sorting them, processing which belong to her own unconscious and which to the other's psyches. Some new ideas occur to her. Once again she realizes the richness of the process, recognizing something else at work in the universe besides her own ability and insight, both of which grow daily.

The room is set in order, the cushions put away, the heat turned off, the lights out. It is now time to return to her personal life, renewed also by working with other people's dreams.

It is still a great mystery.

Some Issues on Group Dreamwork

The Meditative Setting
From this basic description you can, we hope, feel some of what happens in dream session. Few groups, we suspect, keep a meditative atmosphere in working with dreams and the unconscious. Evaluating the quality of dreams shared at the Institute leads us to feel that working ritually does evoke more healing and more spiritually oriented dreams in the sense that strong healing elements seem to be in most dreams. For contrast to the dreams and dreamwork reported in this book read the dreams reported by sleep researchers from their laboratories. Basically, what we may be doing is evoking more strongly the central archetype of the Self.

Dream session is an experience of beauty and of numinous and meaningful powers at work in people's lives. Even many religious services may not give the introverted spiritual experiences which a full dream session can evoke.

Also we do remain open to changing the ritual and structure of dream session. We also occasionally enact rituals which come through dreams.

Group Size
Any dream group with more than four or five participants limits very much the full processing of a dream by each member. I have had up to eight in an introductory group and I had to move extremely quickly to make it possible for everyone to share.

Group vs. Individual Dreamwork
There is a value to working with dreams in a small group which is not present

working one-to-one. This is the value of enriching your own unconscious by participating in how others express the unconscious. We gain in the group a greater sense of both the personal and the collective unconscious. I can follow in the personal unconscious how your parents affect you and you can follow mine. I can also experience through your major archetypal symbols symbols which do not seem to appear in my own dreams.

The small size of the group and the task orientation of the approach go a long way to preventing the excesses of a group experience. These excesses are group merger where your dream becomes mine and mine becomes yours, and before we all know it we are swimming around in the unconscious together. Another excess is my projecting out inner contents onto your dream and leaving them there for you to deal with. If the structure only allows me to give task suggestions and not interpretations then I am more forced into dealing with my own projections. In fact, the great danger of the interpretive approach to anything is that we project our own material through our seeming rationality, then try to get the 'dumped upon' to deal with our stuff!

One-to-one

The value of working individually with one's dreams is that a person gets more time and the dreamwork can be more individualized. Also, the sharing is usually more intimate in one-to-one than in a group.

A dreamwork group is not necessarily introductory for later working one-to-one. Some people stay in a group many months and never do go into individual work. Probably the basic criterion is whether you feel successful in what you are dealing with or not. Do you need the greater support of a one-to-one therapeutic situation? One of the main goals of Jungian-Senoi dream groups is to teach participants the techniques for working on their own dreams. People do get task suggestions from the leader and to a lesser extent from other participants. But basically they do their own work, an achievement sometimes difficult to get those who work one-to-one to accomplish.

Transference

The task orientation and the group setting help much of the healing energy to stay focused on spiritual symbols and the dreams themselves, rather than on the dream leader. The leader will still get projections but, keeping the focus always on the dream and its dreamwork, allows projections to be integrated more easily. Also, teaching clients how to evoke healing for themselves helps prevent the prolonged transference relationship sometimes experienced in traditional therapy.

The Jungian-Senoi Task-giving Sequence

What follows is the typical sequence as it occurs during dream session, and with modifications and variations, of course.

— The dream sharer holds the pouch and either reads or says from memory the full dream as it was originally remembered. The person does not have to use the present tense since this may feel artificial. We have found that, unlike the Gestaltists contend, a person does not need to say the dream in the present tense, as if it is happening now, to feel involved in the dream. All dreams from a single night are usually asked for. What needs to be watched is that the person does not, while telling the dream, start elaborating on it. The other thing is that a person floating in anxiety may start reading the dream too quickly and needs to be asked to slow down in order for all to feel the dream as it is unfolding.

— Then any personal comments, feelings or associations may be asked for from the dreamer. He or she may also be asked what they have done with the dream so far. At this point the dreamwork leader usually does not do anything with the associations. Unlike most other approaches, the associations are not the jumping off place. They are asked for to give clues and to provide a basis of contrast with later dreamwork and for what the dreamer does not know about the dream. As the dream is objectified, what develops will usually be in contrast to the dreamer's own associations.

— As the dreamwork leader has been listening to the dream, sometimes with eyes closed, the leader is doing two things. One, opening up to any intuitions or feelings from the unconscious, and, two, analyzing the dream for its internal dynamics. Both these levels provide clues for the suggestions for dreamwork tasks. The leader does not usually elicit the dream's dynamics fully with the dream sharer. There simply is not time. But the leader may choose certain key issues and dynamics to bring out into the open. This is the stage of objectifying the dream. This stage basically focuses on helping the sharer get clear on major internal dynamics of the dream.

— Then the leader suggests at least four and possibly up to eight different tasks. The goal here is to suggest dream tasks which can actualize various levels of the dream. What are the outer issues? What are the personality issues? What are the dream issues such as the need for development or resolution? What is the personal level? What is the objective or collective level? And so on. The dream sharer writes the tasks down as they are given. The emphasis is on choice. Do not necessarily do all the tasks but do the ones which you have the most energy for. Also a large number of tasks at different levels are suggested in order to prevent the subjective bias which would be there if the dreamwork guide had given only one or two tasks.

— At the end the leader may ask about the person's response. Does the dream begin to make more sense to you now? Do some of these task suggestions feel right to you?

— A variation on the above involves the leader suggesting that they do a dreamwork task together right there. This may take the form of guided re-entry into the dream or acting out briefly some action in the dream. Direct process is chosen when the person is felt to need support or initiation into the technique. Or process is carried out when the person seems too rational.

— Other participants in the group, usually after the dreamwork leader is finished, may give a task suggestion or two. But this is limited so as not to confuse the person with too many different tasks, some of them possibly contradictory.

— At the end when the tasks are written down, the pouch is returned to the centre and after a little silence the next person chooses the pouch and begins to share a dream.

Sharing the dream tasks in the following week's dream session usually includes this sequence:

— The dream sharer may briefly outline the dream again for everyone and then say the tasks worked on and describe what happened. It is usually more important that the dreamer go with the flow in doing tasks, rather than stick to the literal description of the task. Anything the dreamer does is a response.

— The leader may then help clarify points if this is needed, or help establish relation to the original dream. Often nothing need be said in response, especially if the dreamwork is full. The results of doing the tasks is really said into the mystery. The leader is not the evaluator of the tasks. The leader may appreciate, give support, clarify, add information and even suggest new tasks. The focus is self-direction in doing dreamwork. The leader avoids being the authority in the situation. The leader is the facilitator for the process, not the recipient of the process.

— As a person works in dream group, the leader and other participants will be building up a store of information. Thus the leader may point out relation to themes in previous dreamwork or dreams. This helps create the fabric of one's personal myth and a stronger base for the individuation process.

— A leader analyzes and works with dreams, not personalities. It is important to keep the focus on the dream and its dreamwork and not to use these to leap off into someone's personality. It is questionable whether anyone can really diagnose or evaluate another person without bias and putting them into little boxes. Where personality information seems relevant relate it to the dream. If a person seems to have an anger problem which is showing up in the group relate it to the person's dreams and dreamwork. If someone seems on the verge of a mental breakdown, is this appearing in the dreams? The leader may also need to suggest an individual session to find out what is going on.

— Some dream tasks are fun, and even good to eat, and thus add to the personal relatedness in the dream group.

Leading Dream Groups

Leading dream groups, I have found from my own experience and from training others, is a difficult art. It should not be undertaken without commitment and self-knowledge. But one destined for such a role should not avoid the role out of fear or a sense of imperfection. You may be awkward and terribly inappropriate at times. This is the risk you take to also function magnificently in tune with what is going on. The leadership role is healing as well as inflationary. What follows is a series of working principles which can be adopted by anyone leading dream groups or working individually with clients. You can return to these principles over and over to help process your experiences. And you may also want to formulate additional principles of your own.

Dream Group Structure

From reading the chapter of the Jungian-Senoi Dream Session, you will have gained, hopefully, a sense of what one style of dream group can be. The basic structure we have found most effective is to begin with meditation, do some simple ritual like lighting a candle, and then have people share the dreamwork they have done between dream group sessions. Next, each person shares a new dream and receives task suggestions from the leader, and sometimes from

group members, for re-experiencing the dream during the week. Some dreamwork process may also be initiated during the dream sharing time. Dream session is brought to a close meditatively with silence, a circle of hands, and the blowing out of the candle. To allow each person to share fully, the group usually has no more than five to six members. Our groups have a maximim of four. The leader needs to be sensitive to the structure and its transitions so that the structure itself will be a containing base for people's work.

The Leader's Qualities and Role

Outer roles are the creative structures for containing and evoking archetypal energies. The leader's role can often evoke in people their own inner spiritual functions which have not yet been fully developed. The leadership role can also evoke positive and negative parental energies. Thus roles are constructed to deal with projected energies as well as to embody a directing function within the group. Roles can also protect an individual from a group's energy.

The danger of assuming a role is that the individual may easily identify with it and become inflated by its power, thus becoming an archetype rather than a person. Group members can sometimes encourage this by exaggeratedly complimenting a leader. Excessive gratitude may be a manipulation done to inflate the leader and keep him or her docile toward the gusher of compliments. Here, then, are some working principles.

— Do not let stand someone else's description of you said in a group. Give your own description of yourself as a response. You thus are asserting your own right to evaluate yourself.

-- Do not usually deny someone's description of you. He or she may need to project onto you before the projection can be taken back.

— Become increasingly aware of your own assumptions and wanting to guide the process your way rather than the way the process itself seems to want to go.

— To avoid power struggles between yourself and others, continually check as to the effects you and the process are having on them.

— When a conflict develops between the leader and a dream sharer, almost always let the sharer have the ascendancy.

— You are responsible for part of the process, as are those in the group. And God or Source is also responsible for the process. Differentiate continually who is responsible for what.

— When you get into difficulty, maintain consciousness, let go of everything, and let a healing source emerge which you choose to actualize.

— Be aware of yourself at all time, but be focused also on the larger process of which you are only a small part.

— Let your own dreamwork help you make conscious how you are carrying the leadership role.

— Be willing to be alone and different from the group.

— When you are not in the leadership role, drop it completely. Play with it as you use it and you will be much less subject to identification and inflation.

— Live yourself what you teach. We lead others because we are ourselves in need. Leading others can evoke our own growth if we honestly take back what we give away.

— Be willing to be continually guided by those you teach and by other sources, inner and outer.

— Discover, evaluate and create choice with those principles and attitudes which influence your leadership behaviour. How consistent are they with all that is going on in the group? Record your central principles.

— The deepest process happens when one becomes a channel for what is really at the core of a dream. To do this, practise clearing yourself of outside concerns before dream session begins. Also do meditation and other centering practices to connect yourself to deep sources. Preparation may also involve reviewing appropriate chapters in the manual, such as the flow chart, in order to gain a perspective. And, after dream session, clear yourself by meditating on the process and your part in it. Basically, *prepare before and process after*. Acknowledge what has happended to you and the group. Dreamwork leadership can be a profoundly spiritual practice.

The Basis for Suggesting Dream Tasks

As has become fairly obvious by now, we try as much as possible to give people things to do with their, dreams rather than give them cognitive interpretations. Thus, suggesting dream tasks is fundamental to the actualization approach. Basically, we translate methodology into specific suggestions relating directly to a particular dream.

This is the *usual procedure* to use with every dream. Learn it well and you will be more able to bypass it when appropriate.

1. *Hear the dream* while it is being said at as deep a level as possible. You might even close your eyes.

2. *Obtain* any immediate *feelings or comments* from the dream sharer. Do not go into these much or you will be drawn away from the dream itself.

3. *Objectify the dream.* What, briefly, is the dream ego doing or not doing? What are the major contrasts and similarities in the dream, and how do they interrelate? What sequences are present in the dream? What are the major symbols and relations between symbols? What dynamics are revealed by generalizing the symbols? What is the dream ego's relation to the major symbols? What are the issues, conflicts and unresolved situations in the dream? What are the healing factors in the dream? What relation does this dream have to other dreams? What are the possibilities for relations and resolutions which have not yet materialized in the

dream? Sometimes the leader will help the sharer to develop the connections by asking questions, and sometimes the leader will quickly make the connections in order to save time.

4. Next, *focus* in *on one aspect of the dream* and develop it further. We narrow down to go deep and expand out. Following this general procedure grounds both the leader and the sharer in the dream itself. Establish a basis of choice with the dream sharer. Of these issues and symbols, what seems most key or central? What do you now most want to work with?

5. *Clarify and develop* further what the person chooses to work with through questions, interactions and mini-processes done during dream session.

6. Out of what has happened, *suggest tasks* to do during the week. Translate the methods outlined in this manual into the specifics of the dream itself. Often, tasks will be combinations or variations of methods, or they may not be directly contained in any of the methods as such. Sometimes ask if anyone else would like to also suggest a task.

7. Check things out by *having the sharer restate the main tasks* and what he or she has gained about the dream so far. This is essential to prevent 'space out' and to make sure that the leader and the sharer are in tune.

8. Allow a *moment of silence* to assimilate energies before going on to the next person.

Other Working Principles for Task Suggestions

— Let things come to you no matter how wild they seem. Then choose whether they are appropriate and consistent with the dream.

— Develop a varied and large repertoire of dreamwork methods and tasks. Go beyond what works well for you to what is exciting for others as well.

— Make tasks specific in terms of the dream itself and in terms of the methods to be used. Give the task as a question but add to it the method for actualizing it, and sometimes the goal of the process.

— Almost always get feedback on each task suggested. Does the task tune in or create resistance or both?

— Three measures as to whether a task is really appropriate are, a burst of enthusiasm, clarity, or resistance. All are valid.

— When you commit yourself to a process technique in dream session, such as a symbol immersion, move ahead and go into it immediately. To retreat creates hesitation and insecurity.

— Generally, do not answer your own questions. You may rephrase your questions to obtain variety and clarity.

— At the end of an interaction, sometimes refocus with a question such as, 'Out of all this, what is the major energy in the dream for you right now?'

— When a person reads a recorded dream quickly, have them slow down and really read it with feeling. You may also need to probe for feelings around different symbols.

— Choose which methods to suggest based on the sharer's dream and their habitual approach to dreamwork. Balance out their developed dispositions by suggesting the opposite. Do they usually refer their dreams directly to the outer? Suggest then also inner world tasks. Do they usually relate immediately to the symbols in their dreams? Suggest also dream ego work, and so on.

— One central goal of task suggesting is to get to the core of a dream. Why essentially did the person have this dream? What is the basic issue in this dream and what is its relevance to this person's life? What new insight or change is trying to break through with this dream? The point is not to tell the person directly what the dream is about, but to help the sharer arrive at the central place through the dream task work. The leader suggests tasks inspired by his or her intuitions, but also tries to design tasks which the person is moved by. The source of the dream tasks may ultimately be as much of a mystery to the leader as to the dream sharer.

— Dream tasks may be suggested by other members of the group, usually in the form of questions. Train participants not to give interpretations, lengthy comments, strong feelings, etc., but to translate these into questions which leave the possibilities for meaning open. Task suggestions can also be written on slips of paper and given to the sharer.

— Usually have the person write down your task suggestions in the journal while you are giving them. They may be otherwise easily forgotten in the heat of the process.

— Use appropriate humour often. This is serious business.

— When as leader you are at a loss as to what to do next, ask the other person for response. 'What would you like to do now? What is going on with you right now? I'm at a loss. How about you?'

— In doing a dream re-entry or symbol immersion, give some indication of the amount of time you would like to take. Symbol immersion is shorter usually. You need to be careful also not to arbitrarily cut things off. Seek a natural point of resolution or transition as the place to stop.

— Do not comment too frequently on people's responses. An appropriate comment is usually brief, gives the essence and shows caring.

— In giving tasks, suggest goals toward which the tasks are focused. Goals often embody a generalized aspect of human experience: relationship, life meaning, suffering, joy, new birth, crises, etc.

— When there is little time, ground what you are doing in some everyday specific thing that the person can work on.

— Be aware as to whether a person is really responding to your questions or not. Check it out.

— Be aware of your issues as leader versus the issues for the dream sharer. Own your own issues and recognize the other person's issues.

— Continually grow in awareness as to how the forces of the unconscious are affecting the whole process.

— Tension developed by contrasting both sides of an issue may be creatively left until resolution occurs naturally, or it may be resolved through choice, either by saying no to one thing and yes to another, or by choosing a third point which unifies the opposites.

— When a person is hesitant to share, accept their hesitation but coax them a little further by asking them why, or how they are feeling, or by pointing out alternatives and the values for sharing. Maintain the relationship with warmth, humour, and insight. Do not baby people. If they did not want to grow, they would not be there.

— Focus on processing the dream more than on processing a person's reactions to the dream. Always focus and refocus on the dream itself.

Sharing Dream Task Experiences

The first part of the dream session is devoted to sharing dream task experiences done during the week. Each person may share. A participant may remind listeners of the essentials of their dream and give the highlights of the dreamwork experience. The leader can then choose any of the following:

— No verbal comment. The work and the presentation stands on its own.

— A brief feeling supportive comment which is nonevaluative. 'It looks like a lot happened for you. I'm sure we've all been through that one ourselves,' and so on. Not 'You did wonderful dreamwork,' etc.

— A brief comment which gives the essence of what the person went through.

— Key questions which emphasize the value of the experience. 'What is the essence for you here? What might be the next step you could take? How does your dreamwork relate to your original dream? What might you do further?'

— Suggest further tasks coming out of the dreamwork.

— Do not take the other person's experience away from them. Not 'How wonderful!' but 'How do you feel about what has happened for you?' Then after the person's response, you may choose to give some of your own feelings, but also owning them. 'That is exciting dreamwork to me. I'm sure we all can learn from it.'

— Question asking may also be used to clarify points in the person's dreamwork presentation.

— Allow silence between presentations. What is shared is often quite moving.

— If someone has not done dreamwork, they can usually be encouraged to share a comment about the dream.

— The significance and change produced by thorough dreamwork is often amazing. The leader at the end of the task sharing may want to comment briefly on the general meaning of what everyone has shared.

The Dream Vision Quest

In the distance the sheer cliff rises up before the point and the earth falls away to black rock extending out into gravitational waters whose incessant beat upon the shore creates the seascape. But the seascape we see today will be changed by tomorrow.

Somewhere out there down the long, curved beach, we will meet again and form our circle to exchange for the day our worldly names for the spirit names which have come to each of us in our solitary walk.

Spirit Quester . . . Trouble Woman . . . Ramonoa . . . Blue Wing on the Wind . . . Ruth . . . Forever Flowing . . . Ocean Son . . . Earth Clinger . . . and many more. The spirit flows and brings us new wealth. Along the shore the waves have left a full debris . . . empty crab shells, some with beautiful purple interiors . . . old shoes . . . driftwood shaped to figure form . . . rounded rocks, rich in natural tones . . . a fishhead . . . seaweed of many colours . . . And so it goes as we walk letting the eye of deeper awareness find what it has long been looking for to give it spirit.

'Today we will be entering mythic time,' the leader says. 'Let the world speak to you here. Leave everything else behind as you have laid aside your other names and taken on your spirit names. Let us see if we can talk about nothing other than what is here and happening right now. There is no past and there is no future. There is only the eternal moment as it lives now.'

The gifts are offered. We place our found objects in harmony with others on a half-burned stump whitened in the incessant sun . . . A ring of flowers . . . the crab shell filled with the tiniest little shells gathered from the ebb-tide line . . . a great bulbous seaweed looking very much like a snake . . . Each gift in its uniqueness creates the whole, the living spirit permeates this day.

The mandala of our group experience has been formed. We have found a sandy place up from the high tide, a natural amphitheatre within which to enact a primary symbol from one of our major dreams. A large tree has fallen perhaps a year ago under the onslaught of the ocean's rise into shore. Its stump stands rich in dirt and its bare limb makes a natural doorway from which to enter. The sky remains cloudy, but the earth is warm and the wind blows gently on this day.

Choose, choose your place now . . . Eleven sticks have been placed on a rock in the centre, each with its number written underneath. The leader chooses last and receives? . . . number one . . . It is entirely appropriate that he inaugurate the mythic dream drama to evoke the life force; 'We now open ourselves to spirit as we let our chosen symbols live through us again.' The rocks click natural sounds in the hands of the participants.

The leader recites his dream in story-telling fashion. How old is this ritual? It must go back thousands of years. It is of the earth — primal, eternal. In the leader's dream two moons ago, he was given the part in a ceremony of lighting the purifying sage. He went into the sacred hut to learn more of what he was to do and found there the god of that sacred place, a face of wood which slowly moved back and forth. And here it is again, the leader now dream spirit in wooden mask, deer skull and branches, uttering earth sounds and moving slowly in place.

At the end the stones begin clacking again. 'Take only what you find in nature and create your spirit sounds.' The clacking of the sounds evokes eternal time. Moments drown in Oneness and number two is called.

What makes this so alive again? Where can I hide? Where, if anywhere, can I be safe from spirit? No, fear melts in spirit sound, in ocean's wave, in wind over sand, in dreamtime, in renewal and transformation. Again we hear a dreamworld, of crystals embedded in rock which turn to ordinary glass, and we receive new gifts of crystals and journey . . . We laugh with dream enactments of being given a book on what causes smoking, and the feeling spirit figure acting out the compulsion behind the smoking . . . We are frightened by the may-be-poisonous snake found and captured in the supermarket . . . We are scared and laugh at the dreaded lematur who wants to attack nude hot-springs bathers . . . One spirit actor fights his dream monster embodied as the fallen tree roots full of dirt . . . We hear stories of dream re-entries which have transformed nightmares. Each spirit person in turn enacts the drama. It is all our dream now. We clack our rocks at the end of each enactment to integrate the energies evoked.

After completion, we form our circle, sit and share, eating what's left of our lunch food. We have been moved and made joyful by the time together. Fear has vanished into the melting force of sacred time. Intense energy, fun energy, develops for each person's process. It is over. The circle is formed and we let go our spirit names and take on our everyday names again for the walk up the beach and home again to the city.

'I am Strephon. I give back to the sources my spirit name of Spirit Quester, yet I keep it with me also.' 'Janice, Melody, Bob, Henry, Sarah . . .' And so it goes. 'I take with me the spirit óf this place, a new sense of life and joy in symbols. I leave behind what I cannot cling to.'

An occasional person has gone by. One time, also, a dog came close when a dream dog was being enacted. We must seem curious to them, adorned, as we are, in our dreams and symbols. But we are secure enough not to worry. Our gifts in the spirit circle are left behind. Ocean and element are greater than we are. We walk in newness. We walk home in beauty.

PART III
Reflections

Types of Dreams

Including Our Totality

All dreams are meaningful and part of one's totality.

The dreamworld is not embarrassed by our having sex, killing someone, or defecating in public. So why should we feel embarrassed?

We are all human. We are a totality. The dream reveals all. Dreams reveal all sides of ourselves. When we remember all dreams, when we work with all our dreams, when we share all our dreams, as in the dreamwork group, we are acknowledging what the dreamworld acknowledges, our totality and our potential wholeness.

People will often reveal more of themselves through sharing dreams than they would through any other forms of personal contact.

We talk to hear ourselves. We share to accept ourselves.

In a lifetime, most people experience many different types of dreams. In doing dreamwork it is not even necessary to classify your dreams. Yet doing so can help us to keep a holistic perspective. Do I share my skunk dreams as well as my great dreams? Do I share all of my dream or only part of it?

One question which sometimes arises is, 'When I dream that someone is going to die, how do I know whether I have a psychic or predictive dream, or only an anxiety dream?

261

Can we ever tell absolutely? The approach used here emphasizes working with dream content no matter what type it is.

To get clearer on your psychic ability, process your own dreams regularly. When you get clearer on yourself, what your psyche and dreamworld is like, you will be decontaminating whatever psychic ability you do have.

The most common confusion is that between projecting inner content out into the environment and genuinely intuiting a future possibility.

Dreamwork actually seems to help the development of psychic ability by making us more in tune with symbolic and intuitive processes.

What is a Dream?

— A dream is a manifestation of images and sometimes sounds which show common and uncommon interrelations.
— A dream is a mirror reflecting some aspect of life or the unconscious.
— A dream is a call to living life more fully than can be lived just at the conscious level.
— A dream is the creation of night.

In dreams we are always on stage and so usually dreams, like story and drama, have a beginning, a middle and an end. The *beginning* sets the stage of character and situation and often has an image of the dreamer present. The *middle* typically contains some complication, conflict or new development which creates a tension with what occurred at the beginning. Often the dreamer's dream image is itself a central focus of this conflict or tension as it interacts with a challenging 'other'. Then there is the *end* or *resolution* in the dream in which the conflict or complication is terminated by the dream's images moving to various states of completion or at least balance. The final state is of course the *waking* state in which the dream is brought into consciousness by the skilled art of creative dreamwork.

Dream Types

There are many types of dreams that come to one in the night. There are *nightmares*, or extreme *anxiety dreams* in which what one does not face consciously will come up in full force unconsciously and create fear, or perceived danger of annihilation. The task with nighmares is to evoke healing symbols and guides and to deal with the dream situations and bring them to resolution instead of waking up. The other task is, of course, to deal with outer anxiety producing situations. *Anxiety is fear without an object.* To deal with anxiety find real objects for all your fears and use such concrete fears as motivation to change the destructive into the constructive.

Great dreams are those dreams which reflect upon major experiences of our lives and which are full of the essentially spiritual symbolism of the central Self. They leave us in awe at their meaning and provide us with healing directions in life.

The *ordinary dream* is the everyday kind of dream loaded with inner and outer life issues, sometimes presented in a humorous manner by the dream spirits such as this image of an endless pile of wood which needs stacking.

The *skunk dream* is often a *shadow,* or repressed side, dream in which we do something bizarre or messy that we would not do in public outer life. It shocks us with our own hidden messiness or instinctuality, like this image of going to the toilet on the living room table.

Confirming dreams are dreams in which the dream mirrors significantly a new step we have taken in our lives. One person new to the dream group dreamed of leaving a shabby house and finding a dream journal and working in it. The dream spirits liked her decision to learn dreamwork!

Predictive dreams are those dreams which either portray future events or help cause them to happen. We do not know which or if both dynamics happen together. I have had relationship dreams in which the coming together happened first in a dream. Another person dreamed of her room being invaded by angry people and it happened that week.

Prospective dreams, on the other hand, are future orientated but they only portray potentials and alternatives for action.

Psychic dreams involve spontaneous perceptions across time and space which could not be based on outer knowledge. Recently one of the people I work with dreamed two different dreams about my intimate life. I acknowledged their truth as part of the process. Psychic experiences are perfectly natural in dreamwork and developing one's intuitive abilities is one of the benefits of the Jungian-Senoi experience.

Lucid dreams describe the dream state in which the dream ego experiences itself as exerting will power and free choice. Or the dreamer realizes he or she is dreaming, such as observing 'a dream within a dream.' Such states usually symbolize either the need for, or the development of, consciousness. These dream states may also be closer to the central archetype of the Self because of their vividness. Anyone can say they had a lucid dream since no one else is there to observe. Certainly certain dreams are more intensive or vivid than others. And how can we know, really, whether we are in control or truly intentional about anything in this life?

Waking dreams are outer life experiences which are viewed and worked with also as symbolic, or non-literal, experiences. No accidents are accidental. Anything which happens in the outer can have as much significance to our symbolic life as any dream. This seems to apply especially to accidents, synchronistic events, fateful interventions such as rape, bouts of anger, violence, theft or inheritances and other events of positive fortune. We can apply dreamwork methods to any life event to bring out its symbolic values. Dreamwork thus prepares us for a whole new level of consciousness, the symbolic perceptive-interactive level, in dealing with outer reality.

The Functions of Dreams

The Self — Where the Dream Originates

Dreams may not simply be experiences in themselves but hold the potential for meaning because dreams may be *reactions* to the consciousness of the dreamer and to the unconscious dynamics inside the dreamer's psyche. But who or what reacts? If dreams are not simply the unconscious dynamics of the psyche but reactions to them, then what is the origin of this reactive, functional nature of the dreams?

Again it would seem that the *reactor* is the Self, the central integrative factor within the psyche and possibly within life itself.

The Self presents the dream.

The Self works to integrate and transform the dynamics within that have been evoked by how we have been living or not living our lives.

It is the Self that presents the problems of the psyche in some healing context and asks for help from the conscious, or ego-directed, side of the personality.

It is the Self that questions and challenges our awareness, attitudes and choices by presenting other more healing possibilities to our consciousness. It does this through the dream, the dream that shocks, amazes and delights us with possibility.

When we ask, 'What happened yesterday or what is happening now in your life that you would have such a dream?' we are assuming that the Self has

reviewed your recent past, seen the problems in your choices, and presented to you through the dream the way things really are rather than the way you might want them to be.

But we could also ask, 'What needs to happen in your future that you would have such a dream?'

Are we not saying then with this question that the Self not only reviews our past and our present but also intervenes in terms of our future?

The Self knows the potentials, inner and outer, of what is yet still to happen and *desires* that the dreamer choose actively the meaningful potentials rather than avoid or resist them because of personal non-Self-directed attitudes.

What is the evidence that such a destiny source exists? Working with dreams. It is an inevitable experience in looking over a past year's series of dreams to find elements that speak profoundly to where we have come to at the present time, but of which we were unaware and not fully capable of knowing at the original time we had the dream.

The following are the primary functions that dreams seem to manifest. More than one function can be happening in a single dream.

The Compensatory Function

This function is what Jung most emphasized. He postulated that consciousness is one-sided, that the way we see and evaluate things is almost always partial and does not include the whole. Therefore the Self, which sees the whole, compensates consciousness by presenting the other side. If I have a positive self image that I am 'kindly' and 'considerate' the Self will present dreams which show me as 'fighting' and 'greedy'. If I am split and full of psychic wounds the Self will present healing dreams. When faced with a compensatory dream the first response is, 'That is not me. This dream makes no sense.' But the creative dreamwork response is to ask, 'How is what the dream is presenting part of myself which I do not want to face? And what choices can I make to integrate these parts into my psyche, my life and my consciousness?'

The Augmenting or High-lighting Function

Dreams may present us as we really are and think we are but perhaps have not come to terms with enough in ourselves. If I have an exaggerated image of myself I may find myself flying or lifting up a car in a dream. I do think I'm better and bigger than is justified by reality and the Self highlights this image for me so I can see it clearly and choose whether to come down to earth again or remain exaggerated. The dreamer can ask the question, 'How am I being inflated and what do I need to do to ground myself?

This same type of dream can have a compensatory aspect also, since all inflation seems to be compensatory to feelings and states of inferiority. Inflation is identifying with an exaggerated image of oneself that is not consistent with reality. Thus the dreamer can also ask, 'What inadequacy am I caught in that might be causing this exaggerated picture of myself? And how can I deal with it?'

The augmenting function of dreams may also serve to highlight abilities or positive personality qualities which we are not yet living to our fullest capacity. One example might be when in a dream we find ourselves speaking before a large audience to show we have the capacity for asserting our creativity in public. This could also be seen as compensatory if the person does not in fact see him or herself as capable of speaking before an audience or asserting to that degree.

The Reflecting Function

This is when a dream, or part of a dream, reflects a personality aspect or a situation almost exactly as it is. At one level it could be showing that we are perceiving ourselves and outer reality as it really is, that we are in fact in tune. Or it may help us get in tune and accept things as they really are. It would be simplistic to consider that someone whose dreams basically duplicate non-dream reality is really clear and realized consciously. But anything is possible.

There is the issue as to what is the relation of the dream functions to beginning versus advanced states of dreamwork and personal development? I am more interested in the many who are actively working to realize themselves than in a perfectly realized being, which species I have never met.

The Prospective Function

The prospective function, a function described by Jung, occurs in dreams which are future-oriented. In such a dream the creative or destructive alternatives for action in the future are more or less clearly presented so that the dreamer has understanding of the in depth choices available. Such a dream could also be considered compensatory in that a different state from the present state is sometimes being presented. But not all prospective dreams compensate since many show a continuation or developmental process which organically flows out of the present. The dreamworker with a prospective dream is asked not to just live in the moment — and certainly not to live in the past — but to catch up with him or herself by making choices in the present which have as their goal a definite manifestation of certain values in the future. It is only when we encompass the future that our present life direction takes on the quality of destiny.

The Confirming Function

Upon occasion when a dreamworker has really been in tune with the integrative factor of the Self, and has been making choices which acknowledge the opposites, then the Self will present a dream which confirms the choices and the meanings involved. In this sense the least healed and the most healed have profound healing dreams. One dream is compensatory and the other is confirming. The trick is to know the difference. For it is all too easy for a sufferer to identify with a healing dream and assume that the dream is saying one is more healed or together than one really is. It is far easier to identify with a content that it is to do the hard work required to differentiate and relate to that content.

When given what may be a confirming dream the dreamworker needs to check out first whether it may really be compensatory. 'Have the choices demonstrated in the dream already been made in outer life?' And so on.

Why even would the Self 'choose' to confirm an action as a person's life? Perhaps the mystery is that when we respond there is a response from the other side. Often choices, especially choices full of depth and pain, are extremely difficult to make. If the choice is the right, the destiny choice, then confirmation of this choice strengthens it. And this is the substance of the visionary approach to life. Being confirmed in one's essential actions by a healing power outside our conscious control certainly is close to an ultimate experience. And it is the visionary which escalates the passion for life within ourselves.

The Transformative Function

Transformation is when one thing changes into another to produce resolution. In one person's dreams a difficult, unresolved love relationship was pictured as a dance with roses. Something that was split within the psyche was being transformed and brought to resolution in the circle dance of the mystic rose. The transformative function may be one of the most powerful functions manifesting in a dream state and certainly seems to be evidence that a healing source exists. But then what we do with such a dream is still our choice and our responsibility.

The Synchronistic Function

Synchronicity, as described by Jung, is when events coincide relatively within the same period and cluster around a central dynamic or value which gives meaning to the whole. It is not simply events occurring at the same time that creates synchronicity but events occurring in simultaneous relation to each other to produce meaning. A whole is created by a convergence of all the parts to create a centre which is the meaning. In this sense there is the potential for synchronicity in each moment but it seems to occur, or to be recognized as such, only when we need a terrific shove towards consciousness (compensatory) or when we are so conscious and in tune with things as they really are that synchronicity is created in response to our devotion and our choices (confirming).

Synchronicity is also not extraordinary coincidence in itself. Synchronicity is present when the extraordinary coincidence is experienced within a larger context of meaning, both in terms of a person's own life journey and in terms of universal life principles. For synchronicity to be present in a coincidental setting consciousness must also be present. Synchronicity is not the perception of an extraordinary coincidence in the moment. It is when the coincidence in the moment is also experienced within the total context of one's life, past, present and future.

Meaning can be found wherever consciousness is lent to the experience. This is different from simply projecting, or reading meaning into any situation. For using my consciousness to evoke the essence of a situation is also an objective act in which something meaningful happens which could not happen unless my consciousness, my awareness and willingness to act for value, is present. And even for those who are unaware or who avoid synchronicity, when it happens the potential for consciousness is also present, although the act of becoming conscious always remains a free choice.

In a very real sense the dream is 'inner synchronicity'. At other times, as in an accident, the outer events are synchronistic and may therefore be objectified and worked with as with dreams.

But sometimes, and perhaps often if we were more aware, there is a 'spill over' in which the dream permeates the outer life as well as the inner life. This is the synchronistic function of dreams, or when a coincidental unity of inner and outer states and events is created which evokes awe and meaning. We had better be 'with it' at such times or all hell can break loose. For sometimes the weak and simple ego becomes frightened and wants to retreat in the face of such an experience. The challenge is to push on and join the larger picture and find increased life. To retreat when the synchronistic function is at work is to create disasters, little and big. It happens all too often that individuals working for consciousness reach a state in which they know the truth but refuse to actualize it, give in to their fears, and otherwise regress. This syndrome reaches a crisis point which coincides with when the synchronistic function is most active. Retreat at such times — and which is always possible because of a person's absolute power of free choice — may cause reactive events such as accidents, loss of personal property and friendships and a host of emotional and physical ills.

In order to deal with such circumstances when they arise, dreamwork skills and commitments are invaluable. For then one approaches one's accidents, illnesses and losses with the same questions and tasks with which one approaches dreams.

Why am I refusing to accept that I needed to have this accident? How am I allowing myself to be stolen from and attacked in my inner life as well as in my outer life?' And so on.

No accidents are accidental. How do we know this? Only when we approach life in this way can we understand the truth of this statement. Only those who experimentally postulate meaning into any situation can participate in, or evoke, meaning. Rigidified doubt is the greatest turn-off to new possibility.

The phenomenon of synchronicity demonstrates that the centre, or the Self, is not simply within the psyche, the inner life of the individual, but within the situation, the outer life of the individual, as well.

For Your Journal

Describe factually in a page the most terrible accident or life event you have had. Then approach it as a dream and work with it. What were the factors which led up to the event? Why did you need to have this event? What part does it play in your personal mythos, your symbolic life journey? Dialogue with the accident or event itself and ask it why it happened for you in your life. Then evaluate and reconcile yourself to the event for the meaning involved. What life teaching could you have learned in no other way? Do not assume that you will be able to completely answer these questions now. Perhaps only by the end of your life will things have become most clear.

Other ways of categorizing: Dreams can be differentiated by symbols. We might have House Dreams, Sexual Dreams, Out of Body Dreams, Body Awareness Dreams, True to Reality Dreams, Transcendent Dreams, Colour Dreams, Dialogue Dreams, Relationship Dreams, Anger Dreams, and so on. We are collecting dreams at the Institute in various categories for future books involving transforming relationships and transforming anger. We would like to be able to say someday that, to use one example, whenever you have an anger dream this is what you can do with it and these are the possible results you might evoke.

As part of the consciousness process we need our categorizing aptitude. But let such categories be functional and therefore applicable to reality. And let all categories never be taken for truth, but only be indicative of principles, if principles there are?, underlying reality.

A Basic Issue — Can Dreams Be Categorized?

Can dreams be differentiated into definite categories according to their inherent mutually exclusive characteristics?

Or is it the waking ego of the scholar and populariser which imposes categories onto purely symbolic experience not really subject to outside definitions?

And does categorizing dreams serve a functional purpose of helping people work with and apply certain methods to dreams?

An original remembered dream is a symbolic experience, and as such it is so easy to put outside attitudes and contents onto it.

A dream may be a mirror which we look into and see there our reflected, known self. Yet through dreamwork we can look into the dream as mirror and see also reflected our unknown selves.

The message is clear. If you want to discover new material about yourself set aside your categories, even your useful ones, and look at the dream as fresh, original experience.

The meaning of a dream does not depend on your category you give it, but on what you do to re-experience it.

An essential principle is that:

— *No dream is one type of dream or functions in only one way.*

It is the waking ego which categorizes and tends to narrow down, through interpretation, any experience into being only one thing.

The Symbol

What is a symbol?

Is not everything we perceive or engage in a symbol for something else?

How can we work with dreams, a primary symbol-manifesting experience, to get clearer on how our whole reality is symbolic?

What is a book? Yes, a bound number of pages which may convey information through the writings within. But what is a book really? What does it mean when a book appears in a dream? What does the fact that you are working with this book symbolize?

— That you are in need of direction and a higher consciousness?
— That dreamwork is to be a part of your essential being and life?

We ask again, what is a symbol?

— A cluster of images and energy?
— An image which represents something else?
— A manifestation of an archetype?
— An image rather than a concept?
— Anything which has hidden meaning?
— A question in image form?
— An abstraction of some overt reality?

Obviously, the defining of a symbol is a difficult art. Perhaps we can never completely define that which we can never really know. A symbol is the unknowable. We can never capture it within our consciousness. But we can work with symbols to gain meaning. This is our workable goal.

What our own positions are on the nature of symbols, and the archetypes which underlie them, may be crucial, may even be the difference between life and death. How many suicides, broken relationships and accidents have come about because a person remained unconsciously identified with a certain symbol?

Analysts and therapists, the 'symbol workers', have the power to affect a

person's life direction. I work with people who have been in traditional Jungian analysis and whose lives have been narrowed down because of the analyst's symbol system. Years later they come alive and break through their semi-frozen complexes. Where have all the lost years gone meanwhile? Was the former analyst's symbol system partly responsible?

These sections on symbols and archetypes may not be as inspiring as working directly with the unconscious, but they are necessary. It is essential that you learn how to objectify rather than put your own associations onto situations.

The ego is lazy and a natural ecstatic. It does not usually like to think. It knows little about the subtle ecstacy of truly thinking. Rationalizing is far different from true thinking. Thinking takes us to the core. Rationalizing keeps us abstracted and at the surface of things.

In working with symbols in dreams the following questions can be relevant. Do not, of course, expect to answer many of these questions. Let them float in your memory in order to expand your consciousness.

— Is a thing in itself knowable?
— Not only 'what is a symbol?' but how does a symbol function?
— How much do we create what is manifested and how much is it there in itself?
— What is an archetype other than an inference?
— Why do we need symbols to manifest archetypes?
— What is a symbol in a dream? Is there a reality behind the dream manifesting it? How can we tell?'
— What is the difference between archetypal energy and a symbol?
— What are the ways archetypes manifest themselves?
— Are symbols simply projections of inner content onto outer reality?
— Is a dream a projection?
— Is there something there in itself? Is there a hook for projections?
— How can we tell the real from what we project onto it?
— What happens when we put dream actions and images into various artistic forms such as painting and movement?
— Do symbols function in themselves or do they function because of their context? Or both?
— What are the natural boundaries of a symbol as it functions in context with other symbols?
— Does a symbol in a dream represent underlying psychological characteristics of personality? How can we know this if it is true?

What do you perceive as important questions that can be added to these?

We are dealing here with many of the issues underlying the interpretive approach to dreams, which has been the dominant approach in most cultures, ancient and modern.

Is there a place for interpretation? Can we really say, either for ourselves, or for others, that this symbol means this and have it lead to meaning?

Are not the intepreters simply, no matter how disguised in rationality, projecting their own symbol systems onto the material and not seeing the thing in itself?

Why do we even need to categorize phenomena? When we do are we imposing an organization onto the phenomena or discovering its inherent organization? If we are always given the manifestation can we ever get to the essence?

The response is, certainly, that we need to organize our reality in order not to be continually overwhelmed by its multiplicity. And we need to perceive reality more and more as it really is in order to become in tune with it.

Everyone creates symbol systems to organize reality and approach its essence. Zen koans and Sufi stories are not the truth. They are symbol systems. Christianity and Jungian psychology are not the truth. They are symbol systems. Yet what are the various truths of the different symbol systems? How closely does each reflect core reality? How do we know when and if this happens?

The Archetypal Base for Symbol

A working definition of symbol might be stated thus: A *symbol* is an image or cluster of images which evoke feelings, intuitions and concepts. The image or images themselves have an archetypal base. That is, the symbol is itself a manifestation of one or more primary archetypes. *Archetypes* can be defined as the innate essences of existence. At their most basic level they have *form* and *energy* which together manifest as *functionality*.

Symbols can be differentiated from signs. *Symbols* expand the possibilities for meaning, or relatedness, while *signs* limit or contract to one single meaning. The stop sign as a traffic regulator is a sign with a specific meaning. A stop sign appearing in your dream in your mother's bedroom has reverberations for many possible meanings.

The Seven Basic Archetypes Unified Field Theory

In formulating the archetypal unified field theory I went into profound meditation at a monastery for a solid week to get clearer on the possible nature of the archetypes and how they interrelate. Out of this experience there developed a model, a mirror for reflecting the archetypes and their interrelationships.

Certainly Jung rediscovered archetypes but he did not construct a cohesive, unified theory.

Nevertheless, having a model is useful for seeing how things *may* operate. All models are based on inference and their usefulness lies in providing a context within which to process raw experience. Certainly anyone dealing with dreams is faced with hundreds of thousands of symbols. What is to be done?

A *model*, to be usable, must show the differential uniqueness of primary entities, show their laws of interrelatedness, include the whole phenomenological field and be simple in its design. A model should also provide applicability to everyday life.

The unified field theory of the archetypes presented here is not the full description of the model but only enough to give the essentials. The full theory is still in manuscript form.

We have, of course, some major issues regarding the nature of archetypes. How do we know archetypes exist?

Are not archetypes direct inferences from manifesting symbols?

Yes, by definition archetypes are in the *collective unconscious* which is unconscious and can only be discovered indirectly.

Yet we may gain a certainty about archetypes existing through experiencing them in numinous experiences and events. There is no way in the world that the archetype of unity experienced in sexual ecstasy can be considered a willed or only physical entity. Dream and dreamwork experiences as well as certain ritual and meditative experiences may be felt as deeply moving and meaningful. Trance states may be direct experiences of the archetypes. All these experiences are different substantially from just experiencing symbols, although symbols are themselves loaded with the energies of archetypes. It is as if we are able to break through the symbol from time to time directly to the archetype which underlies it. Seeing sexual intercourse can be powerful but it is not the same as experiencing it. When we observe we are experiencing reality symbolically. When we participate we experience reality directly. Each has a particular but different hold on us.

Some would maintain that they can experience the archetypes through a leap of faith to 'God exists' or 'Buddha exists' or 'think positive' and so on. This may be illusionary but brings up the question, 'What is it that can only be known by starting with the assumption that whatever it is exists?' God cannot be known to those who doubt God. And can we live meaningfully if we do not first postulate that there is inherent meaning in all life?

The third way to gain experience of the archetypes is through a philosophic or thinking process. In this dreamwork manual you will find the unconscious process techniques for directly experiencing symbols and archetypes with their full numinosity. But you will also find the more consciously oriented techniques which can draw out the archetypes by good thinking. The unified field theory model is based on the assumption that the thinking process is a useful tool for gaining access to the nature of underlying reality, the archetypes.

We have through all this also the intriguing question. 'Do we have to impose a system onto the unconscious? Or can we discover the unconscious inherent qualities and principles? Can we discover a core or third reality which underlies inner and outer?'

The answer to this question remains paradoxical. For myself I move on the assumption that the core reality is somewhat knowable, both through thinking and through experiencing it directly. I use the model as a system for processing unconscious material from myself and others. And to the degree this creates meaning for me, to that degree I feel confirmed in what I am doing. I also experience confirmation through synchronistic events occurring in the outer.

And now for the archetypal model (page 276). First we see what the model describes in itself and then how it supports working with symbols.

The Seven Basic Archetypes Unified Field Theory Model

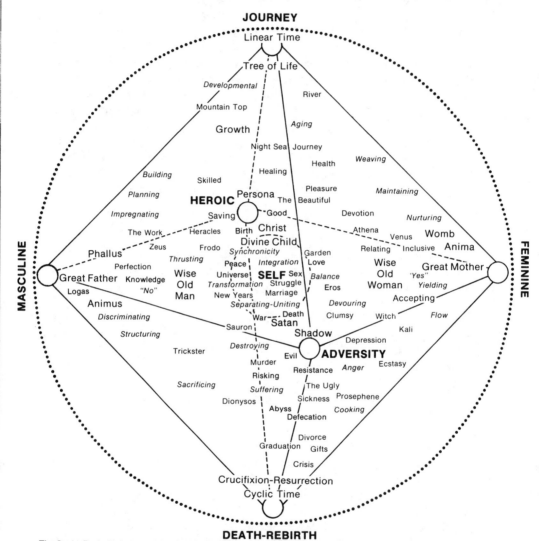

The Seven Basic Archetypes Unified Field Model. The model shows the relationships of the archetypes to each other, and how they manifest as secondary archetypes and functions. Each of the Seven Basic Archetypes has an inherent set of characteristics, or essences, and each stands in a relation of opposition or reciprocity to each other. The Self stands at the center, equidistant from the other six primary archetypes, illustrating how it is the unifying, separating, transforming point for the other archetypes. These secondary archetypes (e.g., wise old woman, great father, trickster, Christ and functions) are here placed between the primary archetypes from which they gain their characteristics. With this model it is possible to see how archetypes, or energy centers of unique character, underlie the major images and characteristics of the psyche and of life. The crystal is itself the universal symbol for total and balanced interrelatedness.

The Archetypes and How They Operate

At the base of all existence are energy clusters of *archetypes* of innate character, energy and function. The most primary of these may be arranged in a crystal, with the Self, the central archetype, at the centre. Surrounding the Self in pairs of opposites are the other primary or basic archetypes of the Feminine, the Masculine, the Adversary, the Heroic, Death-Rebirth and the Journey.

An archetype is an innate pattern within the psyche and within all life. We see the archetypes play themselves out, mostly automatically in our lives. In wars and conflicts there is an enemy and a victor. Male and female embody opposites to each other. People go through a developmental journey process all their lives yet also fall into crises, death-rebirths, and new directions. And at times of real clarity and growth we choose to integrate and transform our lives, as is the nature of the Self.

All great myths and stories are about the archetypes and how they function. We experience archetypes in movies and novels. We experience them also in our own lives in conflicts, love and religious experiences, in fact, in all the experiences of our lives.

An archetype manifests in the following sequence starting at the most primal level:

— The archetype in itself as original *matrix*, or imprinter, and its *energy* which functions in certain characteristic ways.

— Next the archetype manifests as symbol, or images with numinosity or diffuse energy. Naked bodies of young men and women 'glow' when idealized with life force and their respective archetypes. Mandalas, or sacred circles such as the rose windows of Christian cathedrals, 'glow' with symbol energy. This is the level of *Secondary Archetypes* which manifest from the primary archetypes.

— Then we have the archetype still manifesting as symbol, as image, but also functioning as *feeling and emotion*. This is the level of the *complexes,* of semi-autonomous personalities in the personal unconscious. The anima as complex is not only the image of the feminine for the man but it functions to excite and inspire his life. *Feelings* are momentary energy reactions, either positive or negative, which motivate actions. ''I like you so I will do this for you.'' *Emotions* are sustained feeling states of long duration not easily within conscious control. These include grief, falling in love, enthusiasm, passion, ecstasy, depression, inflation and anger.

— The final major level of archetypal manifestation resides at the most conscious level of *feeling-emotion* and *concept*. I am not only angry. I know why I am angry and I know what I think about it and I know what it means.

The Seven Basic Archetypes Described

The Self

'Transforming into new being by separating and integrating the opposites which underlie existence.' — S.K.W.

The Self is the separative, integrative; transformative centre within the psyche from which dreams, visions and other inspirations originate. At its centre are the light and the dark, the primary opposites of the universe. The *individuation* process, or evolving individual destiny, originates here. The *opus*, the wholeness process, the work of one's life, is to continually live from this centre so that much or even most of one's totality becomes separated, integrated and transformed. *Transformation* is total revolution in the psyche, is the creation of a new third, evolving point out of the separation and unifying of opposites. It is the essence, perhaps, of most personal spiritual experience.

The Self shows itself symbolically as the *coniunctio,* or divine union, the philosopher's stone of alchemy, the symbolic child, the uroborous or snake eating its tail, the butterfly, the stove, the ring, androgeny and certain other symbols.

Besides dreams and visions the Self manifests especially in life experiences of *synchronicity,* or meaningful coincidence, sexual and spiritual ecstasy, and moments of absolute clarity and action for consciousness.

Its sacred objects and events include the mandala, the temple, the treasure, the book, gifts, the bridge, the star, seeds and eggs, the lit candle, the rainbow, the lotus, Christmas, weddings and births.

The Feminine

'Dwelling within by being perpetually open to all aspects of life and death'. — S.K.W.

The all-inclusive quality of the Feminine creates relationship and acceptance. It says 'yes' to things. It creates also the cave, the womb from which life flows and the tomb to which life returns.

In the woman the Feminine expresses the dominant qualities of her soul. This is a feminine somehow different from man's own feminine, or anima, which is to him an opposite, rather than his own true nature. In both, the in-dwelling of the Feminine rests in substance, in matter itself.

The Feminine is vessel, cave, womb, queen, princess, the goddesses of love and fertility, the well, lake, night, bed, throne, beauty, spider and the like.

In life the Feminine operates to create relationship, flow, beauty and birth. It can also destroy through devouring and formlessness. It nurtures as well as suffocates and is seemingly irrational or without logic. It is mystery. Its festivals celebrate fertility, the erotic, family and divination.

Its sacred objects include the vessel, the gate or the doorway, the scabbard, the throne, the moon, the tapestry and the veil.

The Masculine

'Knowing the goal and doing what is necessary to achieve it'. — C.G. Jung

The Masculine structures, it says 'no' where needed. It thrusts, it penetrates, asserts itself, gets the job done. It is decisive and discriminating and tends towards the rational and perfection.

For the man the Masculine expresses his dominant force or soul, his being out of which he habitually acts and accomplishes. For the woman her decisiveness and discrimination are expressed through her animus, her own form of the Masculine which is coloured differently from that of a man's. In both sexes it is the realm of the spirit, of ideas and values.

Symbols of the Masculine include sword, King, Unicorn, phallus, sun, and the sacred manifests in sceptre, tool, tower and sword.

In life the Masculine shows itself in fathering, making, directing, organizing and building of structures. It initiates and rules the day. It propagates the new life without itself manifesting it.

Its rites are for the creation of power and cohesiveness, for 'firming up', planning and accomplishing goals.

The Heroic

'Achieving mastery by bringing resolution to the chaotic and split'. — S.K.W.

The hero or heroine always faces the difficult and even the insurmountable, the Adversary itself. In the great myths and stories it often conquers, at least temporarily. The heroic functions to achieve victory and healing, to bring resolution to that which is in conflict and chaos. Its energy is positive or outgoing. It surges with nobility, truth and goodness.

Its symbols are youth, triumphal marches, the garland, the spoils, the great heart, the shield, the battle, the message, the hospital and the healing balm.

In life the heroic manifests in battle, struggle, saviour religions and all the general's, the entrepreneur's and the physician's tasks. It saves and embodies the upright life. Its festivals are the victory celebration and the return to healthy life. Great teachers and explorers create new knowledge from its energies.

The Adversary

'That which limits and destroys all things, and is reality itself'. — S.K.W.

Perhaps nothing that exists can exist the same. 'All is change' as the ancient

Greek, Heraclitis, once said. And the agent of change is that which would limit, wound and destroy what has been built up and what is. The Adversary regresses everything. It comes in with the unexpected and ends things. It is death itself.

Some of the most intriguing symbols are in its realm. Monster, witch, tyrant, wizard, demon, psychopath, devil, fool, gangster, the trickster, the murderers, the Grim Reaper. Its sacred objects include the wall, the abyss, the cauldron of magic and the hangman's knot.

Its life experiences include suffering, dying and death. It produces wars, crises, exterminations and defeats. It upsets the human condition with anger, moroseness and murder.

It is celebrated in secret rites of darkest mystery. Its evil remains undefeated forever.

Death-Rebirth

'Crisis and revolution, the transition in which one thing becomes another.' — S.K.W.

Time itself comes back on itself in cycles which continue throughout existence. We return to where we started and know the place for the first time, to use the words of T.S. Eliot. The progression through life is not always steady. The ups and downs mean divorce as well as marriage, the ending of one thing before the beginning of another. The meeting of cyclic (Death-Rebirth) and linear (Journey) time may be described as 'the place where time stands still.' Such events mark the moments of great transition.

Out of crisis and change comes marriage and all the rites of sacrifice and new life.

In Death-Rebirth we celebrate New Year's, Solstice and Equinox. We celebrate in rites of initiation, transition and graduation. The sacred objects of such times are the altar, the clock, poetry, dance, new plant life and prayer.

The Journey

'The way and steadily evolving direction forward.' — S.K.W.

Inherent within the dynamics of all life is a continual movement forward. Inexorably all things, from galaxies to organisms, seem to be in continual direction forward, as secular linear (Journey) time is forever forward. We describe this both as a development and as a diminishing or ageing process. Thus within linear time as it manifests is also the rising and decline of Death-Rebirth.

Birthdays and anniversaries celebrate the intersections of these linear (historical) and cyclic (sacred) times. Each stage of the Journey is built upon what went before, but always the direction is towards the future, except when the regressive pull of the Adversary takes over.

Sacred objects and symbols of the Journey manifest as the Tree of Life, as the winding road, the ascent up the mountain, the staff, vehicles, guides and as rivers and streams.

We celebrate the Journey in vacations, pilgrimages and the Quest.

The Great Dreams of C.G. Jung

'A dream is a little hidden door in the innermost and most secret recesses of the soul, opening into that cosmic night which was psyche long before there was any ego-consciousness, and which will remain psyche no matter how far our ego-consciousness extends.'

So wrote Jung in his book *Civilization and Modern Man* (CW-10). What kind of spirit or consciousness could produce such utterly moving words about dreams? I do not say what kind of person, for our focus is on the *dream* and the *consciousness* to which several immensely creative and destined dreams came. And I do not speak of 'person' here for we shall not be using Jung's published dreams to conjecturally analyze his personality. He is far beyond analysis now and it would be an indiscretion to try and go into what Jung was like as a person by studying his dreams.

Diagnosis or analysis is not the focus here. Consciousness is. What universal dynamics are reflected in some of Jung's great dreams? And how, through a study of them, may we also relate to these same dynamics as they are manifesting within our own dreams and consciousness?

We can, it is my hope, focus on the nature of great dreams, destiny dreams if you will, by relating to the images from the unconscious as they appeared in the sleep of one of this century's most profound psychologists. Another purpose in keeping our focus on the more universal, archetypal aspects of Jung's dreams is to counter the tendency in many of us to whom Jungian psychology is important to project the Self onto Jung. Thus any tendencies to analyze Jung is a passive manifestation of transference. We shall then enjoy dealing with such projections by shifting the focus from a Self projection personified by Jung to Self symbols as expressed in the dreams themselves.

It is fair to consider Jung a gifted and committed man who lived his journey both personally and professionally. Certainly his great dreams reflect who he was. But in the lives of many individuals striving to become conscious dreams of depth can come.

What does not always happen, however, is the individual's passionate and honest devotion to responding fully and consciously to the dream. In the quote above, Jung mentions 'ego-consciousness' which I would consider the creative or uncreative response a person can make to living his or her dreams.

This matter of ego is in my view of tremendous value and Jung writes of the religious function of the ego in his '*Transformation Symbolism and the Mass.*' Ego, as I define it, is the choice-making function within the psyche. It is also the focus of awareness-making and *Consciousness*, 'awareness plus appropriate response.'

A spiritual or *transpersonal* ego is an ego which has committed its choices to following the Self, or the destiny centre and source of meaning within the personality. A spiritually committed ego may also choose to actualize values which originate in the situation, or outside the personality itself.

When we look at a series of dreams from anyone, what do we notice is the most repeated symbol?

Universally the *dream ego*, the image of oneself, is in almost every dream. This is also why I have tried to make clear this matter of ego as we go on to take a look at the archetypes as they manifested themselves in Jung's dreams.

We are interested in archetypes but we are also interested in consciousness. Consciousness is not simply awareness but an awareness which is integrative and serves a larger whole of realizing the full personality in an *individuation* process. We need, certainly, a developing consciousness in order to respond meaningfully to the archetypes without feeling overwhelmed by them.

My own approach to working with dreams emphasizes dreams as a primary source for working towards wholeness and realizing life's meaning. But, in our view the dream initially is often not enough. Having the right dream does not mean the work is now done. It usually means the work has only begun.

Thus we have found in our thousands of hours of working with dreams that dreamwork is as important as the original dream experience. This is why we contrast *actualization*, the re-experiencing of the dream, with *interpretation*, the rationalizing of symbols. To implement the actualization approach we have further developed over thirty major dreamwork techniques as described in our dreamwork manual.

Jung's comments on his dreams are conveyed as interpretive statements which, along with active imagination, was his method. But I have no doubt from his writings and art work in dealing with his own unconscious that he was active in re-experiencing his dreams and not just conceptualizing about them.

The Dreams

A *great dream* in my definition is any dream which evokes especially strong positive or negative feeling in the dreamer and which has universal and transcending symbolism in it. In addition, I would characterize great dreams as having unusually active and responsive dream egos. Part of the awareness of such dreams is that they seem to come at crucial transition points in a person's life. They seem to have a synchronistic quality in which inner strongly coincides with outer. This is one reason I am especially careful to remember the dreams which happen on my birthday or at the New Year transition point. Such a dream would seem to embody often the central myth or journey for a period or year.

Living thus in tune with the 'universal' adds a depth of meaning to one's life not possible otherwise. In this sense, dreamwork becomes soul work. We need no longer concern ourselves with greatness in individuals and focus instead on the greatness of the Quest itself. Without such a shift in focus from the personalized Self to the objective Self and its non-personified symbols, we will never be able to take back the Self projection from our 'Masters' and live the individuation process fully ourselves.

Jung's childhood dream

Jung's earliest remembered childhood dream when he was three or four follows. As you read it, please let the images and your own feelings come alive for you. Do *not* let yourself, if you can, reflect on the man, Jung. Focus more on how you experience the symbols in the dream, as in the questions that follow this dream.

'The vicarage stood quite alone near Laufen castle, and there was a big meadow stretching back from the sexton's farm. In the dream I was in this meadow. Suddenly I discovered a dark, rectangular, stone-lined hole in the ground. I had never seen it before, I ran forward curiously and peered down into it. Then I saw a stone stairway leading down. Hesitantly and fearfully, I descended. At the bottom was a doorway with a round arch, closed off by a green curtain. It was a big, heavy curtain of worked stuff like brocade, and it looked very sumptuous. Curious to see what might be hidden behind, I pushed it aside. I saw before me in the dim light a rectangular chamber about thirty feet long. The ceiling was arched of hewn stone. The floor was laid with flagstones, and in the centre a red carpet ran from the entrance to a low platform. On this platform stood a wonderfully rich golden throne. I am not certain, but perhaps a red cushion lay on the seat. It was a magnificent throne, a real king's throne in a fairy tale. Something was standing on it which I thought at first was a tree trunk twelve to fifteen feet high and about one and a half to two feet thick. It was a huge thing, reaching almost to the ceiling. But it was of a curious composition: it was made of skin and naked flesh, and on top there was something like a rounded head with no face and no hair. On the very top of the head was a single eye, gazing motionlessly upwards.

It was fairly light in the room, although there were no windows and no apparent source of light. Above the head, however, was an aura of brightness. The thing did not move, yet I had the feeling that it might at any moment crawl off the throne like a worm and creep towards me. I was paralyzed with terror. At that moment I heard from outside and above me my mother's voice. She called out, 'Yes, just look at him. That is the man-eater!' That intensified my terror still more, and I awoke sweating and scared to death. For many nights afterwards I was afraid to go to sleep, because I feared I might have another dream like that.' (MDR page 26–7)

— What most strikes you about the dream?
— How do you experience for yourself the descent into the earth from the meadow?
— What do you yourself see there as you enter the underground chambers?
— What is your own feeling reaction to being in that room?
— What do the mother's words evoke for you?
— Now focus directly on the 'I' in the dream. What are its actions and feelings? Why might it be responding the way it is responding?

Readers will have to be referred to Jung's full remarks about his dream in *Memories, Dreams, Reflections*. If you have responded to the above questions you will probably have gained a strong sense of the depth and penetration of this dream on the young boy's psyche. In fact, let yourself be a four-year-old for the moment and you will well imagine the import of what had been visited upon Jung.

In terms of the great or primary archetypes we certainly have the *Journey Archetype* in terms of the descent. *Death-Rebirth* is in evidence in the transition through the hole from upper to lower realms. The archetype of the *Masculine* asserts itself in the erect, fleshy phallus and the king's throne, although we can think of the throne itself as *Feminine* following Neuman as he describes the throne as the lap of the great mothers (Neuman, *The Great Mother*). The personal mother and a more personal masculine as 'man-eater' is also present. The central archetype of *The Self* appears in the 'aura of brightness' and the chamber and throne where the center is. We have a curious absence of the two other primary basic archetypes of the *Heroic* and the *Adversary*. (See my Seven Basic Archetypes model, page 276).

The *dream ego* here in its terror certainly feels the 'man-eater' as the adversary but in itself the 'man-eater' does nothing. And after this dream Jung describes himself as being so terrified that he was afraid to sleep for several nights after. The ego is not very heroic at this early age. What is important is that the dream ego responded eagerly when it discovered the hole. Its fear began in the descent and continued to increase throughout the dream, moving into real terror. Terror here being, in my view, an entirely appropriate response to the numinous. Had Jung not felt the terror of this dream would he have remembered it and become the man he became?

In Jung's writing about this dream he describes how it stayed with him for years as a valid but not yet comprehensible experience. Its greatness, its sense of destiny, comes from its utter contrast with anything in Jung's known conscious world. He did not know about pagan fertility or phallic gods and was already being taught Christian doctrine by his parents.

Dream — The Dead Come to Life
In his late thirties, and after his break with Freud, Jung had the following dream. Again as you read and absorb this dream let its images come alive for you. Then respond to the questions which follow.

'I was in a region like the Alyschamps near Arles. There they have a lane of Sarcophagi which go back to Merovingian times. In the dream I was coming from the city, and saw before me a similar lane with a long row of tombs. They were pedestals with stone slabs on which the dead lay. They reminded me of old church burial vaults, where knights in armour lie outstretched. Thus the dead lay in my dream, in their antique clothes, with hands clasped, the difference being that they were not hewn out of stone, but in a curious fashion mummified. I stood still in front of the first grave and looked at the dead man, who was a person of the eighteen-thirties. I looked at his clothes with interest, whereupon he suddenly moved and came to life. He unclasped his hands; but that was only because I was looking at him. I had an extremely unpleasant feeling, but walked on and came to another body. He belonged to the eighteenth century. There exactly the same thing happened: when I looked at him, he came to life and moved his hands. So I went down the whole row, until I came to the twelfth century — that is, to a crusader in chain mail who lay there with clasped hands. His figure seemed carved out of wood. For a long time I looked at him and thought he was really dead. But suddenly I saw that a finger of his left hand was beginning to stir gently.' (MDR page 196–7)

— What is the central repeat action in the dream on the part of the dream ego and how do you react to it?
— How would you describe in your own words what happens to the dead when Jung's dream ego looks at them?
— What is the significance for you in going back through the centuries? How might you have had a similar experience?
— What for you is the purpose of this dream?

I include this dream because it illustrates for me a tremendously central point about Jungian psychology and its way of working with the unconscious.

What starts to bring the dead to life? Are they really dead? Could this in fact be a metaphor for how the consciousness process works?

The ancestors, the historical, personified manifestations of the archetypes are both dead and alive. Dead in the sense that they are unmoving. They are just there and always there within the unconscious. Yet they are alive because capable of life when focused consciousness is set upon them.

In this metaphor, consciousness by an individual ego is what brings a particular archetypal manifestation alive. Where we lend energy is also energy evoked.

But we now encounter another problem, a moral problem if you will. Is it in fact appropriate or valuable to bring the archetypes alive again? Which ones and to what purpose? Now that we know they are capable of life again, what do we do with such information?

It is well known to any therapist or analyst that some people falter, even stop, when they realize they are, through consciousness, evoking energic entities within the psyche which may have lives of their own. They reason that safety lies in retreat but they sacrifice also, living a life fully rooted in the archetypes. The principles might be stated thus: *Do not evoke what you cannot contain. And be willing and ready to deal with anything in the work with the unconscious.*

From the dream it is not clear what is the valuable way to go. The dream ego is only given solid information as to what will happen if the focus of consciousness is brought to bear on the archetypes. This dream was in fact one of the dreams which preceded Jung's historic drop into the unconscious on the 12th December, 1913, which he describes so vividly in his autobiography.

The Siegfried Dream
As you read and experience the text of this dream, which came also during the period when Jung was initially dealing with his own unconscious, let go yourself to the necessity for relating to it. Jung himself felt a great urgency about understanding this dream.

After your experience you may want to respond to any of the following questions:

— What is the full image and feeling you get about Siegfried here?

— Why, based on evidence in the dream, does Jung's dream ego feel he has to kill Siegfried?

'I was with an unknown, brown-skinned man, a savage, in a lonely, rocky mountain landscape. It was before dawn; the eastern sky was already bright, and the stars fading. Then I heard Siegfried's horn sounding over the mountains and I knew we had to kill him. We were armed with rifles and lay in wait for him on a narrow path over the rocks.

Then Siegfried appeared high up on the crest of the mountain, in the first ray of the rising sun. On a chariot made of the bones of the dead he drove at furious speed down the precipitous slope. When he turned a corner, we shot at him, and he plunged down, struck dead.

Filled with disgust and remorse for having destroyed something so great and beautiful, I turned to flee, impelled by the fear that the murder might be discovered. But a tremendous downfall of rain began, and I knew that it would wipe out all traces of the dead, I had escaped the danger of discovery; life could go on, but an unbearable feeling of guilt remained.' (MDR page 204)

— What are the possibilities for why the dream ego feels guilty? List them.
— What is it about the rain that is redemptive?
— What exactly is "unbearable guilt"?

When Jung woke with this dream he realized that he simply had to understand this dream or grave consequences would ensue.

Essentially he realized that he had the same problem as the German people of that time. He, like them, wanted to achieve heroically by imposing his will. But '... there are higher things than the ego's will and to these one must bow,' wrote Jung (MDR page 205).

What is impressive is that a dominant archetypal manifestation, Siegfried, gets seriously dealt with by a fairly strong dream ego, and that secondly the act of killing Siegfried causes great guilt on the part of the dream ego.

Again, Jung's dream ego is appropriately active and feels deeply the consequences of its actions.

In Jung's comments about working with his Siegfried dream he goes on to describe how 'new forces were released in me which helped me to carry the experiment with the unconscious to a conclusion.' In his killing Siegfried he felt he was killing his ego ideal of power through Germanic domination of reality by the will.

What then would be substituted in the place of ego-control and identification with the Heroic archetype? Identification with the Heroic archetype may be necessary to ego development in terms of a child's dealing with adversity and becoming effective in the world. And, even in adult years, the ego shows a great propensity to identify with archetypes, whether it be the Great Mother or Great Father or any archetype manifestation.

The *persona* is probably created by the ego's identifying with a role, the outward form of archetypal manifestation. In this dream Jung's dream ego takes on the task of killing the propensity to identify with the Heroic, and who does the dream ego have as a companion in the task? The primitive, or what Jung later called the shadow, and which I would say is the natural opposite to the persona, the mask or positive image we show to the world. Thus the shadow is only opposite to the ego when the ego is identified with the persona.

It is important to see here that the creative ego's task is to free itself from identification and domination with any archetype so that it may relate to all archetypes in the service of the Self, the integrative function in the psyche. The ego's identification with an archetype is an unconscious attempt to build persona and breeds projection as well as ego inflation. Thus to deal with both projection and inflation the ego must often struggle valiantly to free itself from the clutches of an archetype.

This is, in my view, the magnificence of Jung's dream ego's accomplishment in the Siegfried dream. I speak only of Jung's dream ego and his own accomplishment in order to make clear that an event happening in a dream is not automatically an event happening in outer reality. But Jung does write of his tremendous struggles during this time in dealing with this dream and other dreams and fantasies.

That Jung was on the right path, the destiny path, can be hinted at in the dream's imagery of the great rain which washes away all evidence of his dream ego's deed. The dream ego will not be faced with retribution or things hanging on. The killing, the work of the choice maker, was a clean killing. The dream ego has done its task well and received confirmation from a still greater mystery, the Self, the non-ego function, in the form of the healing rain.

Let us focus for a moment on the role of guilt in this dream. Does guilt always occur when one breaks out of a dominant archetype? Is this part of what gives the archetype its power? Is guilt an unpleasant emotion that must often be experienced in disidentification? Guilt may be described as the tension felt when the ego seeks to meet its own needs rather than another's expectations.

What follows next in Jung's working with the unconscious is the birth of *active imagination* and *dialogue* as he used it. He pursued his fantasies by allowing his 'dream ego' or 'fantasy ego' to descend down a steep incline where his fantasy ego met an old man and a young woman which Jung later identified as the *Wise Old Man* archetype and the *anima* or feminine soul figure within the psyche.

Soon after this fantasy Jung had the following dream:
'There was a blue sky, like the sea, covered not by clouds but by flat brown clods of earth. It looked as if the clods were breaking apart and the blue water of the sea were becoming visible between them. But the water was the blue sky. Suddenly there appeared from the right a winged being sailing across the sky. I saw that it was an old man with the horns of a bull. He held a bunch of four keys, one of which he clutched as if he were about to open a lock. He had the wings of the kingfisher with its characteristic colours.' (MDR page 207)

Jung painted this dream and also discovered in his garden a dead kingfisher, a synchronistic event confirming the depth at which Jung was working. His dreamwork methods involved both *painting* key archetypal figures and scenes and doing dialogues. They are actualization techniques rather than interpretive ones.

Diaglogue is, of course, an active imagination process in which a person asks an archtypal figure questions and writes automatically the responses heard with the inward ear without censoring them. In one of the dialogues with Philomen, the name Jung gave to the winged wisdom figure of his dream, Jung was told that his ideas were not his own but came through him.

In other words, the disidentification and differentiation of the creative ego from archetypal contents continues and develops after the Siegfried dream. Jung's ego was now able to handle the contents of the unconscious by differentiation which allowed relation to them rather than identification with them.

Do we feel the impact of this event? Jung's was and is still a magnificent achievement, working as he was solely in the darkness of exploring new and original territory. As Jung writes about Philomen, 'It was he who taught me psychic objectivity, the reality of the psyche. Through him the distinction was clarified between myself and the object of my thought.' (MDR page 208)

And we ourselves who come after now have the opportunity to establish a similar, yet always unique, relationship with our unconscious and the healing centre which resides there. Jung had moved from only the dream and its interpretation to dreamwork, the active participation in the events of the unconscious. Thus active imagination embodies a far greater involvement, risk and vitality in relation to the archetypes than does even the most sophisticated interpretation of symbols.

And we must not assume that because Jung did it first that he did it for the rest of us. Each in his or her own way can go through the confrontation and experience the great dream as a living reality.

Of Jung's other dreams much could be written, which we do not have the space for here. One other aspect of Jung's dreamwork which stands out is how he responded to certain dreams as giving him life direction. He reports, for instance, two dreams on alchemy, long before he made alchemy a major study of his life. Again we see that destiny quality and the ego's willingness, even eagerness, to respond. Jung also had certain great dreams which for him foresaw world events or personal events. Obviously, working at the levels he did, made him psychologically in tune. And again we emphasize, not Jung's personal greatness, but the greatness or depth of meaning of the process to which he was so devoted. If we can learn anything from Jung's journey it is that to varying degrees such a journey is uniquely available to each one of us. The method of the approach, as we are deliniating it here, is definitely one of the dream and its dreamwork. That somehow the dream itself and its dreamwork, is perhaps the most potent door to the inward universe and the *via royal* for the process. We come now to a few of the dreams Jung dreamed in the last years of his life.

Dream of Seeing Jung's Wife

As you read this dream, let the images and feeling flow for you. This dream came after the death of Jung's wife.

'I saw her in a dream which was like a vision. She stood at some distance from me, looking at me squarely. She was in her prime, perhaps about thirty, and wearing the dress which had been made for her many years before by my cousin the medium. It was perhaps the most beautiful thing she had ever worn. Her expression was neither joyful nor sad, but, rather, objectively wise and understanding, without the slightest emotional reaction, as though she were beyond the mist of affects. I knew that it was not she, but a portrait she had made or commissioned for me. It contained the beginning of our relationship, the events of fifty-three years of marriage, and the end of her life also. Face to face with such wholeness one remains speechless, for it can scarcely be comprehended. (MDR page 327)

— What values and transformations are being expressed in this dream?

— What kind of resolution or completion might Jung be experiencing in terms of at least the outer relationship with his deceased wife? What resolution to his inner feminine, or anima, might he be experiencing?

— What does this dream say to us about our own feelings around relationship and death? What can we learn from this dream in that regard?

Jung in his remarks about the dream emphasizes the complete objectivity he felt. Objectivity means, I think, in this context, experiencing *the other* in his or her full innateness without contamination through projections of our own onto the object. For what we project we do not integrate. We put out there what is really within ourselves and we even often try to get the object of our projection to act it out for us. Yet projection is a necessary part of the process of integration. For we usually must see an inner dynamic as out there before we can next recognize it as really within ourselves. Projections become regressive and life-defeating when we seek to maintain them rather than do the creative and sometimes agonizing work of integrating their dynamics within ourselves. We might add that working actively with dreams allows us to bypass some of the projection process.

In marriage projecting and integrating projections is a primary process of the relationship. Those who do not seek the way of consciousness and integration seek to maintain the projections by living them out in roles and other behaviour. What a joy it would be to finally arrive at the place where neither person in a relationship is acting out any roles for the other person or even for themselves.

Is Jung experiencing in this dream, and his experience of objectivity about it, the goal and value of individuation as it applies to relationship? To finally reach that place of objectivity and essence in which he sees his wife finally in her own wholeness. And we are left still with a mystery. Is this dream image of his wife's essence or spirit? Or is it about Jung's personal objectivity in relation to her as a person? Or is it about Jung's dream ego's objective relation to the anima? Perhaps all these? And perhaps there is even more within the mystery of what death is and the 'life' beyond.

Dream of a Yogi

We come now to a dream Jung received after his major illness in which he had an 'out of the body' experience and tremendous visions. After this illness, as he states, came many of his principle works. We shall focus on this one dream for its implications about the nature of consciousness.

'I was walking along a little road through a hilly landscape; the sun was shining and I had a wide view in all directions. Then I came to a small wayside chapel. To my surprise there was no image of the Virgin on the altar, and no crucifix either, but only a wonderful flower arrangement. But then I saw that on the floor in front of the altar, facing me, sat a yogi in lotus posture, in deep meditation. When I looked at him more closely, I realized that he had my face. I started in profound fright, and awoke with the thought: ''Aha, so he is the one who is meditating me. He has a dream, and I am it.'' I knew that when he awakened, I would no longer be.' (MDR page 355)

— What are the paradoxes being expressed in this dream?

Paradox is maybe the most effective form of thought process for penetrating into the nature of things. We list first the contrasts in this dream, using the method 'objectifying the dream.'

— The wide view in all directions vs. the focused view in the little chapel.

— The door closed yet ajar or open.

— An altar but without the two great Christian symbols of the virgin and the crucifix.

— Flowers on the altar but in an arrangement.

— A yogi with Jung's face facing his dream ego.

— Meditation vs. worship in the chapel. The yogi faces away from the altar.

— The dream ego's fright produces insight rather than repression. Jung realizes, 'Aha, so he is the one who is meditating me. He has a dream and I am it.' I knew that when he awakened, I would no longer be.'

The great paradox is, of course, who is dreaming whom in this life? Am I in my own manifestation, which I consider real, someone else's dream? Am I the one being dreamed in the same way that I dream the characters in my own dreams? Is it then that my own existence is relative to the existence of some other great entity? Is my life a manifestation of some other greater source than my own ego consciousness and choice-making? If so, what do I have say in, and in what ways am I needed to the process?

One of the great foci of consciousness is 'to determine the object', to become more objectively aware of the reality which surrounds us. But in becoming aware of object must we not also become aware of ourselves? This is the paradox, the impossible task.

It takes ego to reflect on ego. The consciousness process becomes one also of the ego reflecting on itself. How then can 'I' know 'I'? It is not enough for 'I' to come to know the Self, the other, the object of consciousness. It is not enough for the 'I' to become the focus of the Self. *The ego must make an object of itself.* This is a crucial principle of consciousness, as important perhaps as the ego's commitment to knowing the 'not-I' or the Self.

Further it is only when the ego consciousness is able to make an object of itself that it can be known by the Self. For the Self cannot know itself unless there is an 'I' to comprehend and manifest it. Said in still another way, the Self's object is the ego. But in order for the Self to be known to itself, in order for the Self to become an object to itself, the ego must also become an object to itself. The ego frees itself from itself in order to free the Self from Itself. The ego as the greater consciousness, and lesser being, then frees the Self to objectify itself by the ego's lending its consciousness to the Self.

Without the objectification of consciousness the ego would be contaminated and identified with the Self and any manifestation would be unconscious, predetermined and outside the realm of individuation because unchosen. Without objectification as to alternatives and possibilities there can be no choice. Without choice there can be no individuation, the wholeness process of not simply manifesting archetypes but integrating them into totality which has centre.

Philosophy aside, we are suggesting here that the ego's role is to generate consciousness by focusing on and objectifying itself. It disidentifies from archetypal contents. It takes back projections. It works for integration of projected contents within the large psyche. This objectification process then frees the Self to manifest integratively and transformatively because its contents are freed from the vice-grip of the ego and other controlling patterns, or complexes, within the psyche.

In terms of Jung's dreams, Jung's dream ego is as necessary to the process as the yogi, the chapel and the altar are. For without the dream ego entering through the door ajar that yogi and centre would never become known. And without also that dream ego entering into the chapel it itself would never become known to itself. For it is only within the chapel, within the presence of the Self that the ego can become known to itself by knowing it is known by the Self. This strikes me as an extremely profound principle.

For consciousness to develop the ego must become an object to itself by recognizing that it is paradoxically already an object to the Self. In other words, the ego can see itself as the Self sees it, it can become conscious of itself as ego and therefore, and also, conscious of the Self as Self.

Consciousness is not, then, the ego becoming aware of everything which surrounds it and remaining blind to itself as ego. A false awareness sees only the Other as object, as object and never itself.

The harder task is to make of oneself an object, to objectify the process at the core in the centre of one's own awareness. This is why we make the distinction here between Jung as person and Jung's dream ego, the image of Jung as he appears specifically in his dreams. Thus, analyzing one's dream ego in one's dreams is one of the most effective methods for objectifying one's ego consciousness. I have called this method which I have developed, 'Following the Dream Ego'. In analyzing the dream ego we see not only its actions in a dream but can also infer the attitudes or underlying contexts which motivate and produce the actions and attitudes of the dream ego.

In the dream, what are the possibilities for why Jung's dream ego feels fear upon seeing its own face upon the face of the meditating yogi?

Jung states that he knew when the yogi woke up his 'I' would be no more. But what does this mean? At one level certainly a physical death is involved. When the body dies the ego as a direct choice-maker and awareness centre in this world also dies. But, and here is still one more paradox, when the 'I' ceases to exist the Self wakes up. What would it be to have lived life so essentially consciously that at the moment of our physical death the Self is really fully alive. Perhaps this then is the immortality principle?

The ego becomes so completely itself by objectifying itself, that, when it ceases to be an 'I', because it is now objective, the Self becomes fully alive and holds the essence which transcends the physical death.

The ego dies subjectively so the Self is objectively born.

As in Jung's earliest dream, the dream ego reacts to the dream's events with fear. It sees itself and knows it is being seen by the Self. Only the ego feels fear, the perceived possibility of annihilation. Seen in this light, all fear is the ego's anticipation of possible loss and the greatest loss, at least to the ego, is the loss of itself.

It would be instructive for the reader to study Jung's own remarks about his dream. In some ways they are similar and in some ways different to what I have tried to articulate. I am not trying to say what Jung's dream meant to him or even to differ with him. My goal is to open up the content of the dream *in itself* and to articulate more fully the issues evoked. My purpose is to focus on the nature of consciousness, rather than on Jung's life, or even his comments on his life.

Yet, now we come to the final recorded dreams of Jung's journey, dreams which are so extremely moving in terms of themselves and in terms of Jung's life, that I for one certainly hesitate in writing any commentary. I only move ahead because of how much I personally have been affected by Jung's approach to realizing life's meaning.

The Last Dreams
Jung died at age 86, a man who lived a full and richly deserved life. He seems to have been a person who dealt with things as they came along, whether sickness, professional success, intimate relationships, his own ego and the unconscious itself.

What might be the dreams which would come to such a person during the final days of his life when earthly actions, events, and even dreams would be about over for him? What did he think about? What would now be the focus of such a developed consciousness so close to the end? What was there left still to do to complete the life process, to go with it to the end, to even prepare for what was possibly to come next?

It is difficult to put substance to these questions from what little has so far been published about Jung by his close followers and companions. Probably at the end a person's thought and feelings are largely his or her own. But the weight of such a death is a magnificent one. All that Jung had built and developed through the decades of his life was now almost gone to him. True it lived, the psychology, the life stories and the many books, but these lived for others and not for him. I would think, such a man would know when the end was coming and his last illnesses did make it apparent to him that he was near his earthly finality.

These last dreams are quoted by Barbara Hanna in her book *Jung, His Life and Work*. She states that they were written out for her by Jung's nurse and companion, Ruth Bailey. Here are the dreams:

1) He saw a big round block of stone in a high bare place and on it was inscribed: 'This shall be a sign unto you of wholeness and oneness.' 2) A lot of vessels, pottery vases, on the right side of a square place. 3) A square of trees, all fibrous roots, coming up from the ground and surrounding him. There were gold threads gleaming among the roots.'

— What sense of time or timelessness do you gain from these dreams?
— How do you experience these symbols for yourself? What colour and shape for you is the 'big, round block of stone'?
— How do you see the whole scene?
— What is Jung's dream ego doing and not doing in each of these dreams? What does this possibly say about his consciousness at this time?
— How do you experience the square of trees from the point of view of the dream ego in the dream?

The above questions reflect my bias in working with dreams. What we are after here is for each of us to have a living experience of Jung's last dreams, not as he experienced them, for that we can never know, but as we ourselves re-experience them.

Let me suggest here the primary method in the Jungian-Senoi approach, called *Dream Re-entry*. The goal is to actualize, to re-experience the dream, and not to *interpret* it. Thus, I suggest, as a Self-Dream Re-entry, that the reader can choose to put him or herself into a meditative state with eyes closed and visualize, or see-feel the scenes of Jung's dreams.

What do you experience? How do these dreams live for you? What meaning and appreciation do they generate?

We are not saying identify with Jung's dreams or with Jung but just experience them and see what they evoke in terms of your own psyche.

Perhaps you can feel the potential for wholeness present? For myself, I feel the import of seeing the round block of stone high on a bare place. The meaning is universal, yet a significant achievement by an individual has been marked.

The dream ego is present as an observer and active only as the reader of the inscription. How very necessary is consciousness to the individuation process!

This sign of wholeness is not of the dream ego's creation but comes from the mystery, the Other Side. Who carved the inscription? Who or what dares make such a final evaluation? How does the dream ego respond and not respond? The dream ego reads but is to possess nothing. It is a statement of fact and not possession, the ultimate objectivity. It does not say, as Laurens Van der Post states in his BBC film about Jung, 'Take this as a symbol of your wholeness and the singleness you have become.'

When we re-enter the second dream, how do we experience the vessels being on only one side of the square? Are they empty or full for you? I myself experience a felt shifting over to the other side as well as mystery, the unexplainable. Wholeness may not always be symbolized by symmetry and balance.

Nor do I need to create linkings to other myths, such as the Osiris myth, to try to explain the significance of the vessels. That would be interpretation, or the rational linking of a symbolic experience (the dream) to an outside symbol system (myth) not in the dream itself.

When we meditatively re-enter this dream the vessels are wondrous in themselves and full of mystery, even greater mystery because of how they are placed. Who might have placed them there? And what are the possibilities for why Jung's dream ego is not itself in the dream?

The Last Dream

We come now to the final dream in the series. Why not just stay with it a few minutes and let the subtle overtones of its images reverberate in you in your own Self-Dream Re-entry? Do not try to make anything happen. Just be there with the imagery and see what is evoked for you. People will have different experiences of this dream. There are no answers, no 'right' interpretations which 'click'. There are only responses to a mystery.

As I experience this dream the landscape is dark and bright at the same time. My feeling response is grief, is death, is ending. All is not well in this dream. The dream ego is being swallowed by the great roots. The ego is there, perhaps being nurtured, encompassed and devoured in a transcendent womb of life.

I feel it, my ego feels it as an entrapment, as a final limitation, however magnificent, from which there is no escape. It is well to die and to suffer one's death. But the cost is dear. It is the death in limitation of freedom, of choice, of creativity.

Is there an observer ego watching this dream ego at the centre with the trees and roots laced with gold?

I feel the necessity of the dream ego to yield, to go with the process. To be at the centre of the mandala at any other time might be a gross inflation. But at this time, during the last days of life, to be anywhere else but at the centre might be utter regression. There is everything to die for. One has lived well. However one has lived, now is the time to be surrounded by a grave of life. What greater tribute and symbolizing of the resolution to the individuation process could there be?

As a person with ego and life still to live fully, I feel the grief, the 'sadness in joy', of this person's passing. I know him, even intimately, through his dreams. I begin to understand his significance.

Death is a brutal process, as he himself said in one of his letters. The ego stands to lose everything. What is to be gained? Not the everlasting life of the ego, but that which transcends ego and goes right to the Self and the journey towards wholeness. I feel grief.

Is not really grief for others also the grieving for our own deaths? The ego knows its own mortality. It can choose then to take the journey, to relate to that more universal mystery which can give life its meaning.

The yogi is awakened. The Self has come fully alive and the insubstantial ego goes itself into the mystery. The fear experienced in earlier dreams is no longer appropriate. That for which one has sought for so long has been achieved.

> Let us meditate on symbols and things,
> On a great round stone and Kingfisher wings,
> On a fleshy god with its mystic throne,
> On an act of murder and roots laced with gold,
> On a yogic soul whose dreams have been told.

References

C.G. Jung, *Collected Works*, Princeton University Press
              Memories, Dreams, Reflections, Collins
Strephon K. Williams, *Jungian-Senoi Dreamwork Manual*
Barbara Hannah, *Jung, His Life and Work*, G. P. Putnam's Sons

Jung's Approach to Symbol

What follows is a short evaluation of how Jung worked with symbols. When this material is presented in training sessions there can be quite a bit of feeling aroused. For is not Jung the founder and leading light of Jungian psychology? Certainly he was the innovative person who well launched the whole adventure. But he was not a systematizer by his own admission and his ideas were always developing.

Perhaps by now you have recognized that this approach to Jungian psychology attempts to organize and simplify its material down to understandable and usable basic concepts. You do not have to agree, of course, with what is presented here but the issue remains as to whether the realm of human experience can be organized into a usable archetypal theory?

Jung's method for interpreting dreams was to universalize the dream symbol by referring to similar symbols in myth and folk tale.

The basis upon which Jung does this is his assumption that a common ground of the collective unconscious underlies and connects the symbol in the dream with the symbol in the myth. To assume otherwise would be to

postulate that each and every symbol in this universe is completely different from all others. In fact, what seems more accurate is that symbols rest on the commonality of the archetypes but also have sufficient specificity to be considered uniquely different from each other.

Jung assumed that his method of linking dream symbols to similar symbols in myth and culture was amplification. But this can be severely questioned as the following will show. In fact, what I think Jung is doing most of the time is association rather than amplification. This needs to be made clear. When Jung refers to a mythological symbol to explain a dream symbol, he is *linking* symbols according to his own personal associations. In other words, he is doing the same thing as Freud only Jung links dream symbols to mythology, alchemy, and religious texts, whereas Freud linked dream symbols to sexual dynamics. Their symbol systems were different but their methods were basically the same.

In defence of Jung he did believe in letting the symbol speak for itself even though his practice seems somewhat otherwise. On occasion in the transcripts of Jung's dream seminars, we can find him practising amplification as symbol inherency, or discovering the innate qualities of a symbol.

An Example of Jung Working with a Dream

As a case in point of Jung's interpretive approach to dreams we shall use a dream which is both in his collected works and in transcripts of actual lectures using the same material. The difference between the two versions is revealing although the conclusion as to what the dream means is the same in both versions. I cannot quote directly either version here since one is unpublished and only available in Jung Institute libraries. The references are as follows. *Jung's Collected Works*, Vol. 12, pp. 196, 197, Dream 20. The other fuller version is in *Dream Symbols of the Individuation Process*, Vol. 11, Seminar held in New York City, October, 1937, Dream 15, pp. 18-20.

Another significant difference between the two versions is that Jung abbreviated this and most other dream examples and comments in the collected works. It is my observation that in so doing he generalized the dream symbols, he made them non-specific to support his theory that the symbol in the dream was the same symbol as in myth. There may be a common and universal archetypal base to both the dream symbol and the myth symbol but this goes too far.

We are challenging the approach to get clearer on the issues and so dreamwork people do not try to slavishly follow Jung. He was obviously masterful in his ability to use the world's symbolism to get across his point. We might even state that Jung's psychology is based more on culture and mythology than on dreamwork.

The Cave — Jung's Dream Example

Jung gives a dream about a cave with two boys in it. A third boy falls through a tube from the ceiling of the cave. This is all. There is no mention of the dreamer in the dream.

In his interpretative remarks Jung likens the boys to a 'dwarf' motif, or little men who are always helping out in folk tales. He likens them also to the *Heinzelmaennchen*, or little men who appear in mines. They are to Jung alchemical spirits or personifications of vapour from melting metal. In folklore Jung says they also appear on ships as a bad omen. Therefore they represent split-off parts of our psyche and always show a certain dissociation.

What is Jung doing here? Amplification or association? Did he stay with the dream or did he immediately leap off from it? How did three boys in a cave become dwarfs of bad omen indicating splits in the psyche?

Obviously, Jung is associating and not amplifying. He goes from one symbol to another and another and quite quickly we have left the dream far behind.

Jung, then, goes on, after another fascinating digression into folklore, to state that what were originally boys have now become to him fragmentary souls which are in fact also Jungian typology functions. Jung has taken still another symbol system besides folklore and imposed it onto the dream. Is there anything within the dream which indicates that these boys are functions? No, there is nothing overt which indicates this.

What do you think the dream is about?

Are there methods for getting at the meaning of such dreams?

For one, we do not have the dreamer available to interact with his own dream in actualization tasks, which is the Jungian-Senoi approach. Jung did not even work directly with this particular dreamer but only had him record all his dreams.

Using the Jungian-Senoi approach we might do amplification as in the following questions.

What are the general characteristics of caves in outer life?

What is a tube? What is the effect of the combined image of cave and tube?

How would you characterize the possible qualities of having a boy come through a tube into a cave and join two other boys?

What are the positive aspects of this dream in itself? And what are the possible negative aspects?

Jung seems to have taken the dream as a metaphor to process his theories about typology and psychic dissociation. It might indeed be a metaphor for the dreamer's psyche dissociating and dropping out of sight into unconsciousness. But it might also be a metaphor for new birth with the seminal organ penetrating the womb and depositing new potentials for masculinity. There would be other possibilities for processing as well.

In the Jungian-Senoi approach we would also use unconscious process techniques, such as dialogue and symbol immersion.

Why not dialogue with the boy and find out why he entered the cave? Also ask the cave for its reactions to this event.

Or we might have the dreamer enter the cave imaginatively the same way as the boy and describe how he feels and what happens there.

Thus symbol amplification itself is not necessarily the best technique to use with this dream.

Jung in his later writing actually points to this in his discovery of active imagination (CW-XX, 400). He set his 'patients', as he calls them, the task of developing some dream symbol or association in fantasy. The results were often remarkable and sometimes contained spontaneous healing images. Jung was hesitant to interpret these fantasies and felt that in some ways they went beyond interpretation. In fact he goes so far as to state that active imagination to some extent takes the place of dreams.

In our experience at the Jungian-Senoi Institute we have the dream sharer go back into the dream symbol or dream itself in a re-entry and let it come alive again. We do not usually take the symbol out of context but have the dream itself, and all its dynamics, become more fully present.

Also we feel it essential to ground the experience of the unconscious with specific tasks for changes in consciousness and life situations. Thus, not interpretation, not fantasy, but action is the final testing ground and commitment to the whole dream experience.

Amplification has value in opening up the possibilities for meaning in a dream. It broadens out the possibilities.

It may, however, rob the dream of numinosity, or archetypal energy. This is why unconscious process techniques, which preserve or increase the numinosity of the dream experience, may be preferred.

Amplification is a necessary skill for dreamwork leaders in order to be more objective about the dream actualization process. As I hear a dream from someone I am automatically amplifying it for its possibilities. However, I may often choose not to use this process directly with the dream sharer. I may offer dream task questions which deal directly with the dynamics inherent in the symbols. I may also suggest unconscious process techniques to have the dream come more alive for the person. My amplifying ability helps me maintain a more objective point as I enter into some unconscious process technique with a person.

The Senoi People's Dreamwork

The Senoi, according to reports by the American psychologist Kilton Stewart, were a people in Malaya who worked actively with their dreams each day and had a very low incidence of mental illness and crime.

Today, apparently, their culture has been largely changed or destroyed by outside political events. Recently some investigators have wondered whether the Senoi people ever did work with their dreams extensively. Kilton Stewart, the author of the classic paper 'Dream Theory in Malaya', is deceased and there is some question as to whether or not his paper is partly fiction.

Thus today, the Senoi seem to be largely a mythic people who worked with dreams in essentially two ways.

— They worked to change the dream state while dreaming.
— They did dreamwork projects using dream material to alter their lives for the better.

In the Senoi tradition children were taught to stay in their dreams, even under scary conditions such as falling, and to experience the dream state as one capable of being controlled. And adult dreamers shared certain dreams in tribal council, especially those in which they received new dances, songs and even practical ideas.

Whether or not a dream-based culture ever really existed with the Senoi, we do know that in most earth-related cultures around the world, dreams were shared and worked with in the community. The Iroquois Nation had a dream-sharing gathering every winter. In ancient Jerusalem there were twenty-four professional dream interpreters, and if you did not like one interpretation you could go to someone else for another. In the Islamic culture dream interpretation was an everyday practice. The greatest healing cult of ancient Greece, the Asclepian, lasted for a thousand years and used healing dreams as central to their rites.

It is only today in our culture made shallow by materialism that we have neglected, even shunned, the importance of dreams with our emphasis on outer life to the neglect of the inner.

The Jungian-Senoi Institute uses this name to show its link with these two traditions, although in a sense we represent neither tradition. In some ways we have had to innovate and develop dreamwork further. In essence our approach is experiential and broad. It has now come time to make dreamwork extremely practical so that dreams and their meanings are again within reach of everyone.

What follows here are key ideas of Kilton Stewart's paper about the Senoi paraphrased and simplified. In effect what follows is a very interesting list of attitudes about dreams and dreamwork. Why not use these attitudes to develop your own? The Institute takes a matter-of-fact approach to Stewart's principles. Which ones might actually be relevant to dreamwork and the journey?

For instance, a major principle from Stewart is that he says the Senoi believed in confronting adversaries rather than running from them. At the Institute we have found this a very helpful practice, especially in dealing with nightmares. But we do not go along with the 'Senoi' contention that in confronting dream adversaries one should try and kill them. Our view is that it is usually more productive and healing to relate to adversaries rather than kill them. The Adversary archetype is, has, and always will be present in this universe. So let us not waste good energy slicing vapours. And we do see where it can be a valuable action for someone's dream ego to kill in a dream to express that energy.

The issue here in part is what principles and values apply on the inner level and are these necessarily the same as those which apply on an outer level? We do dreamwork in fact to distinguish the difference between the two worlds.

And now here is what Kilton Stewart reports about the Senoi. His original paper may be found in Charles Tart's *Altered States of Consciousness*.

— When a total community works on mastering the dream state, and integrating dream with waking reality, the incidence of asocial behaviour is relatively insignificant.

— Dreams are the expressions of external forces internalized. If these internal forces are not harmonized, the person's internal and external life is adversely affected.

— Any person can learn to become master of his or her dream universe and utilize all the beings in it.

— One can change one's dream state towards enjoyment and spiritual power by changing one's fearful attitudes into ones of assertion and acceptance.

— Dream anxiety can be changed into joy and acts of will through dream relaxation and pleasure.

— The dream ego should always attack and kill hostile figures, calling on help from other dream figures if necessary. This will result in the essence of the hostile figure becoming a dream ally. Dream figures only seem negative when we fear them.

— Sexual dreams should always be carried through to orgasm, and a gift demanded of the lover in the form of a poem, song, skill, dance, etc. This is then shared with one's waking group. A rich love life in dreams indicates the favour of the beings of the spiritual universe.

— Negative personal behaviour in dreams should be compensated in outer life with positive interactions with those whose images appeared in the dream.

— One can make decisions and arrive at resolutions in one's night-time thinking as well as in that of the day. Thus, one can assume a responsible attitude towards all of one's psychic reactions and forces.

— One can better cope with one's psychic reactions by expressing and dealing with them than by concealing and repressing them.

— Our most creative powers and deepest self are revealed when our psychic processes are freed from outer world focus.

— One's dreamworld, and how one works with it, is to be shared with a responding group for support and community enhancement.

— The bodily state must be relaxed in order to have pleasurable imaginative dreams.

— Social approval of the outer responsive group is used to support active dealing with negative and positive elements in dreams.

— Negative dream situations can form the basis for increased positive interactions in outer relationships.

— Negative behaviour on the part of the dream ego is changed to positive behaviour in the outer situation.

— Outer reality negative situations can be changed to positive ones in the dream state.

— Dreams can provide solutions to outer problems.

— The more one works with one's dreams the less irrational and the more like reflective thinking the dreams become.

These main concepts of the Senoi peoples require careful analysis. Perhaps you have had a number of feeling reactions to them? Why not pick out the concepts which most appeal to you, or turn you off, and create a specific

dream task for yourself to do while dreaming? You can also do any of these tasks through dream re-entry, which is often easier than direct dream change. These are some of the issues involved in the Senoi approach:

— How consistently can I change my dreams while still in them?
— What group is there which can support me?
— How much of this really works? Does it take years to become effective? Can only a few 'masters' accomplish this?
— Do we want to learn to 'master' the dream universe or to 'co-operate' with it?
— Do we need to kill our dream adversaries or can we simply confront them and demand help? This latter is the preferred position of the Jungian-Senoi approach, and has worked a number of times.
— And what would it be like to have dreamwork as one of the essential ingredients of community life?

How have your own attitudes been challenged by considering these Senoi attitudes towards dreamwork?

The Relation of Consciousness to Healing

A question was presented to me recently, 'What is the relation of consciousness to healing?' We could also ask, 'Why is consciousness necessary to healing?'

There are few more fundamental questions than these. Who is there who is not in need of healing in some form? And who is there who is not caught in a sea of unconsciousness about what is really going on in one's life?

Consciousness is awareness which leads to appropriate action.

Healing is the balancing out and integrating of one-sided energies. It is the bringing to resolution of conflictual states.

It is not enough to be aware, to have insight, to obtain knowledge, to figure things out, to have intense experiences, to even feel things in their realness.

Without action, awareness never meets the test, never gets into reality. Awareness which does not compel action is a false awareness, an awareness disemboweled and distanced from life's vital energies.

What would it be to be so committed and so aware that when we realize a new potential for truth we cannot help but act to manifest it?

Of action without awareness we know much. The doers of the world are forever busy doing and undoing the best and the worst that is existence, but seldom knowing why.

We offer a fundamental duality which must be unified if there is to be true healing.

This is the duality of *being* versus *doing*.

Some seek to spend their lives existing in essence. They do not seek the world, the world seeks them. While others spend their time forever in movement and change, they seek the world to create it ever anew.

How can we exist in *being* by *doing*?

Action is the ultimate commitment to a changing reality, while *stillness* is the ultimate stance towards achieving essence.

Consciousness, which is awareness plus appropriate action, is the integration of doing and being.

One purpose of consciousness, perhaps the chief purpose, is to participate in disharmony and one-sidedness and effect and allow healing.

When I experience that I am caught in one opposite, such as love or spirit or any of 'the innumerable', I feel wounded or one-sided. I miss my companion of hate or substance or whatever I am repressing or lacking.

Therefore, people of the light are as wounded as people of the dark. To be one-sided in any one thing will surely evoke its opposite. And the more extremely we sit in one opposite the more extremely will the other opposite arise to overtake us.

Do not trust the good persons, for they are not whole. If you must trust, trust those who express both the light and the dark. For then you will know both sides and can deal with both. And trust even more those persons who are integrating the opposites through conscious realization of life's totality. You will know such persons by their paradoxical natures. They are the many in one, the unpredictable, who manifest themselves at the core of reality.

Flow Chart of the Jungian-Senoi Process

As you will see from the following pages we have taken working with a dream through a developmental sequence of dreamwork techniques.

We have tried to discover and organize the major dreamwork techniques, some known before and some previously unknown, and put them together in the developmental sequence you see here.

We have not included Gestalt techniques, out-of-body, and certain other experiences because our orientation is a practical, everyday framework which nevertheless also helps individuals to tie into ultimate meaning. In the case of Gestalt techniques we have developed different techniques which we feel may achieve similar purposes and yet are easier and more introverted to use. We also put more emphasis on a creative ego than Gestalt process seems to do.

Not every dreamwork method in this flow chart is described in this book due to limitations of space. In the next edition all aspects of this flow chart will be adequately described.

We hope this chart demonstrates the practicality of dreamwork and that there is a complete process for working with dreams.

**Goal: To actualize a dream —
Bring it more alive and put it to use in daily life**

| Dreaming | Remember the Dream | Record in Journal | Write Comments |

Do Dreamwork as follows:

Objectifying the Dream

Analyze Dream Structure

— Locate and title dream segments: Acts 1, 2, 3.
— What are the similarities and differences?
— List repeating symbols or themes.

List Issues within the Dream

— What conflicts are present?
— What is unresolved?
— What questions does the dream leave unanswered?

Following the Dream Ego

— Describe actions of the dream ego. What does it do and not do?
— Define attitudes behind the dream ego's actions.
— Describe feeling states of the dream ego as they are expressed throughout the dream.

List Dream Elements

— Contrasts
— Choices
— Sequences

Describe Major Symbols

— List qualities of each.
— Group if appropriate.
— List contrasts and similarities
— List repeating themes.
— Describe how each symbol functions in the dream.

Analyze Characters and their Actions

— List qualities of each major character.
— Group if appropriate.
— List contrasts and similarities.
— List repeating themes.
— Describe relationships.
— List harmonies and conflicts.
— Describe actions of each major character.

Expand the Dream to Gain Meaning

Applying Key Questions to the Dream

— What issues does this dream raise, both personal and spiritual?
— How are actions or inactions of the dream ego related to my personality dynamics or behaviour in outer life?
— How do attitudes, qualities, or feelings of dream characters show themselves in my personality or outer life?
— How do conflicts or harmonies between characters, symbols, or other dream elements relate to conflicts or harmonies in my personality or outer life?
— What does this dream want from me?
— What would I like to avoid about this dream?
— Why has this dream come to me now?
— What is this dream's relation to other dreams?

Dialoguing with Dream Images

— Visualize any character or object from the dream and ask questions.
— Wait openly for the reply.
— Continue dialoguing until you feel a resolution.

Questions concerning the Dream

— Who/what are you?
— What have you to tell me?
— Why are you in my dream?
— Why are you doing what you are doing?
— What would you like to have happen?
— What do you want from me?

Questions concerning outer life

— How do you relate to my outer life?
— How would you like me to handle this outer situation?

Characters can dialogue with one another to get more than one point of view.

Expressing the Dream in Art Forms

— Poetry
— Drawing, painting, sculpture
— Dance or movement
— Music and song
— Enactments

Explore Symbols as Archetypal Manifestations

Locating Primary and Secondary Archetypes

— The Seven Basic Archetypes
— Anima, Animus, Shadow, Persona, Child, etc.

Symbol Amplication

— What are the object's (person's) inherent qualities?
— List its characteristics and functions in outer life.
— List its characteristics and functions within the dream.
— Reduce qualities to their essence.
— Compare, contrast and blend inner and outer characteristics.

Symbol Immersion

— Meditate on the symbol while deeply relaxed. Let it come alive for you.
— Describe the symbol physically as it appears in the dream.
— Do not let the symbol change, but go into its essential nature.
— How do you feel with the symbol? What does it bring up for you?

— Guided   — Self

Symbol Association

— Find links to mythology, religion, culture, etc.
— Find links to systems of psychological dynamics.
— Find links with personal life, past, present, and future.

Symbol Evolvement

— Meditate on the symbol while deeply relaxed, letting it develop further.

Symbol Regression

— Meditate on the symbol while deeply relaxed, letting it go backwards.

Metaphorical Processing

— Outline how the symbol or dream functions in itself.
— Use this as a context to process personality dynamics.
— Use it as a context to process life situations.

Researching Dream Series

— Research other dreams for recurrent symbols and themes.

Bring Resolution to Dream State

Dream Re-entry

— Revisualize the dream in a relaxed meditative state.
— Let go to any images or dialogue which might arise, staying within the original dream structure.
— Carry intention for resolution, healing, or positive change.

— Guided   — Self

Carrying the Dream forward

— Re-enter the dream at the end and allow it to flow spontaneously until a point of resolution is reached.

Method of the Four Quadrants

— Divide the paper into four quadrants.
— Draw the dream in three acts.
— In the fourth quadrant, imagine and draw a resolution.

Dialogue

— Dialogue with dream characters until resolution occurs.

Working in Art for Resolution

— Use drawing, painting, sculpture, poetry, drama, music or dance to represent the dream and bring resolution.

Rewriting the Dream

— Rewrite the dream making creative changes: resolve conflicts, make the dream ego more assertive, complete or change actions, etc.
— Rewrite the dream as story. Include character descriptions, dialogue, and fuller action.
— Rewrite the dream as folktale or parable. Depersonalize elements to reveal underlying mythic structure and meaning.

Meditating to the Dream

— Hold the dream in its unresolved state in meditation each day, until it spontaneously resolves.

Dream Changing

— Using work you have done on this dream, decide on changes you would like in future dreams: more assertion, more acceptance, more resolution, etc.
— Go into sleep carrying this intention for your dream.

Dream Incubation

— Meditatively, before sleep, ask for a dream on a given subject, or a dream gift, or an answer to a question.

Bring Dreamwork to Personality and Outer Life

Changing Attitudes

— Use dreamwork to identify existing attitudes — see 'Following the Dream Ego'.
— Accept new possibilities for attitudes which dreamwork might bring up.
— Use intentions, affirmations, or actions to change negating attitudes.
— Watch for affirming changes in later dreams and in life situations.

The Choice
Making Decisions and Solving Problems

— Use insights gained from dreamwork to help clarify issues.
— Consider new alternatives suggested by the dream or dreamwork.
— Consider wisdom statements as a possible source of guidance.
— Remember that dreams and dreamwork can only offer alternatives and suggestions. You must ultimately make your own decisions and act to solve your own problems.

Developing Insight from Dreamwork

— Apply key questions:
— What am I hiding from myself?
— What are my hopes?
— What are my expectations?
— What are my abilities?
— What are my values?
— What are my insecurities?
— What centres me?

Doing Outer Life Tasks

— Create objects from the dream.
— Try out new styles of behaviour suggested by the dream or dreamwork.
— Enact specific tasks or projects suggested by the dream or dreamwork.

Relating to the Waking Dream

— See major outer life experiences as symbolic.
— Use dreamwork techniques to process outer life events.
— See archetypal patterns underlying outer life.
— Change or bring to resolution outer life situations as you would a dream.

Use Dreamwork to develop the Spiritual Life

Key Journey Questions

— Where does my dream come from?
— Where does my dream lead me?
— What healing does my dream evoke?

Creating Consciousness

— Use dreamwork to clear one's consciousness for increased openness to a source other than ego.
— Use dreamwork to develop attitudes, commitment, and experiences of manifesting Source.
— Use dreamwork to face ultimate questions.
— Collect and use dream wisdom statements.

Developing Relation to Centre

— Manifest healing symbols through art, meditation, and action.
— Use dreamwork to tune in to the life source which manifests uniquely within your life.
— Use dreamwork to bring out the spiritual significance of any life event.
— Use dreamwork to transform your personality and life into a meaningful whole.
— Develop rituals and meditations from dreams and dreamwork.

Relating to Synchronicity

— Become aware of meaningful coincidences between dreamwork and outer life.
— Respond to negative synchronicity with dreamwork and life changes.
— Acknowledge positive synchronicity as confirmation of dreamwork and life change.

Using Great Dreams

— Develop or experience dreams with major spiritual symbols, guides, journeys, etc.
— Develop or experience lucid dreams with heightened vividness and consciousness.

Psychic Awareness

— Use dreams and dreamwork to develop and become clear regarding psychic abilities.
— Use dreams for intuitions about people, time and events.

About the Author

Strephon Kaplan Williams is a practising Jungian therapist-analyst whose interest is innovation and spiritual searching in the areas of transpersonal and holistic healing. He is the founder and director of the Jungian-Senoi Institute in Berkeley, a centre whose main focus is developing further the methodology of dreamwork and training people, professionals and lay alike, in dreamwork and Jungian psychology.

Strephon's professional life is a combination of working directly with people in the healing process and in writing about the journey towards wholeness. His writings include meditations, peotry and articles in Jungian psychology. See especially his article, 'Jungian Psychology', in the *Holistic Health Lifebook*, And/Or Press. Strephon is also the creator of the Choice Cards, a revolutionary new tool utilizing synchronicity and psychic intunement for making meaningful and effective choices.

As a therapist Strephon specializes in guiding people through intensive personality transformations using dreamwork and other primary healing processes. He has worked therapeutically with the severley disturbed, with children and with adults in crisis and transition.

Strephon is also an instructor in transpersonal dreamwork and Jungian psychology at John F. Kennedy University. He is a frequent presenter at workshops and conferences and has had numerous appearances on radio and television.

As a writer, Strephon comes from a literary background which includes being the son of a well-known poetry anthologist and poet, Oscar Williams, and the poet and painter, Gene Derwood.

His central perspective, as may be obvious from this book, is on continually expanding his consciousness and choice-making and in relating to sources more central than ego. Full creativity, caring and meaning are as well part of the quality of what Strephon seeks to actualize in life.

Meditation for Creating Dreaming

It is time. I have come to the end of my day. But my life is not finished at this point. Only the outer tasks are laid aside to be taken up again tomorrow. Now as I let the cares and the joys of the day's experiences drain from me in a last rememberance and a letting go, I prepare myself for a new life.

As I enter sleep my new day begins. When my eyes close my consciousness of eternity awakens. I am a journeyer, a traveller in a direction unknown before me. I move forward knowing that I do not control my future but only my choices. And the gift I bring as I approach the Other is my choice for openness, nothing more.

The ship awaits me at the quay. It is masted with many sails or only a slim and sleek few? My ship stands before me as I see her now with my inward eyes. I take only the essential. The journeyer's staff, sandles, pouch and cloak. How do I see myself with these as I prepare to embark? What gifts and simple substances for my needs do I take with me in my pouch on this night sea journey?

And now I meet my captain. Is she man or woman? How arrayed? And how strong and capable of destination? And what will be my part in this voyage? What is it that only I can do? What is it that only my captain can accomplish?

Somewhere, somehow now we are embarking and the mists of time flow in to meet us as we set sails into the wind.

My own thoughts are like flurries occurring almost at random. But wait! What is my question as our boat leaves shore on this journey of ours?

If I may have one question to fling across the tides this night what will it be?

May my question be simple and born of feeling? May it be specific and full of my passion for healing and for meaning?

May I ask only that question for which I am ready to receive the dream as response.

The mists enclose me now. My ship is safe. My captain strong. My devotion secure. My question is now a song sung over and over until I am no more and the dreams begin.

The Night Sea Journey fills my being. I will awake when the ship has reached that further shore.

I will awake. I will awake to the dream. I will awake to the night before the day. I will awake recalling, writing my dreams as flow, as wind sweeping in from the sea. I will awake bringing a gift from the eternal sea.

The Journey

'And so here are the white pants. Wear them and sometimes everyone will try to talk to you. And often no one will talk to you. You'll be alone, stand alone, and really have a chance to grow and feel your potential.'

— Directive in a dream

Each individual has a journey to fulfill in life. Whether this journey is lived consciously or unconsciously seems to make a crucial difference. If we remain unconscious of our true selves we live as the plaything of fate often tossed by superior forces from within and without. If we choose and work to become conscious of who we are, we are still subject to our fate but that fate can now be turned into a destiny. By becoming aware of what really is we greatly increase the range of our choices. And by becoming aware of what we are meant to do in life, as well as how we are to be, we actualize personal fulfilment which is also the fulfilment of the Self. Through consciousness and devotion to direction every action, reflection and choice can be woven together towards some larger, more ultimate purpose for our lives.

Each person dreams all his or her life even though most never remember and never use this source. What remains unknown to those who stay thus asleep is that the journey towards wholeness comes out of active actualization of the Source. There seems to be an innate direction moving through the dream and moving through life. But it can only be known with a developed and higher consciousness that originates in the ongoing and committed working with source expressions of the Self, such as dreams, intuitions, insights, projections, visions and certain primal and meditative experiences.

In terms of the larger journey, perhaps the fundamental issue for the dreamworker becomes the gradual giving up of rigid control and then entering into a balanced co-operation with the Self. But much dream interpretation is done with little or no yielding of control to the Self. Clients and analysts alike, as well as dream group leaders and their participants, often fall into this fundamental assertion in favour of the ego.

For whoever attempts to interpret the *symbols* of dreams literalistically as in such statements as, 'this means that... or 'what does this mean to you?' is rationally trying to turn a symbol into a sign.

A symbol is a question, not an answer. We attempt to control the symbol, and source behind the symbol, when we make the symbol into an answer. Is it not more true to the purpose of dreams to ask, 'What questions is this particular symbol posing for me now? And what can be my response to such questions?'

Behind some people's resistances to doing dialogues and other process techniques with dream figures is the issue of control. We remain in control if we tell the dream spirits what they mean. We share control and creativity if we ask them directly who they are and what they want. When we do this latter we assume the journey, we assume that we are not the centre of the universe but a partner in its evolution. We do not know what our dream spirits will say back to us but we do know that it will be a shove towards a possible truth which sometimes we will or will not like. Within the dreams we see this issue of control or being controlled over and over again in scenes of battles, chases and encounters with superior beings, positive and negative. And it is the dream ego, the dreamer's image, which is often the direct participant in all this inner conflict. Many times the ego image does not do so well with the co-operative endeavours in the dream. Often the dreamer's dream image is being dominated in so many ways. Is this the compensatory side of an over-controlling consciousness that simply will not let the journey in, even though it sees it well enough?

We must struggle with a false assumption that 'if I give up control I will be controlled.' Whereas in point of fact all those who control are being reactive, are being controlled by deeper forces than they know. How much better it is to establish a true democracy of the inner spirit in which ego and archetype each exist in their separate and different functions but struggle to create and to co-operate.

And finally the gifts, the rewards, are far greater when we sacrifice control in favor of co-operation. For the journey is the 'Tree of Life' which bears its fruit if it is allowed to grow rather than stagnate because its roots remain unfed out of fear, envy and repressed insecurity.

Resistances and regressions exert their power as part of the process and so the need for commitment, for enduring and staying with a value within time in order to develop the skills and experience necessary for dealing with the total process.

The journey will go on whether we are consciously part of the process or not. Yet all fails when we fail. For to each of us to whom the journey becomes known is given the journeyer's staff, sandals, pouch and cloak. Whether we use these or not when we come to the crossroads is solely our affair. Some let resistance and regression overcome them and throw all away. Some stand at the crossroads but do not let the darkness take over and then they move on. It is to these latter that the journey becomes a living reality, the jewel that has been found and cut by the play and work of a true centeredness and devotion.

Index

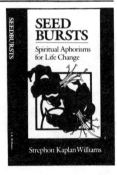